Building Mission-Critical Applications with .NET 10 and C# 14

A Guide to Engineering Modern Cloud-Native .NET Applications with Less Pain

Afzaal Ahmad Zeeshan

Apress®

***Building Mission-Critical Applications with .NET 10 and C# 14*: A Guide to Engineering Modern Cloud-Native .NET Applications with Less Pain**

Afzaal Ahmad Zeeshan
Almere Buiten, The Netherlands

ISBN-13 (pbk): 979-8-8688-2346-6   ISBN-13 (electronic): 979-8-8688-2347-3
https://doi.org/10.1007/979-8-8688-2347-3

Managing Director, Apress Media LLC: Welmoed Spahr
Acquisitions Editor: Smriti Srivastava
Development Editor: Laura Berendson
Editorial Assistant: Jessica Vakili

Cover designed by eStudioCalamar

Cover image designed by Pixabay.com

Distributed to the book trade worldwide by Springer Science+Business Media New York, 1 New York Plaza, New York, NY 10004. Phone 1-800-SPRINGER, fax (201) 348-4505, e-mail orders-ny@springer-sbm.com, or visit www.springeronline.com. Apress Media, LLC is a Delaware LLC and the sole member (owner) is Springer Science + Business Media Finance Inc (SSBM Finance Inc). SSBM Finance Inc is a **Delaware** corporation.

For information on translations, please e-mail booktranslations@springernature.com; for reprint, paperback, or audio rights, please e-mail bookpermissions@springernature.com.

Apress titles may be purchased in bulk for academic, corporate, or promotional use. eBook versions and licenses are also available for most titles. For more information, reference our Print and eBook Bulk Sales web page at http://www.apress.com/bulk-sales.

Any source code or other supplementary material referenced by the author in this book is available to readers on GitHub. For more detailed information, please visit https://www.apress.com/gp/services/source-code.

If disposing of this product, please recycle the paper

Table of Contents

About the Author xiii

About the Technical Reviewer xv

Introduction xvii

Part I: Thinking Software 1

Chapter 1: .NET Ecosystem 3

Development Experience 6

Community 10

Hosting Platforms 12

Assessment 15

Chapter 2: Languages Spoken 17

Speaking C# 21

Assessment 24

Chapter 3: Development Environments 25

Environment 26

Assessment 27

Part II: Software Architecture 29

Chapter 4: Kinds of Software 31

The Need 32

Entering the Known Platforms 33

Migrating to .NET 34

Innovative Cultures and Products 35

Supporting Services and Background Processes 36

Further Reading 37

Chapter 5: .NET Platforms 39

Server Platforms 40

    Enterprise Patterns 42

Consumer Platforms 51

Further Reading 52

Chapter 6: UI-Driven Apps 55

Desktop Apps 58

    Windows 59

    Cross-platform 63

MAUI 63

    Design 66

    Develop 67

    Deploy 68

    Detect 73

Beyond MAUI 74

Further Reading 75

Chapter 7: Working with Data 77

Object-Relational Mappers 79

    Multiple DbContext 83

Micro ORMs 85

Applications with Data Usage 86

    Using Record Types 86

    Field Keyword 87

    Using LINQ 88

Further Reading 90

Chapter 8: Handling Events 91

Program-Space Events 94

Async/Await Nature 94

Events from the Beyond 96

Messages—Serverless, Message Bus, and More 97

Further Reading 99

Chapter 9: Real-Time Apps 101

Polling vs. Server Push 102

ASP.NET Core SignalR 106

Remote Calls with gRPC 107

Hosting Infrastructure Practices 108

Further Reading 109

Chapter 10: Adding Security 111

Master Passwords 114

Further Reading 115

Chapter 11: Defining Contracts and APIs 117

Using XMLDoc 118

Swagger and API Documentation 119

Automating API Documentation 121

API Documentation As a Contract 121

Respect the Contract 122

Further Reading 123

Part III: Software Quality 125

Chapter 12: Building for Testability 127

Bot Limitations 129

Further Reading 131

Chapter 13: The Wild West **133**

Infrastructure Validation 134

    Nothing Is Permanent 135

How Do Versions Help? 138

Further Reading 139

Chapter 14: Third-Party Testing Suites **141**

Bet on Open Source 142

Freemium Scalability 144

Flakiness 144

Further Reading 147

Chapter 15: Question Yourself! **149**

Pipelines 150

Further Reading 151

Part IV: Bundling Source Code Together **153**

Chapter 16: The MSBuild **155**

Further Reading 157

Chapter 17: Build Patterns **159**

Self-Contained 160

Framework-Dependent 163

Multilanguage Solutions 164

Building in the CI Server 165

Parallel vs. Sequential Builds 166

Further Reading 166

Chapter 18: The Basic Build **167**

#1 Restore Dependencies 168

#2 Compile the Sources 169

#3 Generate Artifacts 169

Further Reading 172

Chapter 19: Managing Dependencies 173

Third-Party Dependencies 174

Private Dependencies 175

Further Reading 176

Chapter 20: Artifacts Caching 177

Invalidating Cache 180

Chapter 21: Supply-Chain Security 183

Development 185

Quality Control 186

Delivery 186

Further Reading 188

Part V: Going Live 189

Chapter 22: DevOps and Infrastructure 191

Uptime vs. Downtime 192

Infrastructure Management 195

Chapter 23: Infrastructure As Code 199

Terraforming the Unknown 199

Going Beyond the Infrastructure 201

Infrastructure Lockdown 203

Chapter 24: Development Machine to Production 205

GitOps Pro Max 208

Chapter 25: Environments and Promotions 213

Feature Behavior 214

Hop, Hop, Hop 215

Environments in ASP.NET Core 217

Chapter 26: Distributing Platforms 221

Customer-Owned Platforms 224

Part VI: Observing Apps **225**

Chapter 27: Understanding Your Apps **227**

Further Reading 230

Chapter 28: Monitoring vs. Observing **233**

Start with Monitoring 235

Enter Observability 236

Cardinality 237

Continue with Monitoring 239

Further Reading 241

Chapter 29: Traceability and Telemetry **243**

Traceability 244

Further Reading 249

Chapter 30: Visualization **251**

Application Maps 255

Further Reading 256

Chapter 31: Adding Alerts **257**

Alert or No Alert? 259

Programmable Alerts 260

Part VII: Firefighting **263**

Chapter 32: Firefighting Rules **265**

Further Reading 270

Chapter 33: What Defines an Incident? **271**

Navigating an Incident 273

Further Reading 274

Chapter 34: Identify the Root Cause **277**

T-0: The Downward Trend.. 278

Fix the Code 280

Prioritizing Incident Management 282

Further Reading 284

Part VIII: Repeat **285**

Chapter 35: Monolith vs. Microservices **287**

Breaking Points 288

#1 Teams and Team Size 288

#2 Multiple Products 289

#3 Separate Roadmaps 290

#4 Regulations and Compliance 291

#5 Best Language Choice 292

Further Reading 293

Chapter 36: SQL vs. NoSQL **295**

PostgreSQL: For the Win 297

Short-Term Critical? 297

Further Reading 299

Chapter 37: WebViews **301**

Ionic Framework 302

What Is Wrong with WebView?.. 303

When Should I Use WebView? 303

Further Reading 304

Chapter 38: Machine Learning **307**

ML.NET... 307

Azure AI Services 309

Azure As Machine Learning Platform 309

Notebooks on Azure.. 310

Further Reading 310

Chapter 39: Open Source and Community **313**

Incoming Open Source 314

Outgoing Open Source 315

Contributing a Project 316

Contributing to an Existing Project 316

Community 317

Further Reading 318

Index **319**

About the Author

 **Afzaal Ahmad Zeeshan** is a Developer Advocate currently living in the Netherlands and likes to use .NET Core and Node.js for normal everyday development. He enjoys Cloud, Mobile, and API development. Afzaal has experience with the Azure platform and likes to build cross-platform libraries/software with .NET Core. He is an Alibaba Cloud MVP and has twice been awarded Microsoft MVP status for his community leadership in software development, four times been awarded CodeProject MVP status for technical writing and mentoring, and four times been awarded C# Corner MVP status in the same field.

About the Technical Reviewer

 **Sourabh Mishra** is an entrepreneur, developer, speaker, author, corporate trainer, and animator. He is a Microsoft guy; he is very passionate about Microsoft technologies and a true .Net Warrior. Sourabh started his career when he was just 15 years old. He's loved computers from childhood. His programming experience includes C/C++, Asp.Net, C#, Vb.net, WCF, Sqlserver, Entity Framework, MVC, Web API, Azure, Jquery, Highcharts, and Angular. Sourabh has been awarded a Most Valuable Professional (MVP) status. He has the zeal to learn new technologies, sharing his knowledge on several online community forums.

Introduction

For a developer, a new framework or a library, or a runtime is always an interesting new specie to explore and experiment with. We wear our invisible lab coats and dive into the new libraries as soon as they are released. Most of us even go as far as developing production applications with the release candidates, trusting that the only thing left is ironing and not deprecation of incomplete features. Over the last decade, I've grown to learn

- Never trust the day-one production readiness of anything.
    - Games?
    - New phones?
    - Frameworks?

Only get them on day-one if you're reviewing them.

- Just because a feature is available does not mean you should use it.
    - I cannot emphasize enough how much I am annoyed by the overuse of null check operator.
- Don't upgrade to the latest version the day it becomes available, and don't wait until the last day either.
    - It hurts if you upgrade to a broken version; it hurts more when your system gets hijacked because of a vulnerability beyond the support timeline.

The new versions always bring an excitement because they are packed with opinionated frameworks, libraries, and simpler SDKs, or features that you had to write yourself—all bundled in the new framework.

It is all fun, until this very new framework that you just integrated with your production project is already reaching its end of life. That is what happens when you use a non-LTS version, or when you attempt to use this version to test something, but before you deprecate or obsolete the new app or feature, you move onto something else.

That contributes excessively to the overall tech debt of your business. What I always found fascinating was how you have to update to a new version of the framework every few years. Why can't we just have something work for at least five or six years? The framework should be responsible for maintaining the internals. But hey, it's a new major version and I cannot complain that it breaks a few things here and there.

This book is for you if you also find learning technologies very interesting, but always take new products, new frameworks, and new runtimes with a grain of salt before adding them to your production environment. The current development experience and developer productivity landscape is changing rapidly, the framework you learned two years ago is no longer the shiny one today, and today a new library is replacing that. Take a look at the JavaScript ecosystem; they have a new library for everything. It would not be cynical to say that it is possible to glue together a handful of libraries and get a working program with less than 20% of your own code. While that does translate to "productivity"—especially when these libraries come from your own enterprise and you are only writing the business logic for your module—it does bring a lot of responsibility on the developers or the team.

- How do you contain the impact that each dependency has?

- How do you decide to obsolete a dependency?

- How do your developers know what is internal vs. external? Do you block all external dependencies by default?

Quickly this becomes a cultural question and not a technical one. And most decisions are either enabled or blocked by this thinking activity. You either allow too much, or you block too much. And both ends of the spectrum contribute to engineering challenges, technical debt, cross-team communication problems, and incidents.

The way I see things, the question is never "should we allow this framework?", or "should we migrate to this library?". Instead, it is always "in which environment can we use this framework?". That difference in the approach helps engineers understand what the acceptability of the framework is, what is the risk appetite, and what happens if we either like the framework too much or we dislike it too much.

This book contains several similar questions and scenarios that you should use to be clear with your peers to clearly explain the objectives and outcomes. Even though I am a .NET engineer, I can get the same outputs using Java, Python, Go, yeah maybe even Perl. When you frame the question as where you would use this language, the answer is easier. And another reason why a question posed at environments is easier to answer is because environments change frequently. Today, you may have development, staging, beta, and production, and a few quarters later you may have an extra QA, or canary, or I don't know, but you get the point.

Last, but not least, this book is not a cookbook, it is not an Essential .NET-style content either. This is a set of questions, scenarios, answers, and dilemmas to use when you go about developing. The core of the book contains material to help you decide when .NET makes sense and when it does not. .NET 10 brings a lot of improvements and features to make .NET and C# feature-compatible or may I say purpose-compatible with other languages. Each feature also brings a new way of thinking for a .NET program, and how your "Enterprise" solution should be broken down and rewritten.

In the end, I expect that by the end you will have more questions, more curiosity, and more urge to open the hood—LINQPad (`https://www.linqpad.net/`) is amazing at that—and read more about what's actually happening. And, if you learn something, please teach me as well @afzaalvirgoboy. :)

PART I

Thinking Software

CHAPTER 1

.NET Ecosystem

It is unfair to call .NET just a framework anymore; it is an entire ecosystem of platform, frameworks, libraries, communities, products, services, and concepts that enable organizations across the globe to translate their ideas and goals into realities. Oh, and it has been doing that since the early 2000s.

For decades, Microsoft .NET has been a go-to standard for enterprise application development for organizations. Since its first introduction, Microsoft .NET has impressed developers with its maturity in software development. It has one of the best development experiences, tooling, documentation, and the community. It is plausible how Microsoft has invested in the framework as a product. For a framework, the audience needs to know how well the framework has been documented, how easily they can get started if they need to pay to use the development framework, and if they stumble upon a problem, how quickly they can find it a resolution, etc. The biggest question is, does the parent company dogfood themselves? Do they use the framework for their own products and services? For Microsoft, that has been the case for years as they helped put the .NET framework on the face of the development landscape. Microsoft has invested in the evangelism roles with thought leaders and community experts to drive the community around the .NET framework for years.

Note   I am a fan of the .NET framework and have used .NET Core since the early beta days. This book aims to be less opinionated and contain information that you can use to build your enterprise applications using the .NET framework.

.NET has evolved from a language for console-based, web-based, and graphical application development choice for Windows applications to a broader clientele. Part of this success is kudos to Microsoft for investing heavily in a framework as a product and to the community of developers and experts who supported their years in the technology. As part of this journey to celebrate the .NET 10 release, this book will take you on a

© Afzaal Ahmad Zeeshan 2026
A. A. Zeeshan, *Building Mission-Critical Applications with .NET 10 and C# 14,*
https://doi.org/10.1007/979-8-8688-2347-3_1

journey as a .NET engineer. You will get hands-on experience on how a .NET engineer builds software application and then uses the IDE and language practices to make the application scalable, more readable, easy to maintain, less verbose, well documented, and less in published archive size. Chapter 2 looks at some of the improvements to the C# language in the 14th version and how that impacts the .NET 10 applications. In that chapter, you will learn about the new constructs announced as part of the language. Then, from there we will build the most used concepts of the .NET framework: web development. In Chapter 3, I will help you understand how ASP.NET has evolved into one of the most scalable, elastic, developer-friendly frameworks on the planet. I will use the examples and real hands-on demonstrations using the Visual Studio (and Visual Studio Code) IDE to showcase how to build web applications. Throughout the chapter, you will learn how to build microservices that are well-integrated with each other using common communication patterns, such as HTTP, message bus, queue, etc. Chapter 3 and onward takes a more hands-on approach to guide you through the application development practices in .NET 10 and use the features of the framework and the language to enhance the developer as well as the customer experience. .NET 10 is not just about building web applications, or console applications. Using .NET 10 you can build, manage, and maintain your enterprise's data services and sources. The Entity Framework offers services and features that you can use to design, deploy, maintain, update, debug, and fine-tune the data layer for your enterprise. Even if you do not want to use ASP.NET for the web application, you can use the Entity Framework to build the data layer. Entity Framework offers a code-first and the database-first approach to connect your database and the .NET code. In Chapter 4, we will take a look at the code-first approach to design the database schema, test it, and then create the migrations to deploy the schema on a production cluster. You will also learn the new features that are introduced with the latest version of Entity Framework for .NET 10.

Entity Framework can be used for web applications and for native offline applications such as WPF or Windows Forms. Moving onward, in Chapter 5, I will demonstrate how to build Windows applications using .NET 10. Microsoft has announced its plans to offer a cross-platform solution to building the GUI applications. For now, the GUI features are limited to the Windows platform only. The WPF framework is open sourced and has received a lot of community interactions and contributions over the past years. You will learn how to build the Desktop applications that connect to your web services and Web APIs written in ASP.NET Core. I will also demonstrate what .NET 10 has in store for the Windows Forms lovers. Windows Forms is a very old technology but very impressive in what it has to offer. You can build a basic Windows GUI application that captures data from a Web API and shows the result in a list in under one hour and deploys it to your customers. WPF takes the GUI performance a step ahead, and you will learn how to use the WPF framework to build applications that make use of the best of the .NET 10 and the DirectX framework.

Another interesting area that .NET provides a lot of services to is the mobile development. The Xamarin framework that Microsoft has provided to the developers is powerful. It has a powerful engine that helps build native applications on all the major platforms, from Windows, to Android, to iOS or macOS. Xamarin has evolved into the Multiplatform App UI, simply called MAUI, which aims to bring the XAML experience on all the platforms, cross-platform, and supports Windows, macOS, Android, etc. When using the MAUI, your .NET code can provide native experiences for your GUI applications on every platform. In Chapter 6, we will take a deep dive to look at what Xamarin is, how .NET supports mobile applications, and how you can fine-tune the applications. Remember, mobile applications are not just the user interface. A mobile experience requires offline support, various screen resolutions and interfaces, connectivity with the network, and more. Although we will not touch upon all the features, we will look at the most important additions to the framework that make it easier for everyone to deliver their applications at scale and speed.

Modern applications are smart. An application often uses a very powerful backend service that responds to every request a user makes. Often that service is integrated with the application and runs on the device itself. If you are into machine learning, you know that Google's TensorFlow is one of the leading frameworks for machine learning. TensorFlow models can be compressed to run on mobile devices. For the .NET world, for years there have been community contributions that make it possible to train and use the models in .NET applications. I still remember using the Accord.NET framework to train Apriori models to build basic recommender systems. The Accord.NET framework is amazing and offers many algorithms you can use to build models of the type you need.

Microsoft has their own machine learning framework, CNTK, but in this book we are not going to dive into Python-based machine learning frameworks. Instead, we will explore the .NET machine learning framework developed and maintained by Microsoft. In Chapter 7, we will explore the machine learning framework ML.NET and see how it helps us build models and train them in our applications.

Most of the frameworks and dependencies you will see can be accessed from the NuGet package manager. The NuGet is the well-known package manager for .NET environment. If you have experience with the .NET applications, you have already used the NuGet application to download and manage the dependencies. In Chapter 8, you will learn how to build and deploy the packages to the NuGet instance. You will learn how to configure the package to provide details. Next, I will wrap up the book by teaching you about the deployments and publishing of the application packages. In the Chapter 18, The Basic Build, I will demonstrate how DevOps works with .NET 10, how you can use the scripts to build, test, and package the applications. Different application models require a different deployment option. You will learn how to package the console or the Desktop applications and also how to package the web applications to deliver and deploy. In this chapter, you will also learn how to use DevOps tools and platforms such as Azure DevOps, GitLab, or GitHub to run the scripts whenever a code base changes.

Development Experience

The early versions of the .NET framework were released along with a Visual Studio IDE version. This purposefully demonstrates Microsoft's tight integration for the .NET framework and the IDEs and development platforms. As this is not a history lesson, I will aim to deliver the toolchain introduction for the .NET 10 and onward platforms. As the global development communities move toward a more open culture of engineering, .NET and the related IDEs have joined the revolution. Now the .NET framework is an open-sourced product by Microsoft as .NET Platform. One by one, the frameworks that are a part of the .NET ecosystem are moving toward an open-source first development model.

The .NET framework has a unique engineering experience compared to other frameworks and languages, such as Django, Spring, C++, or PHP. The .NET framework contains the resources you need to manage and maintain the application life cycle. In this book, you will learn some of the best practices you can employ while developing the application on a massive scale. As you will learn in the book, the .NET framework is not limited to web applications. You can use the same code and experience to develop, debug, deploy, and maintain the applications for embedded devices, desktop apps, Serverless processes, machine learning, games, and console applications that run as services.

Starting a project with Visual Studio on any platform and extending it to other platforms is possible with a single Git repository. Visual Studio and the application life cycle management tools, such as Azure DevOps, enable developers to work on the projects in any platform, location, and operating system. On top of that, Azure DevOps and Microsoft Azure will allow you to test, debug, and deploy the applications on various platforms and operating systems.

Note   Today, the topic of cloud development environments or CDEs is very hot. Every enterprise and startup is discussing how these platforms can enable our developers to quickly work on what's important. Not just the code preview or review, but the ability to write code, perform tests, and code coverage and go beyond the capabilities of an online text editor. Notable service provides such as Gitpod, GitLab, GitHub, Visual Studio Code Workspace, and more are all battling to become a crucial part of the software development life cycle. The software engineering industry prefers remote work because anybody can work and solve complex problems from any location in the world that has a good internet connection. The cloud development environments take away the hardware complexity for the software, and you only need a computer system, an internet connection, and a payment method to get a subscription. DevOps and Agile practices are already decades old, enabling the code to build and integrate in parallel and background.

The overall development ecosystem that the .NET framework offers will be beyond the scope of this book. I will try to cover the maximum pointers you should know regarding the experience that the .NET framework enables for your enterprise. Microsoft actively listens to the feedback that the community has to offer. They trust their MVPs, partners, Regional Directors, and employees to share the feedback that drives the overall technology. I have enjoyed building applications with .NET Core compared to other languages. When using .NET Core you can

- Use type safety, as C# is a type-safe language so you can avoid bugs caused by a program's type mismatch.

- Use extensions and packages that are made available as part of the language ecosystem, such as LINQ, Entity Framework, etc. to improve the development experience and speed up the software delivery.

- Extend the language using custom constructs. C# can be extended and secure using the Roslyn compiler platform. Many static code analysis tools have been written using the Roslyn compiler platform for the C# language.

- Build the applications that adhere to each other, are compatible, can be packaged as libraries, and imported into other projects. NuGet can help streamline the software packaging and delivery within and outside your organization.

- Review the best practices to use when writing applications with the latest versions of the language and the framework.

It is valuable for organizations to reuse the code that they have written in various deployment targets. For example, if your organization sells a proprietary version of code, it would be valuable for the company to reuse the source code in as many deployment channels as possible. With .NET, you can generate libraries that target .NET Standard and use them in web, Desktop, and mobile applications. With .NET 10 that goes one step beyond, removing the need to target .NET 10, you can directly use the .NET 10 as the target for your libraries. The don't-repeat-yourself principle comes to help your software engineers by ensuring consistency in your applications.

One thing that I would like to mention here is Conway's law.[1] In simple words, the law states that the way your organization communicates is the way that the components of your software communicate. As we will build scalable solutions and try to dissect the solutions into elastic components, I will highlight how and where Conway's law will have an impact. Normally speaking, it will be best if the developers are allowed to think of the solution that best mimics the organizational communication structure. For me, this is a very interesting research topic, so I would not want to spoil it all here. Again, Conway's law applies to large-scale applications; a simple 2-page mobile activity might not benefit from the law.

---

[1] Conway's law is an inevitable law in computer science. It is best to accept the law and use it to your advantage than try to prove it wrong and hurt yourself. Read more on the law on Martin Fowler's website: `https://martinfowler.com/bliki/ConwaysLaw.html`.

Throughout the book, I will help highlight how Conway's law impacts how we design the software and what would have been done in case the organizational size was different.

If your organization is split into regions, development experience is more important than ever. When your teams work closely, for example, in the same region or in a single office. It is easy for everyone to sit together and discuss the solution's architecture. As your teams grow and people move into different locations, it is less easy for everyone to be able to communicate and question about the decisions that are made. This is even difficult for new joiners. Every new joiner has to understand how the software is "done"[2] in the company. The software development process needs to be reviewed to ensure everyone feels easy and comfortable working with the project. Maybe it is the documentation, perhaps the code base is not well structured, or maybe the performance of the source code is not good enough. All these questions build an engineering culture that fosters innovation in software development.

That said, as part of developer experience, it must be easier for developers to migrate to the .NET framework from other programming languages. The .NET framework offers programming languages out of the box: C#, F#, and Visual Basic. While the .NET framework can be programmed with either of these languages, we will focus heavily on the C# programming language in this book. Various language constructs are enabling developers from other languages such as JavaScript, C++, and Java to use their knowledge and write the programs that work cross-platform. As the developers bring their knowledge from other languages, they should be able to take some key concepts and apply them to other languages. One of the most beautiful distinctions between a Java code and the C# code, for example, is how much one[3] depends on the design patterns and heavily architected software. Developer experience goes beyond knowledge sharing and also includes how quickly can a concept be taken from the source code and applied elsewhere. If your enterprise uses Java, JavaScript, or Python, for example, then building the minimum viable products (MVPs) using .NET framework makes very little sense if the programs are difficult to reverse engineer, or to allow the concepts to float into a different language.

---

[2] The software is a living, breathing object in an organization. It is not just a code that is written or an application executable that is sold. It is part of who the enterprise or the organization is, what its people stand for, and who their customers are. New joiners need to understand what it is, to be able to have an impact in the culture.

[3] Can you guess which is which?

In this book, we will explore how we can use .NET framework to build the applications that are

- Easy to port to various customer and device markets, extend by adding more features and integrating with the framework as needed

- Tested and validated against code quality and the standards of code practices for your organization

- Supported by the modern techniques and technologies, such as cloud-native, intelligent, cross-platform applications

- Developed on any platform, on a cloud, in a virtual machine, and also using any development editor

Remember: Happy developers write code that works. Just because it doesn't rhyme doesn't mean it's not true.

Community

The revolution to move the .NET Framework from a Windows-based framework to an open-source, cross-platform, community-led framework was a win-win for Microsoft and the community. It is not that .NET Core was the first attempt to bring the C# language and the .NET platform to Linux (or macOS). As soon as Microsoft .NET Framework was launched, a community-led effort was made to bring the .NET framework and the C# language to Linux and macOS platforms. The project is known as the Mono Project.[4] The Mono Project was developed by Miguel de Icaza, who also founded the Xamarin Platform to develop cross-platform native mobile applications using .NET Framework. The Mono Project uses the Common Language Infrastructure, published as an open standard. Miguel and Xamarin later joined Microsoft when Microsoft bought the Xamarin platform and open-sourced the code framework. The Mono Project is an exciting intercept between what the community expects, runs, and distributes. Microsoft made a move to offer .NET Core as an alternative to the Mono Project.

---

[4] The Mono Project was introduced as a community effort, and it still is a community effort to this date. The Mono Project maintains their website at `https://www.mono-project.com`, and lists down the active development. Although the IDE that Mono Project provided (MonoDevelop) is still available, Microsoft recommends to use Visual Studio as an alternative to develop solutions on .NET platform.

For the community aspect, on top of the framework itself, I include

- The framework documentation that helps customers use the product in their projects.

- Examples and sample demonstrations of the usage of the platform.

- Guidance material, such as books, courses, and learning guides.

- Local workshops including community-led speaking events and public sharing sessions with partners.

- The customers' ability to contribute directly to the mainstream product life cycle and future plans.

- The integrated development environments and the application life cycle management tools.

- Forums, meetup groups, and official support from the parent company that help with any unthought-out challenges during the development.

- Application deployment platforms that support operations and smooth migration from other hosting environments.

- Availability of the platform on major deployment targets. For example, if you provide software for the embedded devices, you will only want to invest in a framework that can be deployed to an embedded device no matter how performant, easy, or scalable the framework is.

The drive for .NET Core received a lot of help from the communities and open-source enterprises. Individual contributors have also contributed a lot of open-sourced packages to the ecosystem. Moreover, the packages written for different languages and frameworks have been rewritten to support the .NET Core ecosystem. This has enabled the .NET Foundation to expand the deliverables' scope and target environments. Today, .NET Foundation is fostering open-sourced, free to use and contribute frameworks, libraries, and dependencies for

- C# language platform, which includes the C# standard, the C# compilers, etc.

- Data management; the most notable example is the Entity Framework Core by Microsoft.

- Identity and access management.

- Machine Learning model life cycle management frameworks.

- Graphics management and manipulation libraries.

- Web API and Web Services (the old, legacy style SOAP-services).

- Mobile development frameworks.

.NET Foundation is always welcoming new projects and frameworks that can be fostered. For example, recently, a new project was included named TorchSharp.[5] TorchSharp enables .NET engineers to use the PyTorch framework for machine learning, bridging the communities and their knowledge.

By enabling the community to collaborate with Microsoft, .NET framework has reached a milestone that might not have been possible with Microsoft's efforts alone. This approach had its down sides as well, for sure, but bringing all the ideas and suggestions to the table and working on the problems together is always sustainable and more friendly.

Hosting Platforms

An important aspect of the framework is where you can deploy the applications and services you develop. Microsoft .NET for web application development has been supported by all major platforms and hosting environments. This might not be a very important factor for large enterprises with their own data centers and managing their on-premise servers. Investing in an infrastructure that supports the frameworks you use to develop the applications is very important for small to medium-sized organizations. A hosting platform that supports the framework of your choice will help you

- Support the latest version of the framework quickly.

- Adopt the latest changes and features of the language, runtime or the framework before your competition.

- Be sure that the engineers of your hosting platform are aware of any security and hotfix patches and that they apply them quickly.

- Release software quickly and build a mesh of software that uses the same technology.

---

[5] TorchSharp can be reviewed at `https://github.com/dotnet/TorchSharp`.

Having a hosting platform that supports the required runtimes for your business operations is extremely crucial.

It is still unsure why .NET Core or the open-source frameworks, especially .NET 10, which supports open-source deployments, is not made available on specific platforms. For example, even to this day, the Heroku[6] platform has not enabled official support for .NET. It is one thing that a platform doesn't support proprietary platforms but not support an open-source one? At the point of writing this book, .NET has been open-sourced for more than five years, and Heroku decided to not keep it in their officially supported SDKs and frameworks. But that's their choice to make.

For the early days of .NET and the ASP.NET web applications, hosting platforms offered direct support for ASP.NET deployments. Then, Microsoft Azure came along and changed the game; AWS started the whole revolution. The cloud platforms enable enterprises to build an elastic, scalable, modern infrastructure. The infrastructure provides advanced features such as blue/green deployments, monitoring of the application instance, and automatic application of the SSL and TLS certificates. All these features and more are required for a secure and scalable ASP.NET Core web application. In later chapters of the book, you will learn how different infrastructures offer these services.

The hosting platform also enables or disables the services that you can offer from your ASP.NET Core web applications. For example, if a hosting platform does not allow socket connections, you cannot efficiently use the SignalR services. Other services offered by ASP.NET Core that depend on the hosting environment include, but are not limited to, HTTPS by default,[7] sticky sessions,[8] and more. This book aims to understand how we can use the platform to build scalable web solutions. We will use the platforms that support these advanced features. It would be fun to explore the options that do not

---

[6] Heroku platform's official buildpacks can be found here: `https://devcenter.heroku.com/articles/buildpacks#officially-supported-buildpacks`. It would be great to see this page reflect the support for .NET Core.

[7] HTTPS is a must. Period. You cannot have your web application deployed to the public and not have an SSL certificate. Today, there are various methods by which you can receive a free SSL certificate for your website that builds trust between you and your customer. Read more on how ASP.NET Core enforces HTTPS: `https://docs.microsoft.com/en-us/aspnet/core/security/enforcing-ssl?view=aspnetcore-8.0&tabs=visual-studio`.

[8] Sessions are supported in ASP.NET Core out of box, so you do not have to configure anything. Some configurations that enable sticky sessions can help optimize the customer experience in stateful web applications. For more on this topic, read `https://docs.microsoft.com/en-us/aspnet/core/fundamentals/app-state?view=aspnetcore-8.0`.

offer these services and how to overcome the challenges of not having them enabled but still providing a nice experience. But that is not the scope of this chapter or this book. Most cloud hosting platforms offer all these advanced features for your web applications. If you want your application to be scalable and elastic, consider paying for the better service. The book does not help you decide which service to pay for but helps you understand what you need to enable your solutions to be scalable.

More and more hosting platforms are moving toward the cloud. If you want to be competitive in nature and provide solutions that customers want, you need to evolve with the platforms. Using the latest technologies enables your team to

- Focus more on the business value that needs to be generated instead of patching the virtual machines or looking into crash logs.

- Build relationship with infrastructure experts, without having to hire, employ, and manage the people who are expert at infrastructure management.

- Pay for the resources and compute devices your solutions need to provide the services to. Do not get me wrong, having your own data center is good, if you can afford to maintain and scale it. Making a huge investment is not a good option if you are just starting in the market.

- Utilize the latest features on the hardware and use the compatible software features that provide more performance and speed compared to older and legacy software.

At the end of the day, your hardware can only support you so far. It is the software that you write that is going to control the hardware and get things done. Think of your database hardware, caching cluster, message bus or queue performance, and more. Often your hardware is performing the best it can, but your software is not optimized to fully utilize the potential of the hardware. Maybe your architecture is not good enough, maybe the algorithm that your engineers decided to use was not the fit for that particular use case. Various reasons can make your solution slow. Note that the performance of the entire solution matters and not just a single method. You can monitor a single method all you want. Your competition wins if your customer is not getting the response in time. When it comes to the performance of your applications it can be the network layer that is not performing good, for example. Selecting a hosting partner that works "with" you and not "for" you matters. Do not trust a hosting platform that works "for" you. There is no such thing. Every business that is making dollars out there, is working for them. At best you can find a partner that works "with" you! When they work with you, they aim to improve their own services while including your business needs in their goals and missions. I am not going to name any single one of the hosting providers because it depends on industry, regulations, compliance, and laws. It is best to have a legal advice before deciding to go ahead.

Finally, in the book, you will learn how to fine-tune the application while extending the capabilities of your solutions. You will learn how to keep track of the performance and identify the bottlenecks as they appear in the pipeline.

Assessment

The .NET framework has been available on multiple platforms. Which platform do you think has the best integration tools, development experience, and support for IDEs today? Note that there could be multiple correct answers. The answer to this question is not the one posted on Stack Overflow or Microsoft Docs. The answer is the platform that you feel most comfortable in. As part of this exercise, I need you to research what is supported for your favorite framework and prepare the development environment before we start the next chapter.

Do you know which server is used by ASP.NET Core by default to host the web applications? Is this embedded web server good for production releases? Based on the platform of your choice, what features does it have to offer?

Web applications in .NET 10 can be developed using Visual Studio and Visual Studio Code. Which one do you prefer? Do you have everything set up for the IDE of your choice? If not, make sure they are. For Visual Studio Code, we need the proper extensions downloaded. Check out the Microsoft docs to prepare the environment.

CHAPTER 2

Languages Spoken

One of the most important elements of a framework is that the users are able to communicate[1] with the framework. If you are using a framework that provides services to data scientists, but a data scientist is unable to communicate properly with the framework, then the framework is useless because it only contributes more cognitive load to the team.

Topics covered in this chapter:

- How do Engineers translate their thoughts?

- What does .NET framework offer?

- Why .NET shrunk the language support?

.NET framework is one of the oldest frameworks with an active community and a large contribution group. In such a scenario, such a large community causes the "culture" of a framework to be diluted. New concepts, new languages, and new constructs are added to the vanilla framework that a particular group enjoys and prefers. This increases the friction in the community as the framework turns into an opinionated choice by a few enthusiasts. For .NET framework, this has happened various times. When Mono Framework[2] was developed, it was done so to support non-Windows environments while using the benefits that C# language provided. But not all the changes are good in nature, or beneficial in results. At the end, what a language must do is

---

[1] The term communicate is defined as "share or exchange information, news, or ideas," and in this context, it would be the ability of a framework to express its functionalities to the engineer, and an engineer's ability to be able to master and use it to their craft.

[2] Mono Framework is a prime example of a platform envisioned by community and then accepted and owned by the original implementer of a framework. Check: `https://www.mono-project.com/`

- Enable the Engineer to express themselves and get the computing platform to do what the business case or value is.

- Abstract complex behaviors and scenarios that would otherwise be a concern for the Engineer.

- Allow the Engineer or the team of Engineers to collaborate on the solution as a single unit of work.

While in humans, a language plays a part in how we express our emotions, for a machine, that is not particularly important.[3] Let us explore these three core points.

Just like humans, a machine follows what it is told. Like the arrow of time flows in a direction, the machine continues reading the commands, scripts, and continues running in a linear mode. As the programs and the source code become complex, the execution on the computer remains linear.

Note   Speaking in terms of computer hardware. CPUs execute statements in a sequence. It reads a statement, executes it, saves the output, and repeats. Simply speaking, this is everything that a CPU does. Enter GPUs. GPUs enable parallel execution of code. Thus, simply speaking, a GPU reads multiple statements, executes it, saves the output and repeats with the next batch. The emphasis is on batch. However, GPU also executes the commands in sequence.

This is where the language enables an Engineer to guide the computer through various steps and get a job done.

Over the years, various languages have been added to the Microsoft stack of technologies, especially the ones that work in close collaboration with the .NET framework. For the Universal Windows Platform,[4] initially there was support available for JavaScript and the applications could be developed using HTML, CSS, and JavaScript. While the JavaScript platform enabled various developers to quickly port their existing

---

[3] Domains of artificial intelligence, machine learning, and other statistical contexts have enabled computers to reason. A lot of startups have been founded that enable computers or programs to exhibit emotions. But those emotions are equivalent of what a punctuation can do in this book. A simple comma-placement in a sentence will raise your brows similarly.

[4] Universal Windows Platform is seeing less and less traffic from developers and support from the community. See here: `https://learn.microsoft.com/en-us/windows/uwp/`

web-based applications to a "native" Windows experience. It was not a pure native[5] experience and was adding the dilution that I mentioned above.

Luckily, Microsoft has now trimmed down the list[6] and we have the top three languages that you can (and you should!) use to do the development.

1. C#

2. F#

3. Visual Basic

In this book, we will use C# language to explore the .NET framework and build our solutions on top.

F# is an immensely powerful language with its roots in functional programming.[7] While C# is an object-oriented programming language by default, meaning, it allows you to define the nature of programs as objects interacting with other objects. For example, a customer (object) depositing (interaction) their money (the payment details are described as objects in a transaction) to their bank account (another object) owned by a bank (yet another object). In a functional programming language, you treat everything as a function. Functions take an input and return an output. Simple.

---

[5] In this book, when we talk about the term pure native, it means a framework that is a first-class citizen for the platform. For Windows, such as framework is Win32 or MFC-derived application development environment. .NET framework also uses Win32 (via methods of P/Invoke) and thus tangents the pure native concepts. Although the just-in-time compilation and IL pushes it away from a pure native experience. A WebView-derived platform that Microsoft has often invested in is not a purely native experience. Which is why, if you need a pure native/native experience, never trust a WebView-derived framework.

[6] Check this list on Microsoft's official website to learn about the current supported languages. `https://dotnet.microsoft.com/en-us/languages`

[7] Read more: `https://softwaremill.com/what-is-functional-programming/`

If you are writing applications that encapsulate objects and their behaviors, use C#. But if you are building applications that are stateless in nature, and the systems do not have side effects[8] then you need to use F# as it will enable you to express yourself clearly, quickly, and simply.

Finally, Visual Basic. Visual Basic offers an easy syntax and enjoyable experience when building visual applications. In this book, we will not explore Visual Basic as a language. In the author's humble opinion, use Visual Basic if you are supporting a legacy app built with Visual Basic.

These languages are an abstraction over the underlying .NET framework that powers the applications. Using C#, you can tune the .NET framework to get the business jobs done in an object-oriented manner and F# allows you to use the .NET framework and treat everything as a function.

It is interesting that we have a limited number of languages that can be used to program an underlying framework. Call it an opinionated approach, I like to call it keeping it tidy. In general, it might be possible to define a separate language that offers a specific use case.

- A language[9] that allows Engineers to query the databases and parse/process the data and the entities stored in the database.

- A language that is specialized in writing the building scripts, and allows Engineers to script a pipeline to manage project dependencies, source-code build, artifact generation, code deployment, and more.

---

[8] Side effects are when a method changes the state of a system outside the scope of that method. For example, when you buy a ticket for a bus, the ticketing system depends on external sources that are beyond the input of the customer. In such a scenario, an object-oriented language is helpful as it allows you to express a system that has various state stores. In functional languages, your methods cannot mutate the external or outside states and their behaviors are not influenced by external stores. For example, if a customer buys a ticket and the inputs are in valid state, then the method will return a ticket. For a functional language to use the external database or a table as part of the function body, it would need to accept that function as an argument. Read this article, `https://www.c-sharpcorner.com/article/functions-in-functional-programming-vs-procedural-programming/`, and `https://www.datacamp.com/tutorial/functional-programming-vs-object-oriented-programming`.

[9] Actually, there is one such feature available in .NET that we will explore in the later chapters in the book.

- A language that specializes in generating the UI elements and translating those to the underlying framework calls.

- A language that helps in writing secure code, handles cryptographic and encryption modules, and avoids the object-oriented nature of .NET framework altogether.

Allowing the framework to be open to any language proposal promotes competition and Microsoft believes there is a huge win in being open, transparent, and available to anyone. Microsoft drives the adoption and development of C# and F# in communities across the globe and that brings a unique perspective to developing software and solutions; like a hivemind.

With all that said, if you do wander around .NET framework you will find a similar thing happening across the ecosystem. There is a huge plethora of community-driven languages and abstractions over .NET or CLI (common-language infrastructure, a reference specification of the .NET framework by Microsoft) that allows programmers of other languages to program against .NET framework.

Speaking C#

C# is a mature programming language with modern-traits and advanced performance and behavior. If you are new to the language, you can easily and quickly start with the language. I prefer and always recommend the official documentation for .NET framework and various components available as part of the framework. For C#, head over to the official C# getting started page (`https://dotnet.microsoft.com/en-us/learn/csharp`) to learn more.

Note   In this book, we will not discuss and explore the basics of C# or teach you how to write a basic C# program as the goal of this book is to help you understand how to best use .NET framework in real-world scenarios. We will, however, mention various elements of C# that have been improved and matured over time in the last 3–5 years.

If you have even written a program in C-like programming language such as Java, then C# will be easy to get started with for you. In fact, .NET framework and other just-in-time frameworks such as Java's JVM share various common elements so you can get started quickly.

C# language is simple by design, and the compiler platform is open source so it can be extended to add services or features. One of the best feature implementations is the out-of-box static code analysis. C# is statically typed, meaning for each variable or parameter that you define you need to mention what type it can hold at runtime. Believe it or not, this directly contributes to runtime performance and lower-memory overhead.

Note   In dynamically typed languages, such as Python, a simple object such as integer could be large as the variables store extra information as an object. Read this Stack Overflow thread (`https://stackoverflow.com/ questions/10365624/sys-getsizeofint-returns-an-unreasonably- large-value`). The method `getsizeof` in Python, for example, returns the size of the object in memory. Unlike `getsizeof` in Python, in C#, the `sizeof` operator returns 4 (on a 32-bit system) for an integer variable. This extra memory overhead must be considered when deciding the language of choice for your next project. To learn more about the strange intricacies of `getsizeof` (which are sometimes also found in other dynamically typed languages), please read this blog post (`https:// nedbatchelder.com/blog/202002/sysgetsizeof_is_not_what_you_ want.html`).

Knowing what you are speaking, and having the guarantee that the framework understands you exactly how you expected it to, helps write the software in a much scalable manner. Not to forget, a solution is rarely developed by a single Engineer. When working in a system where multiple Engineers collaborate on various modules, it is promising to have a statically typed language. That is what C# provides. In C#, a `System1.Customer` is different from `System2.Customer`. Meaning, that while the name of the type itself is same, their contracts[10] can be different. And this helps minimize accidental errors, where you wanted to use one type but used another. Or, as in some

---

[10] A contract is what you agree on with the system. Loosely speaking, contract is a term often used for interfaces and abstract class types that a type inherits or implements.

other languages, you receive `undefined` on a type when you try to access a field that you *believe* was sent. Beyond this, C# (or a statically typed language) provides various benefits, such as

- Ability to catch code problems during the build-time and helps you ensure that what you expect in your program will be provided during runtime. For example, when you request a name as part of the Customer contract, you will either receive it on the runtime (empty string, null, or invalid characters is a different problem) or you get a build-time error indicating that the type that you have added as a parameter does not have a name field on it.

- Language abstracts away noise and verbose syntax for the type-definition using the keyword "var". Although now every modern language supports this feature, a few years back, it was a luxury offered by C#, C++, and a few other high-level languages. Java was an exception where you still had to define the variable type at declaration.

- Recently, C# has received a lot of syntactic sugar as an additive. Starting from C# 10 onward, there have been a lot of improvements to the language that enable C# Engineers to write code that is at par with other simpler languages such as Python, etc.

  - Range operators (`https://learn.microsoft.com/en-us/dotnet/csharp/language-reference/proposals/csharp-8.0/ranges`)

  - Top-level statements (`https://learn.microsoft.com/en-us/dotnet/csharp/fundamentals/program-structure/top-level-statements`)

  - Records (`https://learn.microsoft.com/en-us/dotnet/csharp/fundamentals/types/records`)

  - Pattern matching (`https://learn.microsoft.com/en-us/dotnet/csharp/fundamentals/functional/pattern-matching`)

  - Deconstructing an object (`https://learn.microsoft.com/en-us/dotnet/csharp/fundamentals/functional/deconstruct`)

- Discards (`https://learn.microsoft.com/en-us/dotnet/csharp/fundamentals/functional/discards`)

- The language features can be overridden to match the need of the business. Roslyn (the compiler platform) can be extended to control the behavior as needed. For example, recently, C# supported the null-forgiving operator that allows you to pass a null to a value that does not allow null.

We will explore most of these features as we explore what C# has for the real-world applications in the later chapters as we apply C# to the common problems faced by the Engineers.

Now to the answer the idea we opened up with at the start of this chapter. We see that .NET allows us to, out-of-the-box, express our business cases and values to the underlying machines and run it. .NET languages allow us to communicate and translate our thoughts, while still validating if the programs would work on runtime. The connected pieces of the .NET foundation[11] allow us to use best-in-class data access, security, cryptography, user-interface, website, web server, and productivity development features and build what our businesses and customers expect.

Now in the next chapter, we will focus on the development environments that are available for .NET and C# developers. While some languages can be coded with text editors and without autocomplete support, most applications in .NET would become very difficult to program and maintain without an integrated development environment.

Assessment

Which language is the most used language when programming .NET framework?

Read Microsoft's strategy for the C# language: `https://learn.microsoft.com/en-us/dotnet/csharp/tour-of-csharp/strategy`.

---

[11] .NET Foundation is an independent body of .NET experts created by Microsoft to drive innovation and improvements in the .NET ecosystem of technologies. Most of the members are veterans of .NET technology and includes .NET experts such as Microsoft MVPs who drive the innovation in .NET technology ecosystem along with the .NET Foundation board.

CHAPTER 3

Development Environments

What differentiates .NET framework from other similar frameworks and language runtimes is that every part of the ecosystem is well connected and orchestrated. A developer, as a consumer, is aware of when to use what and how.

Topics covered in this chapter:

- Code Editing: It starts with a line of code.

- The build scripts, code verification, and artifacts generators.

- Deployment scripts and hosting environments.

- DevOps, DevSecOps, and beyond with Azure DevOps or GitHub.

Development Environments are important for a Software Engineer. While you can write scripts in plain-text editors, for large-scale projects and applications, it is recommended to use development environments that are tailored to provide support and a `co-pilot`[1] experience. In this book, we are talking primarily about .NET framework and the C# language so obviously Visual Studio line of products by Microsoft are best-in-class. Unless you are exploring other ventures and runtimes, such as working with Python (IronPython, for example) or native C++ for low-level programming, it is very unlikely that you need to step outside Visual Studio.

---

[1] Nope. Not talking about that Copilot, just yet.

Note   Visual Studio is used for Visual Studio as well as Visual Studio Code. Visual Studio Code is a lightweight text editor that supports various extensions and plugins. With the help of a few extensions, Visual Studio Code can perform similar tasks that Visual Studio can. For example, for basic C# console or web application development, Visual Studio Code can support you to bootstrap the projects, add code, lint the source code, write test cases, debug the application, set and remove breakpoints, hit the breakpoints, build, package, and deploy the code to the desired environment.

Environment

The tool is called integrated development environment because it is everything that an Engineer would need. This includes the code editors, build scripts integration, feedback from compilers and other build scripts, integrated error, and warning feedback—squiggly lines, and provides enough tools to generate the outputs and binaries to test, deliver, or deploy to the devices.

Visual Studio is a complete suite for Engineers. It is an interesting statement, but Visual Studio is developed using Visual Studio—so that shows how complete[2] this is.

In this book, we will prefer talking about and demonstrating Visual Studio/Visual Studio Code, but it is important to note that we will not use the tools directly since this is not a cookbook or a hands-on guide.

If you are a polyglot Engineer, you would certainly need to work on and use tools, languages, or runtimes that are not natively supported by Visual Studio. A good example is working with Kotlin language. Even though Visual Studio supports MAUI for Android development, but when you need to go low-level, you would need to use an IDE that supports Kotlin or other languages such as Swift on macOS/iOS. In such scenarios, JetBrain's IntelliJ or Apple's Xcode would make sense. Both these IDEs give similar features: you can write the code, build the code, run the code, and publish the code.

---

[2] In all fairness, it is a cheesy statement as well, because the C++ compiler is also written in C++. Computer science is full of these "dream within a dream" conundrums.

The subject of development environments (integrated or not) is becoming very diluted, especially with the advent of Agentic modes available with Generative AI platforms. But, it is still important to note what is needed before you start development.

Now in the next part, we actively explore and review the software architectures, designs, and the deliverables in production.

Assessment

Set up and configure a development environment. For optimal results, either install Visual Studio or Visual Studio Code. If you are planning to develop applications with UI, then install Visual Studio, otherwise, Visual Studio Code is enough for most C# and .NET workloads.

PART II

Software Architecture

CHAPTER 4

Kinds of Software

Software is everywhere. From larger servers, warehouses, to handheld devices and consumer products. Software powers up world economies, enables businesses to operate, and governments to provide a better life for their citizens. Each software has a unique requirement to be designed and developed.

The learning objectives of this chapter include

- The software archetypes that you can develop for publishing with .NET framework.

- How to prepare the development packages for deployment, ideally to any environment.

- Motivations behind developing your software to run as a background service.

Let me start this chapter with a question.

Do you remember the first software you wrote? Do you remember which .NET app you built?

There is no wrong answer to this. For me, it was an ASP.NET Web Pages application with Microsoft WebMatrix. It was a web application enabling friends to collaborate over local network with an embedded SQL Server (SQL Server Compact 4.0). For us friends, a web browser was accessible so the software that I built tailored to that need. As a student, I didn't have access to funds so I could not host the software online and thus had to fall back to my local machine. I hosted the website on the local network using IIS and since the database was available on my own laptop, the website could be easily accessed via local network.

If you notice, there are important lessons to be learned here:

- The scope of the software is not defined by the developer. It is always defined by the customers or the end users.

© Afzaal Ahmad Zeeshan 2026
A. A. Zeeshan, *Building Mission-Critical Applications with .NET 10 and C# 14*,
https://doi.org/10.1007/979-8-8688-2347-3_4

- You can build a top-tier web application, but if your audience cannot access it, then it is useless.

- While ideas are not limited by budget, the projects in the real world always are limited by their budgets and availability.

If you are building a personal project, then sure, you do not have constraints over how you develop, how you deliver and how you make sure the services remain available. If you have users with stake, like paying customers, or citizens of a government, then we have to take extreme care with our planning and execution. Industries also have regulations and legal requirements in place. Financial services, healthcare, government sector, all require your software to follow one or more specific rules when developing the software and when delivering it.

The Need

Often you are confined to the space of delivery. For example, if you are building a mobile application, then you need to be careful with how much memory your application consumes, does it work on all mobile devices that your product is expected to work on, is the user able to interact with the interface, and more. However, the same do not apply in full if you are building an intermediate application such as gateway or an API. For such applications, a different set of rules govern the practices and policies. For an API, while you do not need to put the localization and accessibility in the top priority, you do need to think about how multithreading would work. While stress testing is not important in a UI application—or in actuality, you do not need to conduct a load test as you would conduct it for an API or a server.

The beautiful thing about software is that you can run it on any platform and device. In this chapter, you will learn a few platforms that are extremely crucial in the modern world. Then we will expand on these topics and practices in the chapters that come later in the section.

The maturity of the .NET framework also helps it to provide the best-in-class development experience for all sorts of platforms and developer levels. You can be an individual or a small team building a new product for an embedded experience, or you can be an enterprise working on a microservice-oriented web service. .NET framework has it all.

Entering the Known Platforms

If your target audience is for the known platforms, and by known I mean the regular day devices and platforms such as web browsers and web applications, mobile devices, Desktop applications, and such, then .NET becomes a no-brainer. .NET has supported these platforms for more than two decades now and has been battle-tested to ensure your production environments and applications can rely on the maturity and stability of the .NET platform.

The most used platforms among these is no doubt the mobile platform.[1] Mobile has the biggest potential to enable your business to succeed and .NET framework enables you to provide your applications to customers on the devices that they use. It is no doubt that Microsoft is also investing in mobile-first experiences.

Important to remember: The term mobile-first and responsive-design from the CSS3 world sounds similar. But they are extremely different in how the customers experience them. If your organization focuses on "customer experience" and now just the layouts of the interface then it is very important for you to understand the difference between these. While a responsive layout ensures that your app interface will work on all screen factors, a mobile-first strategy requires a technical change not only on the interface but also the API or the backend servers. Mobile-first requires a change not just in the code but also in how the products are researched, developed, and published. Read more here on the Wix blog: `https://www.wix.com/blog/mobile-first-vs-responsive-design-all-you-need-to-know`.

If you have developed using .NET framework in the last few years, you need to review the dotnet CLI again as it changes a lot. It changes to add more features and services, but also to deprecate and remove older scripts and functions. If you built the applications and/or CI/CD pipelines more than three years ago, you need to revisit the dotnet CLI to learn about the changes as it would have some breaking changes since the earlier releases.

---

[1] Check out the stats for March 2024–March 2025 here: `https://gs.statcounter.com/platform-market-share/desktop-mobile/worldwide`.

> **Tip**   At the time of writing, the comprehensive list of the breaking changes in
> .NET 10 is not ready, but it is available for .NET 9.0. If you're already considering
> porting your applications, you can review the compatibility for .NET 9 on Microsoft
> Learn platform (`https://learn.microsoft.com/en-us/dotnet/core/`
> `compatibility/9.0`). The compatibility for .NET 10 is also available on the
> same page; `https://learn.microsoft.com/en-us/dotnet/core/`
> `compatibility/10.0`. For CI/CD or DevOps pipelines, review the Deployment
> section.

The maturity of .NET framework is also a major reason why all major enterprises offer their SDKs in .NET. From cryptography to observability to fintech to monitoring to geolocation APIs, and more. The community-driven and proprietary solutions enable you to quickly move from an idea, to prototype, to production-ready to customer-loved products. The bootstrapped templates give you a quick start to prepare the authentication-flows, set up the HTTP/HTML mapping, and enable you to create a starter project for your mobile apps. All from within the IDE.

Migrating to .NET

Before we step away, migrating existing applications from other languages and platforms is "possible." However, the complexity of the migration depends on the current stage of the project. If your existing project is in MVP stage, or if it is a prototype that your team developed just to quickly test the waters, then it may be possible to painlessly migrate from other languages or frameworks to .NET.

However, if you are in production or anywhere closer to production, I would recommend against migrating to .NET. In the coming chapters, we will explore what to do in case you have a legacy system that you want to port to .NET, but the short answer is, migrating a legacy system to .NET just because the .NET 10 framework is fresh does not help your team, your Engineers, your customers, your business, and yourself. Do not put yourself in this position. There are common patterns that you can use to gradually move, if you are trying to migrate to .NET, and we will explore those later. In short, you can start with building domains within the software code, and then slowly move less critical services to .NET first.

Innovative Cultures and Products

Today, in 2025, a lot of projects are innovative. This means a new device pops out of the blue at every other big tech conference, whether you're building for handheld experiences, handsfree devices, or smart home platforms. You need a platform that has an enterprise grade maturity and a massive community that can support you all the way. If you are an enterprise with thousands of Engineers, and millions of R&D budgets, you may be able to outsource a lot of elements to a third-party. However, for the majority of the developers that's not the reality. Innovation does not happen when the project is outsourced. Innovative projects are a competitive advantage for your business, your company, and your technical and Engineering department.

.NET projects can be deployed in two ways.

1. **Self-contained**: These executables are archived with the required necessary files as if to provide a "plug-and-play" solution. The challenge is that self-contained executables are created for a particular platform. A Windows-based self-contained package will not work on Linux unless specified in the RuntimeIdentifiers.[2] However, this does mean that the generated artifacts folder would be massive in size, so be careful if your deployment platforms are memory or storage sensitive.

2. **Framework-dependent**: When you want to keep the archive package smaller in size and the deployment environments have their own installed copy of .NET framework, you can use the framework-dependent publishing. These copies are cross-platform as the apps use a locally available .NET runtime.

This enables enterprises to publish their applications in a way that enables their customers to utilize the products. You can publish your applications with self-contained package archives that customers can download and run without having to set up anything on their machines. You can also publish framework-dependent applications that do not contain the runtime binaries but only contain the executable apps and the dependencies that are needed. Your customers or the deployment environments can then provide the runtime binaries.

---

[2] Reference for RuntimeIdentifiers: `https://learn.microsoft.com/en-us/dotnet/core/rid-catalog`.

Publishing the apps to edge-networks, IoT devices, smart home applications are all possible. They are made possible by .NET framework's ability to prepare and archive the applications in a simple manner that enables (1) your developers to release the software quickly and (2) your customers to download the software on their own terms.

You can go down to the hardware level and develop, build, and distribute the applications for your customers. The easy, best, and quickest way to start with embedded development is to use the .NET IoT. The platform enables us to write the software for various boards. Raspberry, Hummingboard, and more are all supported officially. .NET abstracts the underlying concepts of handling the I/O, peripherals, and more. Thus, leaving your developers to do the innovative work. The open source nanoFramework[3] also enables you to do that. nanoFramework goes a step beyond and provides libraries that enable you to perform automation, focuses more on sensors, wearable devices, and robotics.

Tip: In the coming chapters, we will explore templates and different projects supported by .NET and how we can create these projects using Visual Studio or the dotnet CLI.

Supporting Services and Background Processes

In this book, you will also learn about the software that does not have an interface used by the end users.

Tip: Every software has an interface, regardless of the use case or the end user. Some software is used directly by the consumers or customers. However, there is software that does not interact with consumers. Such a software is often called "services."[4] For the sake of simplicity in this part of the chapter, we're using "*does not have an interface*" for the services, even though they do have an interface that can be used programmatically or otherwise.

This background process performs tasks that are crucial to the production stability and reliability of the platform or to make the Engineers more productive. Language

---

[3] .NET nanoFramework and .NET IoT reference: `https://learn.microsoft.com/en-us/samples/dotnet/samples/compare-nanoframework-with-dotnet-core-iot/`.

[4] Read more about Windows Services and their development in the .NET platform: `https://learn.microsoft.com/en-us/dotnet/core/extensions/windows-service`.

servers[5] are a fancy example of such programs that run as a background library in our integrated development environments (IDEs). The Language server for Visual Studio or Visual Studio Code demonstrates how a process processes the language contents of a file and provides feedback; finding references, autocomplete, and more. Our development platforms (environments, or tools) communicate with the language servers to provide productivity features to the Engineers.

Food for thought: When was the last time you wrote a C# program in a Notepad?

.NET provides various packages and extensions that enable developers to write background processes and services. The Microsoft.Extensions.Hosting[6] package provides important and notable classes that enable developers to develop the services, compile, test, and publish the services that can be installed locally, remotely, or on the devices of customers. It is also important to note that this namespace also includes the required classes and types needed to set up the ASP.NET web projects. ASP.NET projects are long-living services that provide an HTTP interface to communicate with customers.[7]

While in this chapter we learned about the kinds and types of software that we can build and publish, in the next chapter, we will explore the options and frameworks that are offered by .NET framework to speed up the development of these software types. Also, we will learn about the specific frameworks that are supported in .NET, but also in the IDEs (Visual Studio, for example) to create the projects, develop the applications, bundle them, and also manage dependencies right from your development environment.

Further Reading

The history of .NET also includes the history of community initiatives to providing frameworks and runtimes where the default framework would not work. The Mono project is a great example of pushing the current boundaries of the framework and then

---

[5] Language servers enable our IDEs to provide excellent productivity regardless of the language we're using. Read how OmniSharp and Visual Studio Code use language server protocols to provide productivity support in Visual Studio Code for C#, and how other languages can use the same functionality. `https://learn.microsoft.com/en-us/visualstudio/extensibility/language-server-protocol?view=vs-2022`.

[6] Read the reference for this namespace on Microsoft Learn: `https://learn.microsoft.com/en-us/dotnet/api/microsoft.extensions.hosting?view=net-9.0-pp`.

[7] Read how you can host your ASP.NET web apps on Windows as Windows Services here: `https://learn.microsoft.com/en-us/aspnet/core/host-and-deploy/windows-service`.

allowing the community to build on top of a solid framework. Read about the Mono project here: `https://www.mono-project.com/docs/about-mono/`, but remember, Mono project is used as an inspiration for .NET Core, so moving forward, we will only talk about .NET Core. .NET 10 is the 10th version of .NET Core.

.NET's primary language is definitely C#, while F# and VB work, the primary language mostly used by .NET developers is C#. C# is a highly interoperable language with other .NET languages, but also non-.NET programming languages. Read this document on Microsoft's documentation: `https://learn.microsoft.com/en-us/dotnet/csharp/advanced-topics/interop/`, to learn about the interoperability features across languages. The key languages that C# provides interoperability with include, but is not limited to, C++, Python, JavaScript, and more. The link explains the interop between C# and C++, check out IronPython for Python, and for JavaScript, check out Blazor project and SignalR to understand how the entire ecosystem comes together.

CHAPTER 5

.NET Platforms

.NET runtime enables our Engineers to provide solutions to common customer problems in a very elegant and efficient manner. The target platforms and environments of .NET enable us to go beyond the mouse-and-keyboard interactions and build solutions that "awe" the audience. From touch-screen devices to voice-enabled automation, and more.

In this chapter, we will get hands-on and explore the frameworks, platforms, and archetypes that are available to us to develop and build our apps. Mainly, we will focus on

- Server platforms and building server-side applications and their different architectures

- Consumer platforms, and how to connect our consumer apps to server-side logic

- The scalability of the architectures, and how we've mostly reached a Serverless milestone

Only when we have identified the root of a problem should we start talking about the possible solutions. In the same way, once we know what we are going to build, or we understand what our customers expect of us, we should start exploring what kind of software we want to build and how that will help our customers.

We can distinguish the apps in two categories.

1. Server-side applications that "provide" services to the consumers

2. Client applications that provide an interface for our customers to interact with our services and products

© Afzaal Ahmad Zeeshan 2026
A. A. Zeeshan, *Building Mission-Critical Applications with .NET 10 and C# 14*,
https://doi.org/10.1007/979-8-8688-2347-3_5

These are unique platforms that can contain the overall types of platforms that are supported by the .NET platform. A simple question that can help answer you navigate toward the right project or template type could be, "are you building a project that allows your customers to reach out to you, or are you using this application to respond to service requests?"

Server Platforms

.NET is designed from ground-up to support server applications. Whether you are building stand-alone server apps or cloud-native applications, .NET has everything you need. Your APIs, web servers, Serverless apps, are the kinds of application that fall within the server category.

Information: ASP.NET Core[1] is an example of a server-platform, but it also includes consumer services. You build the Controllers[2] that act as the server-part of the application and the Views act as the consumer-part of the application. If you are building an ASP.NET Core Web API project, then the same Controller provides the features for both interactions based on the HTTP method verb used.

The folder structure in a project is opinionated and depends on how a team would like to operate and function. In Figure 5-1, a scenario out of many is shown. Some teams prefer to keep each layer separate in its own project. There you will see a separate folder for each layer, including

- Web and web API layer with controllers and request handlers.

- An internal data, models, and data transfer layer. Usually this layer contains data validation as well.

- A business logic layer that contains your own logic to handle the data, its connection between services, and the incoming requests.

---

[1] ASP.NET Core official website: `https://dotnet.microsoft.com/en-us/apps/aspnet`.

[2] Controllers in ASP.NET Core: `https://learn.microsoft.com/en-us/aspnet/core/mvc/controllers/actions`.

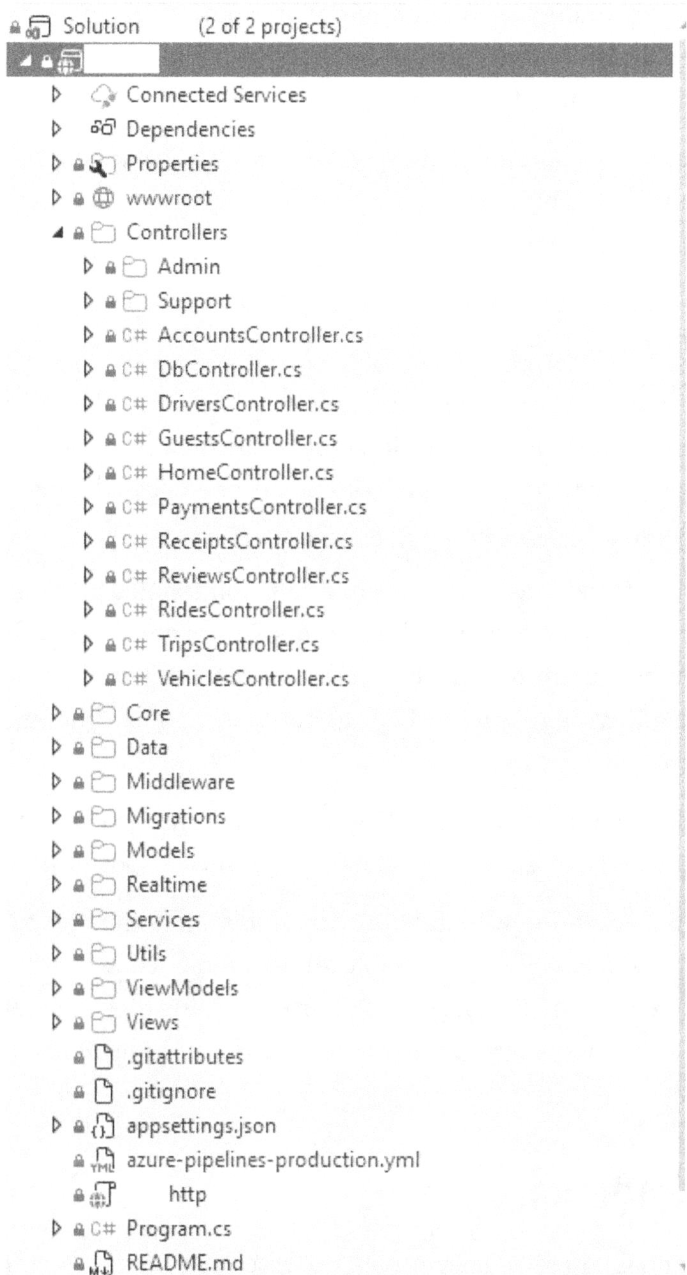

Figure 5-1. *An ASP.NET Core project with controllers, views, and models created in their own designated folders*

Usually such structure starts to show up when your project grows beyond a certain maturity. Starting with such a complexity is only expensive because

- You end up adding dependency graph to a project that has a handful service. Handful services (e.g., less than 10 services in total) can be managed in a monolith easily.

- Your build time and the artifacts size can grow if not managed properly. That is because each project is an identity and must be built again for every change.

Depending upon how critical and how crucial your web application is going to be, you can choose between

- ASP.NET Web apps; which entails, Model-view-controller (MVC patterns), Web APIs, and develop them either as a big monolith if your application does not have complexity or you can deploy them as microservices.

- Serverless workloads. Serverless in a very opinionated approach to deploying your services and the benefits are not always guaranteed. You can benefit from using the Serverless approach in some cases, while in others, it may come back to bite you big time; "hint hint" *cost optimization.*

- There is a new approach, .NET Aspire,[3] an opinionated framework for apps and service discovery, orchestration, and composition.

.NET Aspire is a new framework that provides tools and templates to get started with the projects that are observable, composable, discoverable. These are benefits only for the apps that are new, or you are just getting started. Adding these to the production-ready apps is no easy feat but also is not guaranteed to continue to deliver the values for the next five years.

Enterprise Patterns

A server application is composed of various processes that interact together to act as a Product for your enterprise. The more complex a Product, the more services and processes it requires to function and be able to remain available, reliable, stable, and interactable. Enterprise patterns is a common set of practices that have emerged in

---

[3] .NET Aspire official documentation: `https://learn.microsoft.com/en-us/dotnet/aspire/`.

various languages, frameworks, runtimes, to demonstrate the good practices to build scalable applications. Without going into specifics of the languages, or the authors and original implementations, enterprise patterns are a few dozen patterns that help you write solutions to common problems that are only faced in an enterprise solution. These include, but are not limited to

- High volume and high velocity data traffic.

- Applications where applying a patch with zero or minimal downtime is crucial.

- Data integrity and consistency requirements.

- Lazy loading, pagination, and data transfer caches.

- Object-relational mapping, patterns to capture and commit the data.

Also, the enterprise patterns (as the name suggests) are patterns for enterprise application and are agnostic to the type of app you are building. The enterprise patterns for server apps are different from the enterprise patterns for client apps. For anyone that wants to start in the design patterns, especially for enterprise applications, I highly recommend this website as a research and learning tool: `https://www.enterpriseintegrationpatterns.com`.

Tip: Microsoft Publishing provides Enterprise Application Patterns for MAUI Apps which talks about the patterns for enterprise mobile development. Get the book from here: `https://learn.microsoft.com/en-us/dotnet/architecture/maui/`. As for the server-apps, one of the most trustable sources is from Martin Fowler's website, you can read more about those here: `https://martinfowler.com/eaaCatalog/`

#1 Microservices

There is an ongoing debate in the Engineering world about the use cases and future of Microservices, their adoption in the Enterprise worlds, and how they assist simplification of complex workloads. While, the challenges that are outlined in these outrages is true, it is not a problem created by the Microservices pattern.

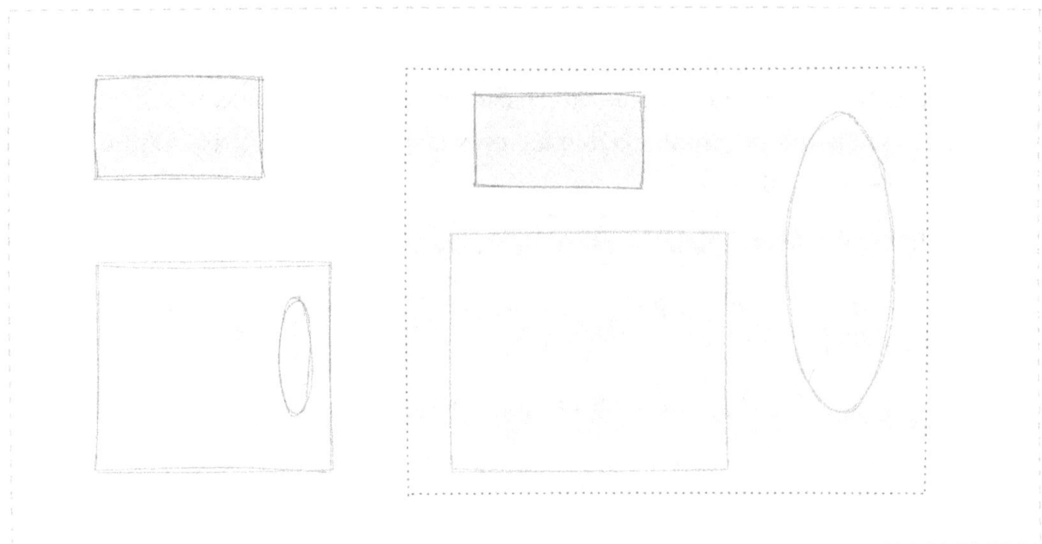

Figure 5-2. *The goal of microservices is to break the big monolith structure into self-composed, independent, and isolated services that each have their own life cycle and can be maintained and updated on their own. Note: the diagram is conceptual and not labeled*

Here are a few threads that you should read to learn why you should avoid using Microservices:

- When we should not use Microservices? (link: `https://stackoverflow.com/questions/48616949/when-we-should-not-to-use-microservices`)

- You probably don't need microservices (link: `https://www.thrownewexception.com/you-probably-dont-need-microservices/`)

- When Microservices Are a Bad Idea (link: `https://semaphore.io/blog/bad-microservices`)

The problem is the usage or adoption of Microservices, the problem is always unknown, unwarranted, and unplanned adoption of Microservices.

You are sitting in your office on a Monday. You have a few Jira tickets on your hands that are the last ones for this sprint. You hear a few Engineers talking about an awesome talk they heard from a speaker at a conference the last week. While you are having a hard time listening in to what they're saying from your desk. You walk over to the coffee corner to get a better chance at hearing the conversation, and the first surprise you hear is:

Engineer 1: We can improve the build times by adopting the Microservices pattern.Engineer 2: We also need to make our databases scalable as a platform and remove the current flow of ticket-based database creation flow. Engineer 3: We can start by removing our existing edge traffic to Microservices first to avoid any disruption in the entire platform.Engineer 1: Welp, the speaker said we could use Serverless for one-off event-based traffic.

You grab your coffee, come back to your seat and continue working on your tickets because you know Jira is reality, patching the existing systems is reality, perfectly written software crashing for unknown reasons at unwanted times. Post-conference-hyped-up-gossip is for fun. Only.

The entire dialogue above is a routine dialogue which happens in every organization. There is no problem with the dialogue, or to talk about what can and what should happen. The problem is when you bring your coffee chats and commit to them religiously. Without reviewing or addressing the technical challenges of your current tech stack, and how the modern (or potential, future) tech stack would impact your development life cycle. The only problem I see is that the dialogue does not have the context that the speaker might have shared. A TL, DR, or a disclaimer indicating that Engineers must take the shared information carefully as not everything applies to their application as well. At a conference, due to time constraints, backgrounds of audience, project complexity, speakers take that audience understand the underlying challenges faced ("problem"), they share their research ("action items") and the results ("presentation") they got. Audience focuses more on the presentation and skip the problem. I believe the problem is more important. In the start of this chapter, I mentioned that only after we have identified the problem that we are solving, should we talk about the solutions.

One of the best examples of teams discussing, sharing ideas, while still staying in touch with reality is to read technical papers, research articles, news, publications, organize watch parties for conference talks.

Now, on Microservices.

- Yes, Microservices are a very big challenge.

- The benefits offered by Microservices are not guaranteed.

- The technical challenge is very time-consuming, and the resulting application architecture and infrastructure is very complex.

- Microservices do not fix the problems that your source code, probably a monolith, faces.

- Microservices do not speed up build just because you created a manifest. The build pipeline also considers the dependencies, test suites, artifact packaging, and more.

That said, Microservices never made any of these promises, with no extra effort. Like the Agile manifesto, or DevOps, the benefits of an iterative product development required frequent and transparent conversations between the Product teams and the Customer. If Product teams continue to work in silos, and customers only join the initial meeting and then show up on the launch day, Agile and DevOps would just be a huge burden with no added value.

In the same manner, Microservices requires a huge change. A change, not in the way the software is built, tested, published, and observed but an organizational change that warrants that teams restructure themselves around their own domains and own it. If you want to gain benefits of Microservices and other modern development practices, I encourage you to pick up the book Team Topologies (`https://teamtopologies.com/`) and read it cover to cover.

ASP.NET enables Engineers to write software that works together with other services and products to provide a solution. Because, at the end of the day, your customers want solutions to their problems. Right? Why should a person ever open your app, or visit your website, or keep your service running in the background if it does not "solve" a problem that they are having. The nature of modern ASP.NET enables us to write Microservices and make less mistakes from a technical standpoint.

#2 Serverless

Over the last decade, almost, Serverless-approach to developing and deploying the "code" has taken almost every industry by storm. The application of Serverless has been a driving force in places, sometimes where it doesn't make much sense either. In short, Serverless, contrary to what the word indicates, is an approach to deploying small, single-objective tasks. The major benefit of developing and deploying as a Serverless is

- You only need to focus on the development aspect of the SDLC.

- You do not worry about the operations.

- The underlying platform is responsible for booting up the process, running it, handling the input and output bindings, providing the response, and cleaning up afterward.

- You can write the script in any language that your development team is comfortable with.

- If you chain multiple functions in a Serverless chain, each of these functions can be written with a different programming language, different runtime, or underlying operating system.

- You only pay for the time that your function is running.

Last, but most notable, if your function does not get executed, you do not pay a thing. Most platforms offer a cherry on top; they offer a set number of initial executions per month as free of cost. Microsoft Azure supports free quota of executions[4] of the function per month for free. In short, if you're building a small contact form for your business and expect to receive a million queries each month, Azure Functions-based deployment should give you a good starting point.

How does this apply to .NET, then, you ask?

Well, the .NET framework is a perfect candidate to write a Serverless program. The modern C# language does not require a Main method definition or all the shebang of a legacy C# program. If you compare this C# to a Python or JavaScript script, the following C# program is equivalent at a higher level:

```
Console.WriteLine("Hello from C#");
```

Read more: To read about the modern C# program and the top-level statements, check out the Microsoft documentation: https://learn.microsoft.com/en-us/ dotnet/csharp/fundamentals/program-structure/top-level-statements.

This simplifies the code that you must write, and the less code you write, the less you need to maintain. The Serverless runtime binds the inputs and outputs as per the Function definition and provides these to your method as input and collect them as an output.

---

[4] Check out the Azure Functions pricing: https://azure.microsoft.com/en-us/pricing/ details/functions/?cdn=disable.

Serverless Inputs

Let's take an example. You have a database or a table and you would like to process once data has been inserted into it. This is a legacy database that you do not want to modify or change because of the business flow that runs on top of it. However, you do need to update or process the data to take further business actions. You can add a trigger for this database to call your Serverless function.

Read more: The input bindings are attached to the source to read the events that your function will be interested in. If you define the input bindings for a database, then the underlying Serverless platform will connect to the source and listen for any changes and, as soon as there is an update, it will run the bound function. It seems as if the function is capturing the input as soon as it arrives, but in reality, it is a reactive program that listens for changes as the underlying platform pushes the new records to the function. Check out all the available functions available on Azure platform and how their bindings can be used: `https://learn.microsoft.com/en-us/azure/azure-functions/functions-triggers-bindings`.

Your Serverless has the bindings to translate the incoming data to runtime objects that your program can read. Note that in a Serverless program, you do not want to be in a position to translate and process the data yourself. You expect the data to be provided to your function fully translated and ready to be used. This means, that instead of capturing the raw database connection, you use relational mappers to capture the C# (or other languages) objects on the runtime to process. Serverless is for the "get working" approach of writing the code. Check out the examples on these Azure Storage Tables binding to the Azure Functions with C#,[5] how the table record structure has been defined in the C# program so that the function does not have to do the translation of raw data to C# runtime objects. Instead, the framework does that for you. You, as a developer, only have to read the data, perform the business operation, and throw the data back into the system.

Serverless Outputs

So, you've processed the data and returned the data from the method body. Where does it go? That is where the outputs binding come into the play. These bindings ensure

---

[5] Check the online tutorial here: `https://learn.microsoft.com/en-us/azure/azure-functions/functions-bindings-storage-table-input?tabs=isolated-process%2Ctable-api%2Cnodejs-v4%2Cpython-v2&pivots=programming-language-csharp`.

that the data returned from the process is mapped directly to the output source. A few common examples include

- Returning the output as response to the HTTP request.

- Adding the processed input as a record to a table storage; Azure Storage Tables, or other type of simple of complex database engines.

- Building a queue pipeline where the output of the process is ingested for further processing or notifications. This helps build an async pipeline of complex but less time-critical processes.

- Binding an external service that captures the result of the function and takes an action; think of something like sending an email, or a push notification.

One of the most common use cases of Azure Functions is to build an API interface for your business. You do not need to create a project, implement business pipelines or processes, to create an API portfolio.

You can create functions for supported operations around your resources. Each function is developed, deployed, and operated in isolation and gives you an ability to scale the functions that your customers consume more. Imagine you have a "pet store."[6] You create a few endpoints to support the customer operations for your business:

- GET[7]/pets

- GET/pets/{id}

- POST/pets

- PUT/pets/{id}

- DELETE/pets/{id}

---

[6] Pet store has become a common "hello world" pattern in the world of APIs, microservices, and operations. Here is an example Pet Store API definition available at the Swagger website: `https://petstore.swagger.io/`.

[7] The HTTP verbs are part of the HTTP protocol and can be used by the server-side logic to perform operations based on the verbs. The common verbs include GET, POST, PUT, DELETE, and more, and can be used to create complex structures while using the same URLs. Read more about the HTTP verbs on the Mozilla Developer Network: `https://developer.mozilla.org/en-US/docs/Web/HTTP/Reference/Methods`.

You need to provide these operational endpoints for your customers to manage their tasks to care for their pets in your business. They can create new records for new pets to automate pet care items purchase and delivery (for the sake of clarity: this part of the business is not listed in the endpoints above). Now, your operations show that the most used endpoint is `GET/pets/{id}` and the least used endpoint is `DELETE /pets/{id}` (phew!). In a typical system, all the endpoints would share the same resources. If your DELETE/pets/{id} endpoint consumes 10% of the infrastructure resources that means your GET/pets/{id} would handle a smaller number of requests than it would handle on the 100% infrastructure. A common approach to tackle this is by sharding the application and moving less used components to a low-resource region, while giving more resources and power to the bread-and-butter regions of your application. Serverless, or in this case Azure Functions, solves this by sharding-by-design. Your application is written as modules, functions, or methods that operate in isolation for a specific input. In our case, we will create one function for each endpoint. Each function would define the input bindings—since these are HTTP methods, the input binding for HTTP would be used. The input bindings would provide the HTTP request to the function body, which would read the input, take action, generate the result, and "return it." This is where the output bindings come into play. Since we are returning a response from the body, our function exposes itself with HTTP output binding which generates the HTTP response and returns it to the client.

Important: For complex scenarios, you can create multiple bindings or inputs/outputs from each Function. However, it is recommended to keep one input binding and one output binding for each function. Also, note that in Azure Functions, bindings are not triggers. A Function can have only one Trigger (remember: every binding is not a trigger), which can be an input binding; as in the example of the HTTP request, the HTTP request acts as a trigger but also provides the input binding. Timer is an example where it provides a trigger but does not provide binding. Read about the Triggers and Bindings for Azure Functions here: `https://learn.microsoft.com/en-us/azure/azure-functions/functions-triggers-bindings`. Other Serverless platforms would have their terminologies, but the concepts are similar.

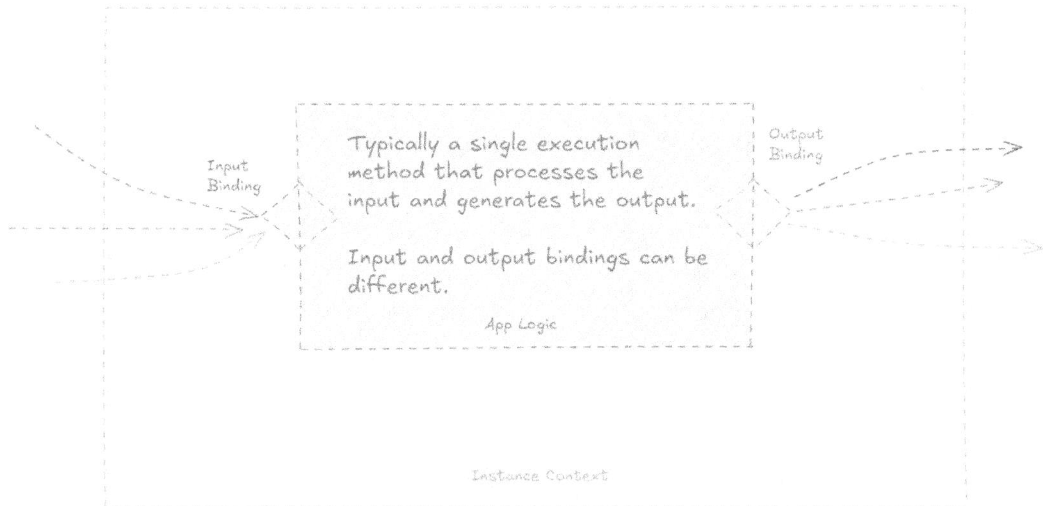

Figure 5-3. *A common execution flow for a serverless instance. The input bindings act as a trigger that run the method with the provided context. The business logic (method body) processes the input and generates the output on the output triggers. The output triggers do not have to match the input bindings; for example, you can send out an email in response to a file change in online storage folder.*

Other offerings of Azure platform, such as API Management, amplify and accelerate the value generation for your solutions.

Consumer Platforms

The apps you build for your customers to use your services, products, features, and APIs, all fall within the consumer platforms. I prefer to group the consumer platforms into three categories:

1. Web applications

2. Desktop applications

3. Handheld experiences

ASP.NET and Blazor cater to the audience for the web applications. The web applications platform, even though it works mainly on the HTTP protocol, the applications themselves run on various patterns and structures. Most projects in ASP.NET start with an MVC approach to writing the business logic, together with the data/model layer, consumed by the views layer to provide the response to the users.

.NET enables you to provide different flavors of Desktop consumer applications. Whether you would like to provide a GUI package or provide a service through CLI, .NET has it.

Fun fact: The most popular WPF framework for the GUI-based Desktop applications supports CLI command execution, so that your application code can be exposed for automation scripts/jobs to make the Power users productive.

Last, but not least, the MAUI platform supports handheld app experiences for Android, iOS, and other supported mobile platforms. While MAUI does allow developing applications for Android or iOS, it also offers delivering the experience to web and desktop users. The key feature here is the code sharing across these platforms. The more code you share, the quicker you fix problems across platforms, and the less you have to run maintenance chores across different platforms.

In short, if I must recommend selecting a platform—provided that your business does not already set a requirement here—I would recommend starting with web applications. Every user has access to a web browser, and if you can provide a mobile-first experience to your customers, they may not have to download your applications or wait for installation. Read[8] about how building your services in a mobile-first approach enables you to provide services to your customers with little to no friction.

In this chapter, we focused on the backend-services (aka, server-side). We touch upon the MAUI/UI-driven frameworks in the next chapter.

Further Reading

Microsoft's architecture center for .NET provides guidance on application, design, architecture, and practicality of the .NET framework. The Modern Web App pattern for .NET is an interesting topic: `https://learn.microsoft.com/en-us/azure/architecture/web-apps/guides/enterprise-app-patterns/modern-web-app/dotnet/guidance`, as it guides you through three important points, (1) the architecture of the application, (2) the code guidance for app optimization, and (3) configuration of additional features such as managed authentication.

The sibling page is also recommended that focuses on Reliable Web App pattern: `https://learn.microsoft.com/en-us/azure/architecture/web-apps/guides/enterprise-app-patterns/reliable-web-app/dotnet/guidance`

---

[8] Article on web.dev: `https://web.dev/articles/drive-business-success`.

Microsoft's UI platforms over the last years have usually come with a UI toolkit. We will explore MAUI in the next chapter, and it is no exception. The Community Toolkit for MAUI (`https://learn.microsoft.com/en-us/dotnet/communitytoolkit/maui/essentials/`) is a good read to prepare yourself for the next chapter.

CHAPTER 6

UI-Driven Apps

Client applications are delivered as either console or service based, or they are delivered as apps with a user-interface "UI," also called graphical user-interface "GUI" apps.

In the last chapter, we discussed the backend-services and how we can build those using .NET framework. Now, in this chapter, we will focus on the consumer apps, and learn about the platforms and frameworks provided by .NET to build the applications that provide UI for the customers. We will focus on

- Desktop apps, mainly Windows, but also how to go cross-platform.

- We will then explore the MAUI platform by Microsoft for cross-platform mobile development.

While the goal of this chapter is to uncover the UI-development with .NET framework, the objective is not to build the apps. Mainly, because this territory of the framework changes quite frequently and by the time the next framework is released, we may be looking at different architecture or code structures.

With the UI apps, the distinguishing factor between server and client apps is often very unclear. What do you call an advertising display? Is it a server-app? Is it a client app?

I think the answer is that it is not important.

The most important and notable feature is that it enables your apps to communicate the business-critical details with the customers with little to no effort. A user does not need to interact with the device to see what is happening. A real-life example can be a weather kiosk at train stations. As soon as your customers get off their trains and go to their destinations, they can review the conditions of the weather for this hour and the hours to come.

In terms of critical apps, or mission critical apps, you have screens and monitors showing **(a)** traffic trends on your website, **(b)** stock market information for the stocks that you are trading, **(c)** the number of patients in the hospital, **(d)** how many devices are connected to our multiplayer game servers, and **(e)** where are the emergency service

© Afzaal Ahmad Zeeshan 2026
A. A. Zeeshan, *Building Mission-Critical Applications with .NET 10 and C# 14*,
https://doi.org/10.1007/979-8-8688-2347-3_6

vehicles present at the given moment. The mission critical scenarios are same as any regular scenario, only that the criticality and requirements for system and platform reliability, stability, and availability are much higher. Also, any problems in system reliability or stability come with not just unhappy customers but also heavy fines.

Mission critical apps are usually built with an API at the backend. The API is controlled, developed, maintained, operated, and made available by the business producing the services.

For example, the only thing common in the UI of a driving school class management system and an emergency vehicle or ambulance management system is that they are both a dashboard with an admin panel. However, if your driving school class and instructor management system goes down for five minutes, ten minutes, or even an hour, the impact is very minimal and not fatal. While, in the other case, a lot of redundancies are put in place to ensure that the system is available 24x7, 365 days a year. This is why your driving school could be hosting the entirety of the system on a single laptop. You can host that on your laptop or tablet, and it would work just fine.

That helps us set a few requirements for the UI apps.

- The UI apps have a graphical interface that allows users to preview the information and interact with it using more than just keyboards and commands.

- Since UI apps provide a visual interface, they have a set of dependencies needed to show the visual elements.[1]

- UI apps do not always require input from the user as they are precompiled to provide the information to the user. Think of most used weather apps or stock market information.

- The environment where the UI app runs should be fault-tolerant, enabling your services and apps to reload in case of any problem. Nobody wants to see a blue screen of death on their kiosks. Do they?

---

[1] This is beyond the scope of the book, but for reference, the visual interfaces run on terminal as well. Your computer's operating system's boot hierarchy has terminal at a lower level that loads all necessary system components and then provides bindings to the higher-level user-oriented programs. You can experience this on Linux distros easily, for example, on a Ubuntu installation you can easily remove a built-in Desktop graphical interface and replace or retrofit it with any other. For more on this, read `https://askubuntu.com/questions/1451210/start-gnome-from-terminal` and `https://askubuntu.com/questions/917320/switching-between-virtual-console-tty-and-gui`.

The apps that we build and deploy using .NET can be deployed in the critical operations. A few notable examples:

- Digital information boards at train stations that update based on the updated information available.

- Digital product information and shelf price labels in supermarkets.

- Updated gas price information at gas stations. Remember: GUI doesn't have to be RGB only.

- Flight information at airports that indicate the real-time status of all the arriving and departing flights.

If we reduce the criticality of the business, we can still have various use cases and scenarios to deploy UI-driven apps.

- Home automation apps, such as smart thermostats, home controllers for lighting, and other devices.

- Productivity apps on your mobile or other platforms, such as TV or car, smart watches, and more.

Note   The most interesting one of these for me is the digital shelf price labels. In the Netherlands, I visit Albert Heijn frequently for grocery and, for the uninitiated, it is very difficult to identify when a label is digital vs. printed. The e-inks enable developers to publish real-time information to these mini-screens. This video on YouTube (`https://www.youtube.com/watch?v=t-rFj54BsDI`) "The .NET Docs Show - Using .NET to build an e-ink dashboard for home automation" by dotnet shares an example of building a home automation system using e-inks and .NET. For the story about Albert Heijn, read the news here `https://www.emerce.nl/nieuws/albert-heijn-digitaliseert-prijskaartjes-winkelschap`.

Note that in the list above we did not mention the apps that require input from a user to form a request/response pattern. Because, for a GUI app, that is not required at all. All the applications above can be services where they pull the information and make a change somewhere else without involving a human. The reason to add this "visual" stage is two-stage:

1. Keep you updated with what is happening and share real-time live updates as they happen in the system or as new data arrives.

2. Enable you to make data-driven decisions to do your job.

In this book, we're looking in the second range of the apps that you build. The apps that enable you, your teams, or your partners to take actions. To take data-driven actions. In the next chapter, we will dive deeper to learn how to connect your data to UI-driven apps. We will demonstrate how the entire SDLC pipeline can be built for a mission-critical platform from web app, the API, the UI, testing, deployment, observability, patching, security (Security needs to be included in every stage. Period.), live customer feedback, analytics, and more.

Tip: The first range of app includes Health services, personal apps, watch faces, reporting apps. This does not make these apps and these categories less critical. Take the Health services as an example. You might be wearing a smart watch today, and your Health Connect[2] services— *sorry, I am an Android person*—provide critical data such as your daily heart rate, breathing rate, body temperature, and more. This data in itself is very critical and when used correctly can lead to better health and lifestyle. But for a mission-critical app or a platform, a certain set of expectations needs to be met.

Desktop Apps

Desktop form factor is the cheapest to start with. Almost every business has a Desktop lying somewhere they use to store the information in. You may be running a barber shop, and you would have a small system in one corner to

- Put on the music for your customers to set the mood.

- Manage the appointments or waiting time for current customers.

- Handle the payments for the customers or print receipts.

- Manage multimedia entertainment, such as cricket matches—I am from Pakistan, so it's a big thing for me.

- Run advertisement on any available kiosks.

---

[2] Read more about the Health Connect services on Android Developer website: `https://developer.android.com/health-and-fitness/guides/health-connect`.

This is a true story. Not just barber shops but other players in other industries too. Back in 2015, I worked with a mobile repair shop where the owner wanted to modernize the experience of their customers. They did not want it to be a mom-and-pop shop but wanted to build and manage a customer experience journey. Their idea was to digitize everything, and my team worked with them to deliver the value. Their requests were unique to their market and region for their size but not impossible.

- Providing self-check-in kiosk to select the device information of the customer.

- Add QR-code functionality for repeat customers to find the available options that the store has for them.

- Self pick-up for the orders placed online.

- Receipt management, not just printing it but also handling refunds where needed.

Out of all these features, the only feature that was not fully contained within the Desktop app was the payment service. Every other component was fully contained within the app and was deployed on multiple Desktops across three locations they had in Italy. The criticality they had was to minimize the friction that a customer would have in buying from them. The digital world has enabled everyone to be able to operate at scale that was not possible in brick-and-mortar world.

Windows

Applications with visual element have been available in Windows since the early days, and Microsoft being a developer-first company has always enabled developers to build apps for the Windows platform. From Visual Basic (`https://learn.microsoft.com/en-us/dotnet/visual-basic/`) to modern Win UI (`https://learn.microsoft.com/en-us/windows/apps/winui/`), the one thing common is to give developers a platform to build applications that offer intractability with device peripherals. In my experience, the design languages, color swatches are just a branding touch, and they are not the super-important element for an application to be a visual app.

Windows Forms (`https://learn.microsoft.com/en-us/dotnet/desktop/winforms/overview/`), as shown in Figure 6-1, a platform released in 2002, is still actively developed and maintained. Microsoft open sourced the framework a while back to bring community on the table and let community drive a lot of aspects of the framework.

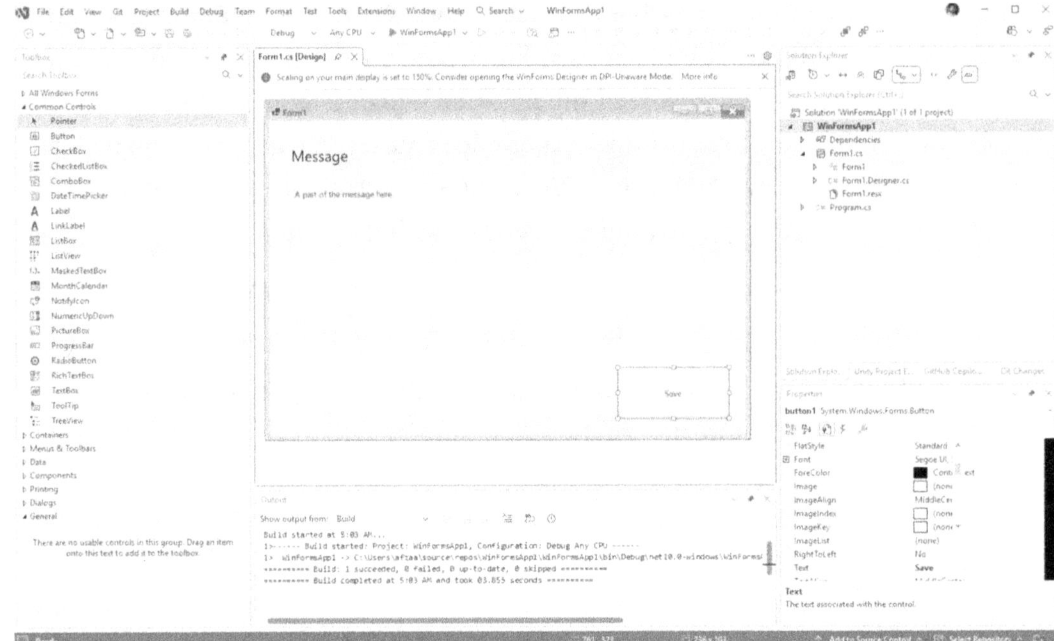

Figure 6-1. *A Windows Forms project open in a Visual Studio window. The benefit of Windows Forms is that you can quickly prototype the project by drag-and-drop components and quickly bind interactions and operations directly through the visual builder*

If you have developed any libraries that work with Windows Forms, at the time of this writing, they will continue to drive value for your business. However, the recommended approach would be to use XAML-driven Windows Presentation Foundation (`https://learn.microsoft.com/en-us/dotnet/desktop/wpf/overview/`) or WPF in short (as shown in Figure 6-2).

- While Windows Forms enables developers to prototype their apps with Windows Controls quickly, WPF offers a greater control over the UI and user interactions.

- Windows Forms supports drag-and-drop UI builder, while the same is also available for WPF, WPF provides framework and toolkits to build responsive user interfaces based on the screen factors.

- If you have never done user interfaces, WinForms may provide a simpler and easier learning curve—due to the drag-and-drop UI builder and ability to attach code to the components and their events from the builder. WPF has a little learning curve, but it pays off greatly in terms of maintainability.

- Windows Forms uses the Windows Components, and thus, depends on the Windows platform to offer responsiveness to adapt to various screen factors and interfaces.

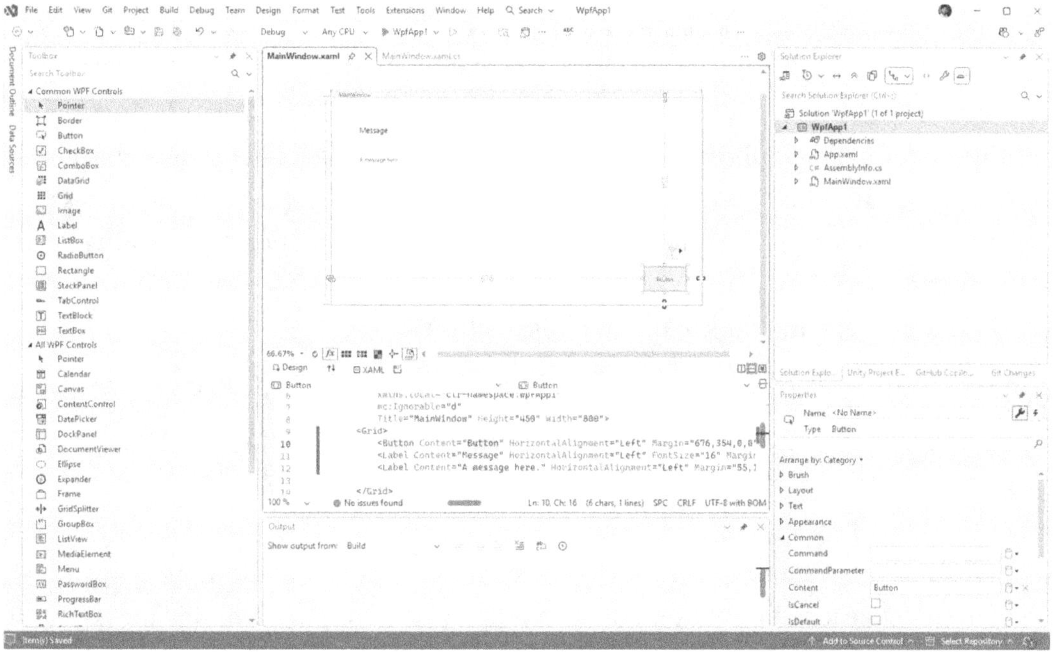

Figure 6-2. *A Visual Studio window showing the Windows Presentation Foundation (aka WPF) project. The WPF projects can be built and developed using the visual builder, or through the declarative UI (XAML). The WPF framework is modern and recommended over Windows Forms*

Moving forward, Microsoft plans to introduce the Fluent design support in WPF. In .NET 9, Microsoft introduced the support to add the Fluent UI support (`https://learn.microsoft.com/en-us/dotnet/desktop/wpf/whats-new/net90#fluent-theme`) and in .NET 10, they are doubling down on this and are adding more features, visual styles, animations, and more to bring the fresh theme to the WPF framework.

If you are starting now, I highly recommend using WPF as your Desktop template. The framework is battle-tested with more than a decade in production, enabling businesses to build mission-critical apps. This huge demand also led to birth of various community-driven and second-party partner frameworks to offer UI, controls, services, and consultancy enabling success.

- WPF apps can be bundled to publish on Microsoft Store for more security, safety, and trust with customers.

- WPF apps can be designed to work on any screen factor and size, including any resolution.

- WPF uses DirectX natively and thus can utilize the underlying hardware acceleration.

Any render-heavy application will get slow and demonstrate poor performance if you have to render a lot of pixels, or update controls on the UI repeatedly, or process tasks that take too long—I/O intensive tasks such as network requests, processing large amounts of data, etc.

There are several patterns to use to mitigate this risk:

- Use built-in patterns to avoid intensive computations. The RecyclerView in Android[3] is a prime example of a pattern that enables developers to speed up the performance of their apps without adding various libraries.

- Utilize lazy loading in your apps. Lazy loading happens when you only load the resources when the user needs them. Lazy initialization[4] is not a practice for UI development but a practice used in programming in general. With Lazy loading, you defer preparing the resources until the user actually needs to use/process them.

- Use asynchronous approach to writing the code that would take **noticeable time** to finish.

---

[3] While this pattern is from the Android development, it demonstrates a useful example where a framework feature is designed as a pattern to overcome the computation need. Read more here: `https://developer.android.com/develop/ui/views/layout/recyclerview`

[4] Lazy initialization is a first-class citizen in .NET, and enables you to build your own custom implementations on top of the native **Lazy<T>** type provided. Read more here: `https://learn.microsoft.com/en-us/dotnet/framework/performance/lazy-initialization`.

I cannot stress enough, that if your UI framework has only one thread, asynchronous programming is a sort of silver bullet that you must use.

Note   While asynchronous programming is a silver bullet, if you put one silver bullet in the chamber with regular bullets, it would not help you. You have to go all-in with the silver bullets. In other words, do not intermix asynchronous code with synchronous code. If you must, write everything as synchronous code. I recommend using asynchronous code as almost all frameworks and UI platforms offer native asynchronous features.

Cross-platform

While the Windows platform is primary Desktop target—and have as the best development experience in the .NET ecosystem. The other Desktop variants, including macOS and Linux, are also supported. The cross-platform support for Desktop apps with user-interface is provided by MAUI.

MAUI

MAUI is the next step in the life cycle of Xamarin.

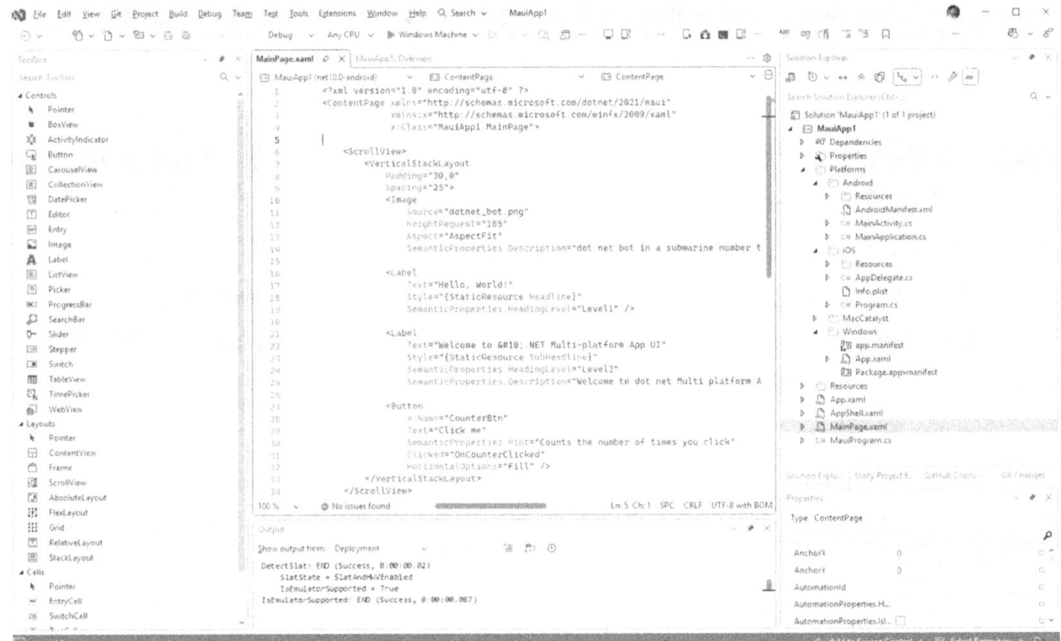

Figure 6-3. *The MAUI projects in Visual Studio do not support visual editors (for XAML), yet. But you can work with the project using XAML (which supports Hot Reload to quickly make changes and review them), and the project structure shows the cross-platform code and the platform-specific code*

The goal of Xamarin framework was to enable cross-platform and native applications to be developed from a single source, and deployed autonomously to the customers. Xamarin framework was developed and released when the Engineering world was using JavaScript-based runtimes to build the apps. These apps were prone to various problems, most notably

- Lack of type-safety. TypeScript did offer type-safety but that would mean extra boilerplate code.

- Non-standard development tooling. IDE was owned by one provider, the build tools were provided by another, online services—logging, authentication, etc.—were provided by another.

- Bloated apps, because the transpilation and underlying runtime would be a huge binary artifact.

- No native interoperability with the underlying platform features.

- Advanced platform functionality would often be locked behind a paid license or a different license agreement; for example, not available to commercial projects.

Xamarin leveled the playing field. Xamarin enabled the Engineers and organizations to write the native cross-platform applications using C#. While ability to write code in C# is not a massive performance improvement, but the ecosystem of C# language, .NET framework, and the development tooling brings a plethora of improvements.

- LINQ[5] in C# enables making data-related queries work like a charm.

- Building event driven systems is a language-first feature for C# and .NET framework.

- C# language is feature-rich, advanced, and since the last four versions it has been introducing features that make it possible to write C# programs as scripts.

- The thread-safety features, newly introduced System.Threading.Lock[6] type provides more control over synchronization.

- Built-in asynchronous programming makes C# a perfect choice for UI-driven apps, where writing unblocking code is crucial and a frozen UI drives customers away from your business.

- Native interoperability makes it possible to write code that can communicate with underlying runtimes and platforms.

On top of these, the development tooling—the main Visual Studio or Visual Studio Code—is a development experience put on steroids. The entire tooling ecosystem and chain is owned[7] by Microsoft. Microsoft tailors the entire software development life cycle,

---

[5] Read LINQ documentation on Microsoft website: `https://learn.microsoft.com/en-us/dotnet/csharp/linq/`.

[6] Read the reference here: `https://learn.microsoft.com/en-us/dotnet/api/system.threading.lock?view=net-10.0`

[7] By "owned" I mean it is developed, distributed, and maintained by Microsoft. Various components are contributed by community and partners, too. There are multiple bodies that drive the conversations at the .NET table, including .NET Foundation. But .NET is a product of Microsoft and Microsoft drives the adoption and development of the platform. In the past, .NET Framework started as a proprietary software development framework for developers and has evolved into an open-source framework that it is today.

from version control system, build and development tools, deployment tools, and observability tools to provide the best development experience to the customers. The customers are not just developers—yourself, including myself—but also the organizations who must build these platforms. If a platform is difficult to build upon, test, or deploy or even patch in case of an emergency or an incident, no customer would want to invest their time in developing for it.

Design

The top required feature or capability for a UI-first application is for the output to be supportive on a wide range of screen and resolution factors. You can call it responsiveness of the application. The design of the application requires understanding of the deployment platforms.

- Is this application going to run a handheld device?

- Does the application show a lot of charts or graphs?

- Do we need the user to provide us with input?

- Is the input text-based or visual?

- Or do we need the user to interact with complex visual components and controls?

  - Are we expecting big screens or small screens to be the default?

- Do we offer screen orientation changes?

Most frameworks offer controls in one manner or another. Even if you do not want to use a feature or provide a layout design today, it is best to check if such a feature is supported in the framework of choice. The images above (e.g., Figures 6-1 and 6-2) show the Toolbox on the left side of the window. The Toolbox window shows all the controls that are available to you to use in the current project. The controls can be native, built-in, or they can be community or third-party installed.

While .NET is used to target Windows platforms mainly, with MAUI, you can also target Android, macOS, and iOS devices, too. In these instances, MAUI does offer scalable UI designs that work on all screen sizes and factors.

Develop

You will find a lot of content on the social platforms where the app development starts in a UI-design platform, such as Figma, or Dribbble. These are amazing platforms, and they offer a huge amount of inspiration for the UI designs. If you want to start with the development of the application, these platforms offer insights into designing the apps that scale.

The development starts with a basic template. At this point, it is important to avoid a "fancy" template for the project which shines and whistles but doesn't scale. For apps that require to be supported beyond the year of inception, use a template that has been available for a while and is planned to be maintained for a few years ahead. Microsoft has made several templates available and taken them back a few times, so be careful, if you would like to scale the apps past just the MVP.

The WPF and WinForms templates are part of the .NET CLI templates (`https://learn.microsoft.com/en-us/dotnet/core/tools/dotnet-new-sdk-templates`) and can be used directly from the terminal window (as shown in Figure 6-4). For MAUI, you need to use the MAUI SDK and MAUI extension for the VS Code or Visual Studio. The templates are shown when you create a new project.

```
PS C:\Users\afzaa> dotnet new list
These templates matched your input:

Template Name        Short Name                   Language   Tags
-------------------  ---------------------------  ---------  ----------------------------------------------------------------------------
.NET MAUI App        maui                         [C#]       MAUI/Android/iOS/macOS/Mac Catalyst/Windows/Mobile/Tizen
.NET MAUI Blazo...   maui-blazor-web              [C#]       MAUI/Android/iOS/macOS/Mac Catalyst/Windows/Blazor/Blazor Hybrid/Mobile/Tizen
.NET MAUI Blazo...   maui-blazor                  [C#]       MAUI/Android/iOS/macOS/Mac Catalyst/Windows/Blazor/Blazor Hybrid/Mobile/Tizen
.NET MAUI Class...   mauilib                      [C#]       MAUI/Android/iOS/macOS/Mac Catalyst/Windows/Mobile/Tizen
.NET MAUI Conte...   maui-page-csharp             [C#]       MAUI/Android/iOS/macOS/Mac Catalyst/WinUI/Xaml/Code/Tizen
.NET MAUI Conte...   maui-page-xaml               [C#]       MAUI/Android/iOS/macOS/Mac Catalyst/WinUI/Xaml/Code/Tizen
.NET MAUI Conte...   maui-view-csharp             [C#]       MAUI/Android/iOS/macOS/Mac Catalyst/WinUI/Xaml/Code/Tizen
.NET MAUI Conte...   maui-view-xaml               [C#]       MAUI/Android/iOS/macOS/Mac Catalyst/WinUI/Xaml/Code/Tizen
.NET MAUI for ....   maui-aspire-servicedefaults  [C#]       MAUI/.NET Aspire/Cloud/Web/Web API/API/Service
.NET MAUI Multi...   maui-multiproject            [C#]       MAUI/Android/iOS/macOS/Mac Catalyst/Windows/Mobile
.NET MAUI Resou...   maui-dict-xaml               [C#]       MAUI/Android/iOS/macOS/Mac Catalyst/WinUI/Xaml/Code
.NET MAUI Windo...   maui-window-csharp           [C#]       MAUI/Android/iOS/macOS/Mac Catalyst/WinUI/Xaml/Code/Tizen
.NET MAUI Windo...   maui-window-xaml             [C#]       MAUI/Android/iOS/macOS/Mac Catalyst/WinUI/Xaml/Code/Tizen
Android Activity     android-activity             [C#]       Android/Mobile
Android Applica...   android                      [C#]       Android/Mobile
Android Class L...   androidlib                   [C#]       Android/Mobile
```

Figure 6-4. *You can also use the dotnet new list command to preview all the available project types available for the .NET CLI. The list generates a lot of output, this screenshot is truncated to fit the space here*

I always consider "testing" to be part of the development process. Testing is your own responsibility to ensure software quality. If you or your team are pushing the testing to someone as a responsibility, you are welcoming a storm of issues. I recommend using xUnit to test the apps. XUnit platform is a little less verbose with less boilerplate code. Microsoft uses xUnit to test their EF Core framework (`https://github.com/dotnet/efcore/tree/main/test/ef.Tests`), which is a topic of our next topic.

Writing the code and writing the test cases that validate the code, in terms of the business requirements is a very big topic. In the next section "**Software Quality**" we will revisit this topic to talk about testing strategies for our applications.

Deploy

Okay, so you have developed the apps, tested it, and I mean really tested it. Manually, with linters, static analyzers, and QA it to ensure everything is as we are expecting[8] it. Now is the time that we build the application and distribute it to the customers.

Build the App

Modern practices of Engineering and DevOps put too much emphasis on continuous delivery state of the software. The continuous integration and continuous delivery are often broken down into two separate phases.

- Continuous integration being the phase where the code is committed to the central repository, repeatedly, multiple times a day by several contributors.

- Continuous delivery being the part of DevOps where you compile and build, scan your code using analyzers, run tests, validate business requirements (BDD, etc.), and ensure the software is in "deliverable" state.

Continuous delivery separates the DevOps pipeline in two manners. On the one hand, it enables teams of any size, any code-submit velocity, and any branch-strategy (trunk-based, vs. master-based, or other Git, GitHub, or GitLab flow) to continue to be able to push the code to a central repository with minimal conflicts. Second, it runs the checks on the quality of the software in parallel.

---

[8] Remember, no amount of software testing will lead to 100% bug-free software. Software crashes in production. Come to terms with this, and own it. You are only in control of ensuring that a software doesn't stay down for too long. Especially since you are building a mission-critical application, your industry, customers, business requirements, contracts, and legal requirements would define how long your software can stay down for. Sometimes, to build a better brand, you need to keep the "downtime" lower than expected. But, to repeat, your software will go down and you will find bugs in production, so do not slow down aiming for perfection.

One major problem with this approach is that it slows down the feedback to the developer. If your code is already merged with the main branch where other contributors also collaborate, then it is already too late. You should review the code, run automated testing, and provide feedback to the Engineer before the code is merged in an upstream branch.

Aim for quick and short feedback loops to the developers and Engineers. In other words, if having two separate pipelines does not really speed up anything or enable the Engineer to make quick changes or decisions, go for just one step; continuous integration is enough to also run the automated testing.

Pro tip: Do not solve the problems you do not have today.

Distribute the App

Distribution of the app happens in two ways:

- Customer pulls a fresh copy of the software.

- You push the fresh copy of the software.

It is as simple as that.

Keeping in line with our scope for the book, ask yourself:

- If your mission is to ensure the customer is using the up-to-date software, push the update.

- If your mission is not to hinder the operations of the customer, have the customer pull the updates.

Let's talk about some examples of these scenarios.

Several financial apps, such as crypto wallets, multiplayer games, etc., all expect the customers to be using the latest version of the software. This is to ensure that everyone has the same opportunity to "win."[9] Various opportunities exist for the apps, such as over-the-air updates (also known as OTA updates, as shown in Figure 6-5), which are often available through marketplaces or stores (App Store, or Play Store), and are also

---

[9] Winning in the general sense of achieving the mission. If the latest version of the game provides better FPS, of course, you are more likely to win the game. For other crucial apps, often, winning could mean being less vulnerable to bugs and critical exploits that hackers and malicious users can use against you. Not being hacked or vulnerable is a win-win.

supported by various frameworks.[10] When you broadcast the updates, there can be client apps that are not updated. This can be for various reasons, the client simply has stopped the app from being updated, the store was not updated, the user's region has not received the update yet, and more. You need to be mindful to allow the customers to access the platform with restricted capabilities where the impact can cause damage to other customers.

---

[10] NetSparkle is an open source software update framework. Read more about it here: `https://github.com/NetSparkleUpdater/NetSparkle`. It supports WPF, WinForms, and community-driven platforms.

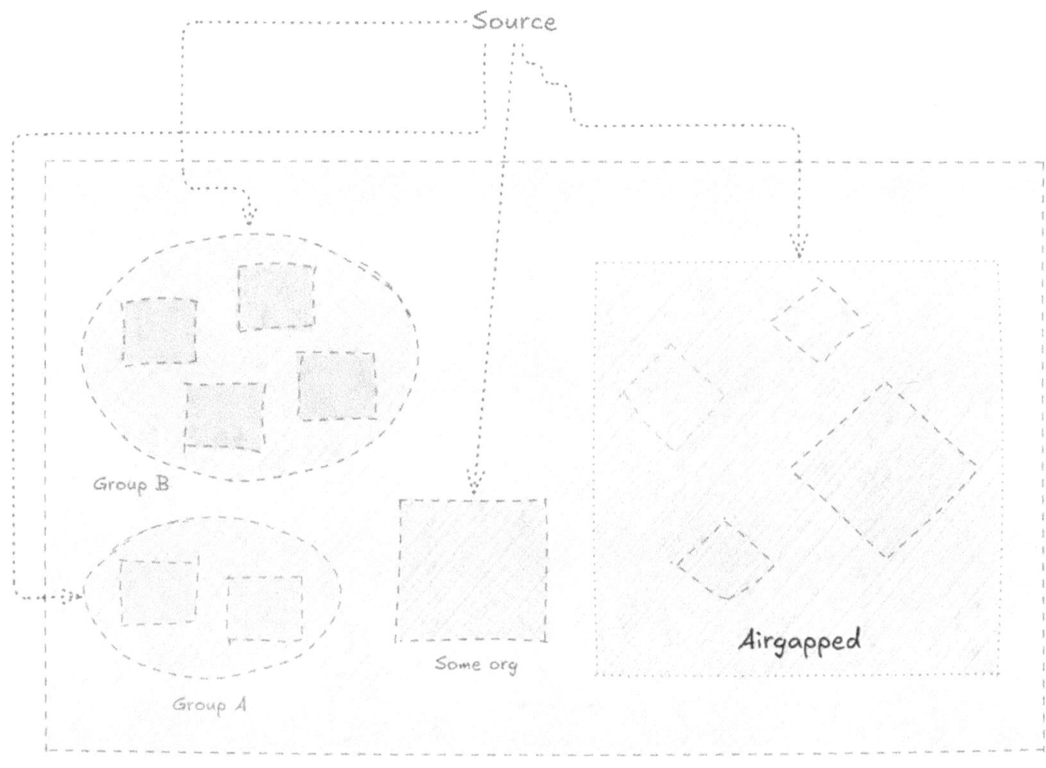

Figure 6-5. *The fan-out updates are usually helpful when you want to make sure everyone accesses your services with the same version. The services can be deployed to beta or tester groups (such as Group A) and other customers can also download the apps on their own. The OTA updates such as from the stores or your website can make sure the services are reliably delivered. In such scenarios there can be cases where some groups cannot access the latest version (such as Airgapped clients), they are often prompted to download the latest version before accessing the services.*

On the other hand, if your software is run on critical components of your customers, such as warehouse, POS terminals, etc. Or other critical locations such as ICUs, or train stations, then you should not touch their operations systems and apply the software update—regardless of how quick and easy the update is. Even the OTA updates. You may end up bricking[11] the system or breaking the flows of your customer's customer. You allow the customers to hold on to the updates until the time that they are ready to apply them (as shown in Figure 6-6).

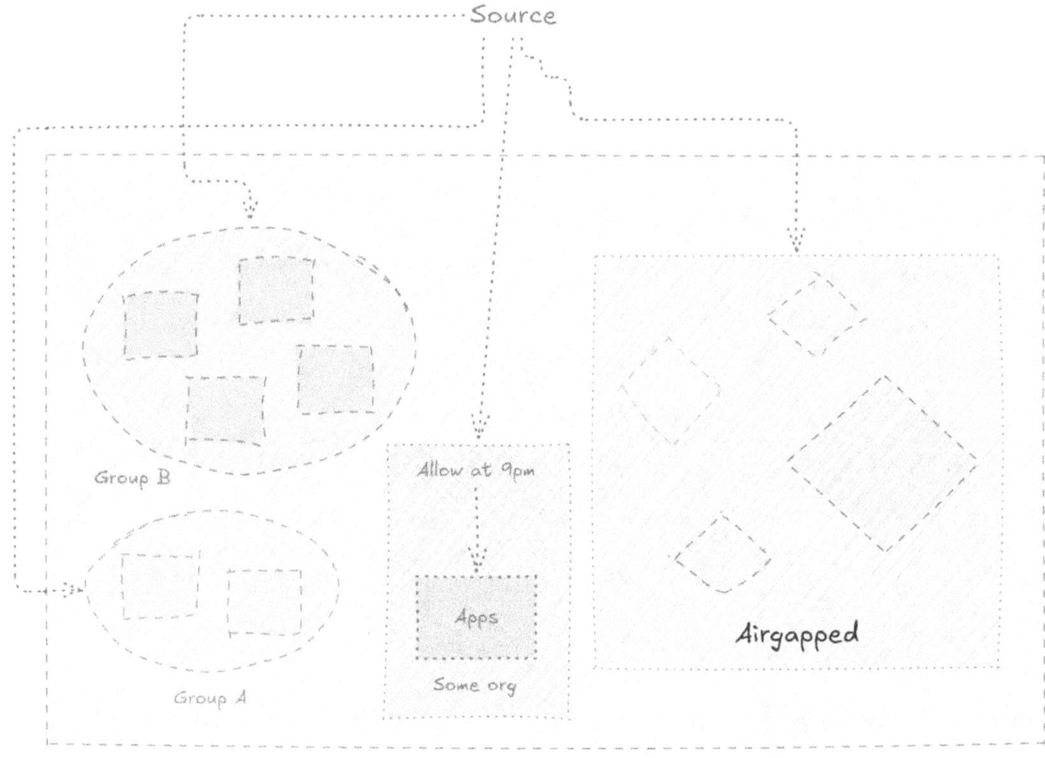

Figure 6-6. *The update flow continues as in fan-out for regular updates, but here you allow your customers with a restricted or critical workflow to be able to hold on to certain updates until they are ready to apply them. You will have to manage and execute the logic.*

---

[11] A bricked system is a device, such as a phone or a Desktop/laptop that does not function because its firmware or kernel has a fault. This happens because of a corrupted firmware software, or data, and when it is not easy to repair or start the device.

Detect

Ohkay, well, you got it. You got your app distributed to the customers and they are using it. But are they actually using it? Are they even opening your app? Are they visiting the page that your team spent three weeks refining, developing, testing, and fine-tuning? How long does it take for your app to load on low-power devices? All these are valid questions. This is where we now need to build a continuous feedback loop with our customers through our application.

Typical observability patterns apply to the backend systems, frameworks that run on servers to serve millions of users. For UI-driven apps, you do not really need to measure the performance in terms of **latency**, **throughput**, or **response time** because all of this will depend heavily on the device itself—which is out of your control. A normally optimized application will work and function decently on any device. But, optimizing the app code any further for a very small audience will not yield dividends in user experience; unless that is your primary audience. But again, if your primary audience is using a low-powered system then perhaps such an optimization should not be a "good-to-have" but a strategy to focus on low-footprint frameworks.

The important metrics to track in the UI-driven apps on the consumer-side are

- User behavior

- User geographics

- App usage

This information helps your product teams devise better approach to handling the customer experience—which is the goal here. The app usage includes, but is not limited to

- How long users interact with your app in the foreground?

- Which pages or screens are used the most?

- Is there any path that the users take in your application?

    - Is that the intended path for your users?

- Which versions of your software are most used or currently installed?

- Which platforms or operating systems are most used?

- Which screen factors or orientations do your users prefer the most?

- What is the application's current user retention rate?

On top of these, various platforms and analytics services also include crash reporting, performance monitoring—for on-device resource allocation and consumption—and custom events and metrics tracking to track customer business logic.

To better understand your customer, and who they are, the user behavior and the user geographics help translate the user audience into user personas.

- Where are your customers located?

- What languages do they speak?

- Does your product target a specific gender, or age group?

In specific cases, you can also learn about the usage pattern of your application. When do adults use your application? In the morning or in the evening? Who uses your application the most? Based on this information you can further devise reports to identify which group is a part of the paying customer group. For non-paying customers, you can also define which groups are more likely to pay and then identify the frictions that these groups experience in paying. Your teams can then devise either marketing campaigns to offer better subscriptions, free trials, or better support plans.

We will revisit the specific details on observing the applications and different services and platforms available to developers to analyze the user behaviors and application performance in Section #6 "Observing Apps."

Beyond MAUI

MAUI has been driving very slowly over the past few years. There are various players in the market that provide the features of cross-platform development, with a developer experience that is at least at par with MAUI, if not better. If we are to scope within the .NET, then community-led and second-party frameworks such as Uno platform or Avalonia enable .NET developers to use the .NET frameworks—WPF, Xamarin, Blazor— to develop and deploy cross-platform apps to non-Windows Desktop environments.

To learn more about these platforms, read about them on their own dedicated websites:

- Uno Platform (`https://platform.uno/`): Build cross-platform .NET Applications in record time

- Avalonia (`https://avaloniaui.net/`): Build apps for every device using .NET

> **Note**   The above list is not a recommendation and is not sponsored in any way.

Microsoft open sourced[12] WPF framework along with various other Desktop development frameworks and platforms. This push enabled the adoption of various second-party platforms such as those mentioned above. I still believe the XAML-based UI controls need to be open sourced, and to be supported on non-Windows platforms too. That is what Avalonia XPF (`https://avaloniaui.net/xpf`) enables developers to do. You can build your existing Windows-based WPF apps and deploy them to macOS or Linux environments.

Another big challenge that we have today is since WPF is Desktop-first platform, the UI and the Controls are not mobile-friendly. Currently, UI-driven apps are supported for Windows, so if your business needs to deploy UI apps to non-Windows environments, the developer experience will take a toll.

All in all, the .NET platform enables developers and teams of all sizes to be able to design, develop, publish, and monitor the applications with interfaces. Whether they are for Desktop, mobile, or custom interfaces. The community-driven initiatives also provide great productivity when it comes to developing and releasing services.

In the next chapter, we will learn how .NET enables us to manage and control the data in our systems, whether they are generated through customer interactions or through partners.

Further Reading

The Windows development platform has come a long way and supports a variety of design and development practices. For the UI apps, read how you can make your Desktop apps responsive to support various screen and resolution factors: `https://learn.microsoft.com/en-us/windows/apps/design/layout/responsive-design`.

Since we will discuss how to manage and control the data in our apps, it is a good moment to review the data flow in UI apps, especially in the context of .NET apps. You can read these resources on Microsoft's website: `https://learn.microsoft.com/en-us/dotnet/standard/parallel-programming/dataflow-task-parallel-library`, and `https://learn.microsoft.com/en-us/dotnet/desktop/wpf/data/`

---

[12] Read more about the announcement here: `https://blogs.windows.com/windowsdeveloper/2018/12/04/announcing-open-source-of-wpf-windows-forms-and-winui-at-microsoft-connect-2018/`.

CHAPTER 7

Working with Data

A program, application, or a service is created of two things: logic and data. Even if your application does not take input from the user and only shows the information to the end user—think of a weather app—it still works with the data coming from the API to help the user perform their operations or get the information they need. Today, data is considered the equivalent of crude oil. But, you cannot just keep the raw oil without processing it and turning it into value—gold.

In this chapter, we will learn about

- How does .NET provide data management services?

- What is a DbContext, and how can you create one?

- How to query databases and data sources without creating DbContext?

Let's start this chapter on a lighter note. For this initial section, let's scope out the user inputs and data coming from the consumers, for now. The programs that we are left with are the applications that provide information to the users without asking for input.

Side Note   Okay tech savvy, even in an API, the user is providing and passing data—the page to request, the product ID, or the session information that includes browser details, IP address, etc. But for the context, we will consider the incoming data as user input such as email address for newsletter subscription, credit card details for order placement, address information for delivery information.

You do not need to use any external .NET packages or extensions to build data integrations. Your console or web applications can natively interact with external and internal data and data sources. While .NET does provide a large set of native data types, in a majority of the cases, they are enough to perform your jobs. For example, a lot of

© Afzaal Ahmad Zeeshan 2026
A. A. Zeeshan, *Building Mission-Critical Applications with .NET 10 and C# 14*,
https://doi.org/10.1007/979-8-8688-2347-3_7

cases that require numerical operations can be performed with the native data types—int, float, double, decimal, etc. For very limited scenarios, where your operations or values in these operations outgrow the native data types and containers, you may choose to use BigInteger.[1] The BigInteger is used to work with arbitrarily large values, signed values, meaning they do not have to be positive-only.

Read more: The built-in (`https://learn.microsoft.com/en-us/dotnet/csharp/language-reference/builtin-types/built-in-types`) data types in .NET provide a data type for every use case. While they are mostly limited to a minimum 8-bit size—including the Boolean value, which is 1-byte—and grows up to 8-bytes for some data containers, such as long or double, they ensure compact structure, proper initialization with default values, and often get allocated on stack to optimize memory management.

The largest number of features and types for data manipulation, generation, and management is available in the **System.Data** namespace in the .NET platform. The System.Data namespace provides all the services, components, classes, and abstractions around the data management. The System.Data namespace includes the classes and interfaces that represent the database connections, database tables, records, and specific fields. Since System.Data is very low-level, it also provides us with the data translation options to capture and read the database values and translate them to the .NET types. Note that the System.Data namespace does not only provide the data connectors for relational databases but various file types—such as Microsoft Excel, or Microsoft Access, etc.

In short, System.Data provides you controls to

- Connect to external data sources using the data source drivers and connectors—such as SQL Server, PostgreSQL, Microsoft Excel, or OleDb.

- Make queries on the data source to fetch the data and perform data creation operations.

- Read the data returned from the data sources and map them to either a default .NET runtime structure or parse the data and translate to a suitable type. This is important, for example, when working with DateTime.

---

[1] Read about the BigInteger here: `https://learn.microsoft.com/en-us/dotnet/api/system.numerics.biginteger?view=netframework-4.8.1`

- Manage the resources used by the data sources, and the runtime objects to represent the data available in the data sources.

- Read each individual column and process the value, or update the values in queries.

- Manage the security, for example, SQL Injection prevention.

- Create and manage the transaction execution, rollback, and commitment.

For any application that requires data access, these are the underlying required actions that every application needs. And since System.Data provides the native constructs from the .NET platform and the C# language, you use the best practices natively, out of the box.

Before we move to the object-relational mappers to learn the abstractions provided by .NET platform to speed up the development, here is an example of the data types (`https://learn.microsoft.com/en-us/sql/connect/ado-net/sql-server-data-type-mappings?view=sql-server-ver17`) mapping between the .NET runtime types and the database data types.

Object-Relational Mappers

Writing and managing the SQL queries for basic to intermediate scenarios is easy and can be done. A good architecture should reuse the queries based on the use cases. For example, a basic CRUD-layer for your services should be responsible for preparing and executing the queries and thus this layer should contain the entirety of the SQL commands in string formats. Each method takes care of translating the runtime objects—the class definitions and structures—into database types that get added to the database tables. As the application grows, you see yourself repeating this simple task.

- Add an extra column to be fetched from the database table.

- Add the parsing to read the value from the record row and then add to the .NET type.

- Add any try...catch blocks or conditional checks to ensure the data remains consistent.

You continue to do this for every added or modified column. If you modify the column in the database, such as changing the data type of the column, you must also translate the change in the class definitions. Changing the class definitions is a breaking change, mostly, and must be addressed. Another breaking change, or at least a crashing change, is when you remove a column but do not remove the code that uses it.

Tip   Since removing a column from the table breaks the code unless you remove the code that uses those columns, it is often a good practice to mark the column as obsolete in the code before removing it from the database table. Once the application stops using the column, you can then safely remove it from the database table.

Adding these changes is not enough. Since you are applying this change frequently, and other Engineers would also be contributing here, it is a must to add test cases. The test cases ensure that your latest changes do not break the business logic, and the customers can continue to operate and get their jobs done. That said, just a simple change of adding a column, modifying a column, or changing the data type of the column requires multiple steps of a job to be done before you can safely deploy the next version to production. Oh, and we have not even spoken about different relational engines. What if you—*due to business reasons or technical challenges*—want to change the underlying relational database engine? From SQL Server to PostgreSQL, or to MySQL? You must change all the code, suddenly and that is not a good application of the Engineer's time.

This is where object-relational mappers come into the scene. The entire scope of the object-relational mapper is to enable you to write the database schema in your code[2] and let the framework handle the data persistence in the underlying store.

Entity Framework Core[3] (hereafter abbreviated as EF Core) is the native object-relational mapper, part of the .NET platform. EF Core is open source, lightweight, and has an excellent development experience. It gets the job done—no matter the size of the

---

[2] This approach is the code-first approach in object-relational mappers. In code-first approach, you write your application's data layer that annotates various objects and defines the database schema. The object-relational framework then generates the database schema, applies the migrations to the database, and handles the data conversion across the database/runtime boundary to provide a simpler development experience.

[3] https://learn.microsoft.com/en-us/ef/core/

job. EF Core today supports more than 20 different sources[4] that each offer a benefit of its own structure and size. Some most notable data sources include

- SQLite

- PostgreSQL

- MySQL

- MongoDB

- Various NoSQL modeled databases:

  - File-based

A lot of these data sources are community-driven or third-party and are maintained by communities or third-party service providers. Regardless of the ownership, the EF Core data sources all provide the same behaviors, features, experience, and tooling, because the entire ecosystem is built on top of the dotnet CLI.

The object-relational mappers (hereafter mentioned as ORM or ORMs) enable your developers to focus on the business requirements and business opportunities while the ORM handles marshalling responsibilities as well as ensuring that the data is consistent across the runtime and database boundaries.

Important: We will not reteach the concepts of an ORM, or EF Core, as it is quite an old technology with a lot of improvements and new features added with each new .NET version. If you are new to .NET or EF Core altogether, the best resource to get started with EF Core is the official documentation for the EF Core framework: `https://learn.microsoft.com/en-us/ef/core/`.

The major benefit of ORM is to translate the data between sources and sinks,[5] but it also ensures good practices are applied. When you are writing the queries to fetch conditional data—the data with the WHERE clause—or when you are inserting or updating the data, if you do not properly sanitize the SQL queries, they are prone to a very well-known SQL vulnerability called SQL Injection.[6] Unsanitized SQL queries can, at the bare minimum, expose your data to the attacker, and in the worst case, completely

---

[4] `https://learn.microsoft.com/en-us/ef/core/providers/?tabs=dotnet-core-cli`

[5] The term source meaning the data sources, and the sinks meaning the controllers or code that uses the sources to process the requests and provide responses.

[6] SQL Injection prevention is the SQL best practices 101. Read more about this very common but extremely dangerous vulnerability here: `https://owasp.org/www-community/attacks/SQL_Injection`

destroy all the data in your database; of course, the minimum and worst case depend on your business and what is more dangerous.[7] Other common benefits include

- Security vulnerability patches and live updates for any zero-day vulnerability.

- Mapping of all commonly used data-types, such as Unicode, to-and-fro between the database and the runtime.

- LINQ can be used to write compiled queries that get translated to SQL queries.

- Usage and definition of index and other database-concepts from the .NET code, the models.

- Managing and applying the database schema migration and ensuring the right model of the database is available on the production.

- Creating the database seed directly from the runtime objects, that get created on the database for testing or development purposes.

- Tracking the changes and the creation of new objects in the runtime before they get created in the database table.

  - You can set custom parsers to process the fields before submitting them to the database, such as setting custom IDs based on your business-logic and not having to rely only on the database engine.

- Run the queries in asynchronous manner, meaning, the result of your query is provided in awaited manner, freeing up your UI thread from being blocked by I/O operations.

The default object-relational mapper in .NET is Entity Framework Core (for .NET Core, and Entity Framework for the legacy .NET framework). We can create the connection between the code and data layer through a DbContext.

---

[7] In many regulated industries, data leaks are worse than data deletion. For example, if you lost the data of your customers, it would mean you have to recapture the data and that would definitely frustrate the customer but not lead to any fines. However, if the data of your customers was exposed to external parties then you could be exposed to various hefty fines. So, consult your legal team on what should be allowed and what must be mitigated.

Install Entity Framework Core (hereafter EF Core) from the NuGet[8] package manager (`https://learn.microsoft.com/en-us/ef/core/get-started/overview/install`), and then create a new DbContext in your project. You can create a new class and then inherit it from a DbContext object. Here is an example of a DbContext that contains tables, and providers configuration to be used to initiate the connection with the data source.

```
namespace TodosDesktop.Data
{
    public class TodosContext : DbContext
    {
        public DbSet<TodosDesktop.Models.TodoList> Lists { get; set; }
        public DbSet<TodosDesktop.Models.Item> Items { get; set; }

        protected override void OnConfiguring(DbContextOptionsBuilder
        optionsBuilder)
        {
            optionsBuilder.UseSqlite("Data Source=database.db");
        }
    }
}
```

This code is shown in full context in Figure 7-1.

This code demonstrate how to create a DbContext (note the inheritance does not require any type assignment, or special attributes here) and then you define tables using DbSet fields. DbContext reads these types and generates the tables for your migration. The OnConfiguring method is used to provide the default connection string. In this instance, we are using SQLite, but you can use other data sources as well.

Multiple DbContext

The database connection is defined as a DbContext within the application. You create the context, connect to it, run queries and operations on it. In ASP.NET Core,

---

[8] EF Core supports various databases and each database has its own unique package that you must use to configure the support. Check out all the official and community-supported packages here: `https://learn.microsoft.com/en-us/ef/core/what-is-new/nuget-packages`.

for example, you can use dependency injection to allow the framework to create the instances of the database connection and provide to your controllers to handle the data requirements of the requests. DbContext can also take care of the connection pooling. EF Core pools the "context connection instances" so that instead of creating a new instance the next time a request requires the content, it provides this reset instance to the request.

One of the biggest challenges is using multiple database connections or different database contexts in the same controller. EF Core and .NET enable you to create as many DbContext in a project and use them in a single controller—the limitation is of course from the infrastructure resources, such as memory, network, database I/O, etc. The more important element to pay attention to from the Engineer's perspective is the domain and the control over the database. In Figure 7-1, you see an example DbContext created in a Desktop app project. The DbContext type is available for all major .NET platforms and not just for web projects.

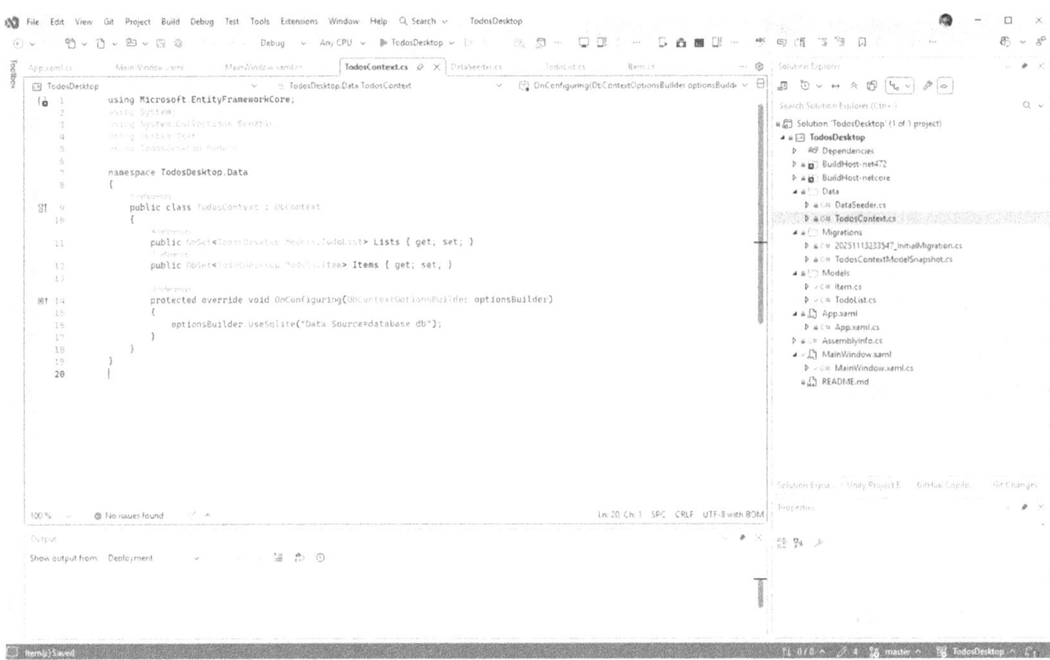

Figure 7-1. *This image shows a DbContext that uses SQLite database for a Desktop app that allows users to create and manage todos. The goal of this project is to demonstrate using and reusing the SQLite databases for local data storage and WPF-based UI generation for the application*

DbContext is a database connection that provides the baseline for the controllers to connect to the database and fetch the resources. While the data can travel and be transferred across the DbContext boundaries, it is often a good practice to keep a single DbContext per "service" offered. If you have an ecommerce web application, it is recommended to keep a single DbContext for the store items and the orders placed, but for the payments and data analytics, use a different DbContext. The product catalog, discovery, and order placement happens in one flow while the data analytics, market research, user behavior analysis happen in a different flow. Why should your controller maintain access to both these DbContexts?

One step above, often the DbContexts are shared between different customers and tenants. Multitenancy[9] is possible with EF Core, but a lot of caution needs to be taken. In my experience, that is the perfect example of "just because you can do it, doesn't mean you should do it." Today, creating a new database instance is just a 5-minute task. If you have multiple customers, never, I repeat, never, share the data for multiple customers in the same database. You are one bad code logic push away from exposing the data of one customer to another. And, if you happen to be in a highly regulated industry, then a few hours away from a huge fine and brand trust loss.

Micro ORMs

If using the ORMs is not possible for your applications—for example, you are using a Serverless platform, or nanoservices; the example of this can be found in the minimal APIs—then you can use Micro ORMs instead of a complete suite of ORM. The promise of Micro ORMs is the added benefit of data translation and marshaling but without the complexity of internal data state management, custom data translation, framework-driven encryption, or other dependencies. Micro ORMs do not generate the SQL for you. This is the biggest challenge for backend Engineers using Micro ORMs; you are expected to know the SQL.

```
var query = "SELECT * FROM Books WHERE AuthorID = @authorId";
var book = await connection.QueryAsync<Book>(query, new { authorId = 1});
```

---

[9] Read about the multitenancy here: `https://learn.microsoft.com/en-us/ef/core/miscellaneous/multitenancy`

To learn more about Dapper, consult the documentation (`https://www.learndapper.com/`), or check out this GitHub project: `https://github.com/DapperLib/Dapper`.

In the end, Micro ORMs are not the best of both worlds but they sit between both worlds. They give you a platform in-between both:

- Micro ORMs use the resources created by the underlying System. Data services, or database connection providers.

- Micro ORMs stop right before elevating the experience to generate the SQLs, cache the requests/responses, validate the SQL, or perform security operations such as SQL Injection prevention.[10]

The choice of using the Micro or regular ORMs depends on how much support you need, and how much complexity you want to include in your project.

Applications with Data Usage

Let's hold the data source data usage, and focus on the data within the application. .NET is a very mature framework and has a tool for everything. But how do you make sure that you are using the right tool for the right job? Let's talk about that scenario now.

Since .NET 6, Microsoft has been adding a lot of constructs to the C# language and the .NET platform in general. Most of these changes were breaking changes.[11] Today, the changes are mostly syntactic sugar around the basic constructs of the language or framework.

Using Record Types

C# is an object-oriented language and every class—in some cases even structures—that you define contain more than just the data. They contain internal representations, states, methods, events, delegates, etc. to make it an "object." Sometimes you just need a "data

---

[10] SQL Injection is possible with Micro ORMs such as Dapper, but it depends on the SQL that you write. If you write a prone SQL, it will be exploited.

[11] Read about the breaking changes in the .NET 10: `https://github.com/dotnet/roslyn/blob/main/docs/compilers/CSharp/Compiler%20Breaking%20Changes%20-%20DotNet%2010.md`

container"; a data-transfer object. You can create a record-type, or mark class types or struct types as records. So, when should you use the record types?

- You want to declare a type-container to transfer the data between objects and services.

- You want to simplify the equality check across objects.

- You want to create copies of objects and mutate basic fields and properties with a simple language construct; the "with" clause in C#.

- You would like to deconstruct the data into fields to read and process the data.

- You want to use the built-in formatting to print the data; this is useful for terminal or console-based apps.

Creating a record is not like creating a class, and vice versa. The record types can be created in-line with all the properties and fields declared with the constructor.

For Engineers coming from other languages, such as Python, Tuple is a great way to return multiple data values from a method. If used adequately, a Tuple type looks and feels just like a record.

Important: I believe the best way to return multiple data objects from a method is by creating a unique data-container that returns the entire object needed by the caller. Returning tuple, or (mis)using the out parameter(s) is not a natural flow of data between caller and callee. This is extremely important when you are developing a library that will be used by other Engineers, or even other organizations. Developer experience is the most important element of your programs. If no one can understand the logic or reasoning behind your program's structure, it needs to be revised.

Field Keyword

Before C# 14, to customize the behavior of the getter/setters, you needed to define an extra member field to store the value.

```
public class Engineer {
    private string _department;
    public string Department {
        get => _department;
        set => _department = value;
```

```
    }
}
```

With the field keyword, you do not need to create an extra member field, instead, you can use the compiler-generated field, which is available as "field" keyword to simplify the class definition.

```
public class Engineer {
    private string _department;
    public string Department {
        get => field;
        set => field = value;
    }
}
```

The example is basic, but you can further customize the behaviors and the login in these setters or getters, without having to generate an additional member.

Using LINQ

LINQ is very big differentiator for C# compared to any other programming language. LINQ provides a very strong language construct to process, parse, and slice the data available to your programs. While LINQ does not guarantee speed or performance boost, the PLINQ (Parallel LINQ) does enable Engineers to spread the compute across multiple cores or threads to run the processes in parallel.

The primary benefit of using LINQ is that you process and operate on the data sources—in-memory, database, file-based data—using the C# language. LINQ query syntax is just like SQL, but provides complete type-safety and can be compiled down for speed optimization on the runtime.

LINQ goes hand-in-hand with the .NET method-based query syntax. This means, that the following codes are the same:

```
// Using query expression syntax.
var linqBased = from item in items
            where item.Name == name
            select item;
```

Now, compare this to the method-based syntax:

```
// Using method-based query syntax.
var methodBased = items.Where(item => item.Name == name);
```

The output would be the same. Let's take a quick example of how to process and crunch the data,

```
var data = new List<string> {
    "John", "Doe", "Dane", "Johan", "Joe"
};

var theJs = from name in data
            where name.StartsWith("J")
            select name;
Console.WriteLine(theJs.Count());
```

The output of this program will be 3"; because three of the records start with a capital J. Here, the code takes the data and operates a conditional on the data source to validate which records meet a certain condition.

As mentioned already, in most cases, LINQ does not provide better performance. The main benefit shows up when your queries and the data sources grow complex. LINQ makes it easier to

- Applying the query conditions on various data elements.

- Sort the items in a natural syntax—sort by ascending or descending order.

- Group multiple sources together—each source can be a table, thus, providing an SQL-like JOIN experience. Do not take it wrong, the method-based approach also gives the same flexibility, but it is more complicated.

- Process and generate the data from relational databases, XML sources, or in-memory/in-process data.

- Create data projections to read the relevant data from the sources and skip the data that is not needed or required.

- Apply .NET methods and extensions to the data sources and data on the runtime.

- Break the larger data sets and run operations on them in a
  parallel manner.

While PLINQ is not a pocket-sized MapReduce, it does enable you to process
multiple files and get the results in a faster time—given that you have multiple
processors for the program to use. The last but most important feature of LINQ is the
dynamic generation of the queries on runtime—which is what powers EF Core.

Note   LINQ is very powerful, very complex, and thus, very complicated. It is not
possible to dive into the LINQ feature of .NET in this book, since we have a lot more
to cover. But I highly recommend reading an in-depth guide on LINQ. LINQ is like a
Swiss army knife and would deliver high returns, if used accurately.

The data is created through the user interactions, and C# and .NET provide us
with controls and bindings that we can use to handle the user interactions. In the next
chapter, we will study how .NET supports events and interaction management.

Further Reading

It is very easy to write a logic that processes hundreds of records quickly, but to scale
your application to process millions of records quickly, you need to architect your
application efficiently. The .NET guidelines around Entity Framework Core are useful
to make sure you get the performance you need. Start here `https://learn.microsoft.`
`com/en-us/dotnet/framework/data/adonet/ef/language-reference/query-`
`execution` and continue through `https://learn.microsoft.com/en-us/dotnet/`
`csharp/linq`.

DbContext is a complex and expensive resource in your application. Recreating the
resource for every new request is a very expensive operation that it will bring down your
entire application infrastructure. The best way to handle this resource is by handling the
lifetime of the DbContext and reuse it throughout your application logic. Read about the
life cycle of the DbContext in a .NET application, `https://learn.microsoft.com/en-`
`us/ef/core/dbcontext-configuration/`, to best utilize the resources used to create the
DbContext.

CHAPTER 8

Handling Events

Events happen all the time. A program handles events that are happening within a process or a thread but also the events that are beyond its control or scope—network events, CPU events, user input events, timers, garbage collection, and much more. While you cannot handle all the events—*errors in an underlying native library, or when system goes out of memory*[1]—you do receive notifications, and your program can use this information to make an informed decision.

In this chapter, we will focus on

- Reactively handling the user interactions and internal program states

- What is a blocked state of the application, and what are the limitations of single-threaded applications

- How to scale the events and messaging systems?

This chapter will set some ground for out-proc (this term means any processing or storage that is outside the context of the process, such as out-proc memory meaning the data that is not scoped and contained within the process-context and can outlive the process life cycle) data transfer and events broadcast.

Events are a natural part of the program that mutate and change the default execution path for the code. C#, Java, C++, and almost every programming language executes the code sequentially. Yes, yes, there are methods, loops, and other structures that change the execution sequence of the program, but in the context itself, the program executes sequentially. In this chapter, you will learn about the events that you must focus on and pay close attention to, and the areas that are perhaps too advanced or complex for certain use cases.

---

[1] Read about OutOfMemoryException in the documentation: `https://learn.microsoft.com/en-us/dotnet/api/system.outofmemoryexception`.

One important aspect to note is that event-driven programming or development is different from handling events. While you do handle events and run the programs and processes reactively in event-driven manner, but just attaching a handler to events and notifications in your program does not make your app event-driven. If you are evaluating the event-driven approach to development, or you need event-driven approach because of a business requirement, you can skip to the last section in this chapter where I talk about using external event storage and notification systems to implement. Also, at this moment, it is very important to mention that the events are different in

- Backend Systems

- UI-driven apps

The application and development of events and handling the events in an efficient manner has a different requirement and a different benefit.

First, let's talk about the backend systems. In a backend system, you have a server that is serving potentially hundreds of thousands of clients per minute. The server can execute the code very fast, as long as the code is available to execute. If your code depends on a resource that is not available or needs to be prepared for the server to read and process, that is wasted time. In technical terms, this is called "blocking." In a blocking, a thread or a CPU process is waiting for a resource to be available for the code to continue executing. Some examples include fetching a large file, or reading an input from a peripheral that takes more than a few milliseconds to respond. This is poisonous for the server-applications. For every unavailable resource that your CPU waits, it makes a client wait—*in practical scenarios, it makes a few hundred clients wait.* This blocking call breaks the performance and efficiency of the server and does not help your business. So, be very careful, never use a blocking call in a request handler—unless there is no other option. And when there is no other option, try to add one.

Backend Engineering has moved toward non-blocking calls, and non-blocking APIs and SDKs that enable your apps to "not wait" for the unavailable data and resources.

- You use async/await keywords that help break the execution flow when a resource is not available and return the control flow to the breaking point once the resource is made available.

- .NET platform provides asynchronous variants for various methods and functions; especially around the `System.IO.File` methods.

Secondly, on the UI-driven apps, even though you do not have multiple users relying on the app at the same time. But, you do have multiple threads running to provide the interface and the services to the users. The biggest challenge with the UI-driven apps is the frozen UI. Your UI apps have main thread, and this thread is used to update the UI controls. This thread is responsible for making sure that the UI is interactive, and that the form fields are accepting the input, etc. You use this thread to update the UI or interact with the app. You also use this thread to pass the data from underlying system to update the UI. All the user input comes from this thread as well. And, naturally, you are allowed to make calls to any services or methods, and these methods can be blocking. For example, if you are reading big files into the memory, then you definitely are making a blocking call. If you are making an HTTP call, you would be blocked until the HTTP response is ready. While this does not cause the problems like a server dropping a few clients, because it does have only one client using the app at a time. But it does frustrate that one client. A lot.

This frozen-UI behavior happens when your app's primary thread is busy handling—or as in case of server-side apps—waiting for a resource to be made available. That is why blocking calls in the UI are also very bad for the performance. When the app is frozen, to the end user it is almost as if the app has crashed even though it is working on the operation requested.

In short: blocking calls are bad for your programs because your CPU waits for the resources to be made available to your CPU before it can continue. During this period, your program cannot continue processing the requests or providing the services.

This is where events come in. When you make a request to capture a resource, instead of waiting, you can just "raise a flag"—loosely speaking—to be notified when the resource is ready. Once the resource is ready, your process is notified to continue executing from where it left off. That is in essence the "asynchronous programming" paradigm. The concepts of the async programming are not very complex, but also not very simple; if you want to dive deeper into the concepts and approach, consult the documentation on Microsoft Learn (`https://learn.microsoft.com/en-us/dotnet/csharp/asynchronous-programming/`).

Program-Space Events

First, let's focus on the events that are generated from within the program or the events that we generate ourselves. The example of the events generated by program include (but are definitely not limited to)

- Memory management events such as garbage collection

- Diagnostics of the system, such as out of memory

- Interactions with the program interfaces—the APIs

- Control flow and changes in the flow state; CTRL + C

- Resource processing, loading assemblies, just-in-time compilation, etc.

- Threads and thread pool events for synchronization or concurrency

- Task management and asynchronous program control flows

The program handles these events for you and provides handlers to attach to. The most notable one being the task management with the async/await keywords—more on this in a minute. But the less obvious ones include diagnostics events, such as memory management or garbage collection. You have the controls to trigger these events but also handle some of these events. The OutOfMemoryException is an example of where you can handle such events and scenarios to handle a safe exit for the application or recover from the system—by removing the unnecessary resources and objects from the memory.

The native C# events and delegates are useful constructs for internal communication. However, with modern programs, complex system architectures, the event and delegate do not play that major of a role. Unless you are building a UI-app, where the events are raised and consumed internally. For server-side apps, consider external event and message queues, which is the last section in this chapter.

Async/Await Nature

The async/await keywords are not new to the .NET ecosystem, and since .NET 8 onward there have been various additions to the platform that make async/await usage with IEnumerable (IAsyncEnumerable) and yield keyword much simpler. Thus, enabling the asynchronous generators.

As mentioned earlier, the most important areas where you must use async/await include

- I/O bound operations where your program must have for the resource to be made available. This includes HTTP resources, large files, or any operation that take double-digit milliseconds to finish.

- CPU bound operations, where the operation would take a long time. However, note that in some cases, it may be better to use native threads instead of the Task API. Also, instead of threads in the ASP. NET Core apps, consider changing the architecture of the data flow here. If you end up creating threads for each request, you will end up consuming too much memory and thus performing worse than ever.

My favorite is to keep the async/await for the I/O bound operations and for the CPU bound operations just keep old school. If there is one thing you should take away, it is, don't mix async/await with the synchronous flow of the code. If you are using async/await, you must do it through the entire pipeline.

- So many times, an asynchronous operation is not awaited, which ends up creating mixed or unwanted changes in the system. There was a scenario where one EF Core method call was not awaited, and that led to very undesired results—not joking.

- In the Tasks API, the flow is managed by the contexts, and these contexts schedule the tasks for re-entry. This context is called SynchronizationContext,[2] which prepares the result expected by the expression and then allows the control to flow again.

It is worth mentioning, overdoing async/await leads to no benefit at all. Note that while C# and .NET optimize the results of the compilation process, a lot of syntactic sugar leaves out bad parts on the generated intermediate code (also known as IL). When you are defining the Controllers in ASP.NET Core, it is very useful in maintaining a good performance by making the action handlers asynchronous so that you can perform database queries, I/O operations asynchronously. But if you are not doing any I/O heavy

---

[2] Read more here: `https://learn.microsoft.com/en-us/dotnet/api/system.threading.synchronizationcontext`

operation, or if the data is already available and you are just returning the response back to the customer then adding the async/await keywords do not add any value. In fact, they do trigger compiler checks and green squiggly lines in the IDE.

Events from the Beyond

A program must be able to handle events that are not part of its natural execution flow—*where natural execution flow means the procedural calls and a routine user input.* This includes, but is not limited to kernel calls, system interrupts, etc. While your program continues the execution of the program code, the program does receive signals from external sources, such as kernel. These signals are often also called interrupts. These interrupts are not always sent to stop the program; such as SIGKILL or SIGSTOP, etc., which are sent out to the program to end the execution of the code. A few examples of such events could be

- Input from the peripherals

- System shutdown or system reboot

- Premature exit for the program; also called control-break

- I/O updates and signals

These events are important for your program to know what is happening outside its own scope and context. Signals and interrupts are an important part of the Linux-based systems, while on Windows .NET platform provides you with exceptions to stop the execution of the code. Starting with .NET 10, the platform will not wrap the underlying signals and provide a .NET signal, instead, you can read this blog (`https://learn.microsoft.com/en-us/dotnet/core/compatibility/core-libraries/10.0/sigterm-signal-handler`) that talks about the impact of this recent change and any actions that you may need to take.

A good example of importance of this input and signal handling is with your apps that are running in containers. In Docker, for example, you must handle these inputs—and on Docker, they are raised several times. In Docker, since the resources can also be restrained, the same application that functions just fine may start to misbehave.

Note   In Java, they have two classes denoting problems in a program execution. Exception and Error. The difference stands in checked vs. unchecked problems. Error is a type of unchecked problem, and the program is less likely to recover from it, such as OutOfMemoryError. The language gives hints to the programmer that this problem falls within the space of an Error and thus proceeding to handle the situation may lead to a bigger problem. Exception, on the other hand, notifies the program of some logical problem such as ArrayIndexOutOfBoundException, which can be easily corrected using the size check of the ArrayList<T> or List<T> instance. I wish C# had that. 😊

Messages—Serverless, Message Bus, and More

When your application's architecture grows complex beyond a few classes that you can count on your fingers and when the consumers of the app grow beyond the size of a cricket team—mainly just you and your friends, internal event management makes less and less sense. For the most obvious reason, internal events are stored in-memory, and you lose them if your program crashes. For two, you cannot communicate internal program state efficiently with another program—I am not talking about JSON or other data-interchange format, I am talking about the intermediary state to be shared across the program for event management, storage, and processing. That is why, using the right tool makes sense.

Azure Queue Storage provides a flexible queue message storage mechanism to enable distributed, asynchronous processing for our events, messages, and data. Azure Queue Storage provides a rather basic implementation of a queue, mature systems are also available. Every cloud platform offers these services and platforms that are ready for scale of 10 users to 10 million. The benefit of using a cloud platform is that you will be building the storage and processing plane within the single platform. If you build the queue on the Azure Storage platform or if you use an MQTT-compliant queue storage, you can connect it to the Azure Functions to handle the events and process them as they arrive.

Read more: for events in the server-side processing, it is very important to maintain the sequence for the events, occurrence of the events, and maintain a log for them. At-least-once and at-most-once are two common requirements for every queue system, which ensures that your message has a pattern of consumption applied to them. A queue that guarantees that your message will be processed at-least-once is useful in implementing a notification system, where you make sure everyone acknowledges the message and receives it once. For consistent systems, or where your systems process further information, at-max-once (also called at-most-once) is used to ensure that a message is only processed once by the consumer. Another protocol which is more complex is the exactly-once, this guarantees that a message will only be processed once, but would definitely be processed. To learn more about these message semantics and guarantees, check out this blog from Confluent: `https://docs.confluent.io/kafka/design/delivery-semantics.html`

Kafka, RabbitMQ, etc. are all systems that provide the message brokerage to store the messages/events, transmit them, or log them internally for audit or replay. Now, I am not saying you need these systems. But if your application is complex enough to generate millions of events per day and you want to efficiently scale your app as the demand and consumption grows, it is better to prepare your app.

.NET is a major platform, and the SDKs and APIs are available for all these message management systems.

One thing I'd like to mention here, do not misuse the system for things that it is not meant to solve. Use the message brokers to broker the messages, and not mimic other protocols, such as a database for data persistence or ticket management system. Trust me, I have seen these and they do not scale, and they do not support the business growth and development.

The events and notifications are a very simple way of handling and updating the state of the program or system. In this chapter, we explored the events and notifications constructs available in C# and .NET. We also took a look at the asynchronous way of writing the code and handling the events and state. If there is one thing that you must take away from this chapter, it is to stick to one paradigm of writing the code. If you are using asynchronous code, stick to writing the asynchronous code and do not intermix it with the synchronous code.

In the next chapter, we will dive into the topic of realtime applications, their support in .NET, and how to build and distribute them.

Further Reading

To go advanced, it is usually a good idea to start at the beginning of the topic. Learn about how .NET handles and serves the events and events programming here: `https://learn.microsoft.com/en-us/dotnet/standard/events/`.

For various complex systems and apps, .NET and Microsoft has a common approach: make things observable and allow consumers to observe the changes and take an action. Read more about the observer pattern on: `https://learn.microsoft.com/en-us/dotnet/standard/events/observer-design-pattern`.

CHAPTER 9

Real-Time Apps

Events happen, all the time. A program handles events that are happening within a process or a thread, but also the events that are beyond its control or scope—network events, CPU events, user input events, timers, garbage collection, and much more. While you cannot handle all the events—*errors in an underlying native library, or when system goes out of memory*—you do receive notifications, and your program can use this information to make an informed decision.

In this chapter, we will build on top of the learnings from Chapter 8 and learn how to build the applications that keep consumers on top of everything that they care about, and it does so very quickly that we can name it "real time." The focus of this chapter is to learn about

- The communication modes and how consumers can stay up to date.

- How does .NET ecosystem provide a framework to build real-time applications?

- What does community have in store for real-time communication and high performance?

We just learned there are several types of events in our programs and several methods to keep our apps up to date. When we focus on the client-side of the applications, then we see a requirement for near-live or real-time information flow. This pattern is not an either-or concept, rather it is a style of communication. The nature of this communication differs from traditional request/response model in that the communication loop is always open, and the messages travel as needed. The clients need to handle the response as they arrive, and the server maintains an active open connection—*yes, this does mean that the server resources are consumed aggressively as more clients connect.*

While both the server and the client play an active role in this communication, this pattern is required on the client-side, to enable the client-apps to work reactively. The servers are already working in a reactive manner; they provide response to the requests that you send. For the clients to also receive the updates as they happen, the server-side technology often called "push notifications"[1] is implemented to communicate the updated data for the clients to render the most up to date information for the customers to see.

Polling vs. Server Push

To distinguish between how real-time apps work, it is important to note the difference between the traditional and modern way of communicating the changes. Imagine that you are working on an application shows the live or most up-to-date information to the customers. A few examples include

- A financial app that shows the live information about the current stocks.

- A sports viewing app that must show the live scorecards and updates.

- News application that must show the live updates as they are happening.

- A traffic app that must show the live information about traffic congestion.

The amount of real-time is also very important. Does your application require updates every second, or does it require an update every minute, or even hour? Every day does not count. In some cases, every hour is also very late for real-time standards. Consider a traffic or bus/train station sign board that updates every one hour. If the train is delayed by 10 minutes, you will not see the change until the sign board updates; which will happen every one hour. If you are watching a cricket match—especially between India and Pakistan—you cannot wait for another minute, you need to get the

---

[1] In the space of web applications, the push notifications are the notifications or updates sent from the server. But the concept of real-time communication is broader than just the web applications. They work on the client apps such as Desktop apps as well.

live updates. Right. Now. For such scenarios, you need to fetch updates at least every 30 seconds. Or 10 seconds. Two ways to implement this fetch/query mechanism are shown in Table 9-1:

1. Polling

2. Server Push

The polling method is used by the client to make a request to the server to fetch the data. The same shebang, you pass the URL, provide credentials—if needed, and server responds back with a response. Repeat. To continuously fetch the live data—cricket match scores, train schedule, stock prices—the client needs to continuously send the requests. The server receives the request and provides a response back to the customer. Now, think about these requests happening every 10 seconds, for every client. Every HTTP request contains the HTTP headers which is extra payload that needs to be transferred with every request—including cookies, browser details, etc. Not only does this consume extra resources, it also adds a lot of boilerplate and verbose data that travels between server and client that does not make any sense beyond the first request.

This is where the server push technology comes into the play, as shown in Figure 9-1. If your client only needs to make the first request and then always expects the response from the server, then you can use the WebSocket protocol to establish the communication between the server and the client. This way, the client connects to the server and servers then uses the socket-based communication channel to continue to send the updates to the client. Prime examples of this protocol include chat applications. For a chat, you must send the message to the consumer immediately—typically within a few milliseconds, like 10 ms, or 20 ms, for a good customer experience. Over a WebSocket protocol this happens immediately with little overhead headers and does not need to close and open connections.

Table 9-1. *The use cases of HTTP polling and WebSocket protocol for communication*

Use-case	Polling	WebSocket
Connection	Uses HTTP-based connection requests that each contain their own headers and must be remade for every new update.	Uses WebSocket protocol to establish a connection and leave it open to receive or send the updates between client/server.
Message format	HTTP is based on TCP protocol and follows a specific message format as packets, and must include headers for message and client identification.	WebSocket updates can be a stream of bytes and updates that can be of arbitrary size and structure. Your server and client must then translate the data into processable format.
State	The requests are by design stateless, you provide information that makes a request "stateful," such as cookies or browser agent information.	While the protocol does not maintain the "identity" or purpose of the user beyond the connection detail, it is possible for the server to attach fields and attributes to each connection object.
Concurrent users	Each request happens between a single client and the server and other clients do not share the same request.	Servers can maintain an active list of listeners via their WebSocket connections to send the updates to multiple consumers at the same time.
Use case	HTTP requests are best for stateless, one-requests, where a client does not need to fetch updates frequently. HTTP requests are also stable and they use the best of TCP protocol to ensure guarantee in the message structure delivery.	Use the WebSocket when you need to establish connection once and send messages frequently at arbitrary intervals. The protocol enables the communication to happen both ways, client can send messages to the server as well.

For further read on the difference between performance of each protocol, check this article on Medium: `https://blog.feathersjs.com/http-vs-websockets-a-performance-comparison-da2533f13a77`.

Important: Before WebSockets, an extended version of polling was used, called "long polling." Long polling was a similar version as WebSockets but worked on the HTTP protocol, and server kept the connection open using the Keep-Alive header (which can be configured based on the request or the client). It worked in a counter-way, because instead of server sending an update, it was client sending a request and waiting until server had something to send back and then repeating the cycle. The modern WebSocket protocols leave the connection open for two-way communication without the need for additional HTTP requests.

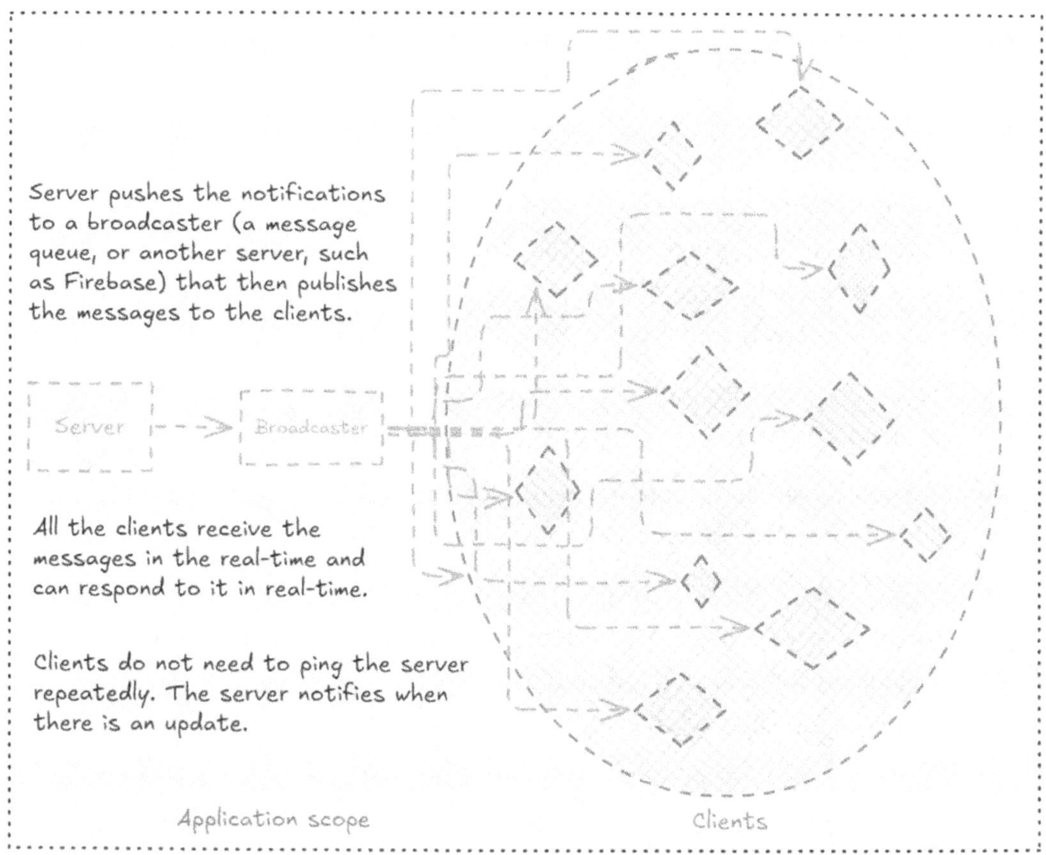

Figure 9-1. *The server sends the notification to the clients through a broadcast server (often hosted on the same server process) to make sure the clients receive the updates instead of clients having to ping the server repeatedly. While this sounds complex and expensive, it is mainly less expensive in terms of compute, because opening a port on any device is possible and a client can leave the port open for longer periods to allow the server to send updates*

ASP.NET Core SignalR

The WebSocket implementation in ASP.NET Core is available as SignalR,[2] an in-house, out-of-the-box solution to implement real-time updates to the clients. SignalR, while a wrapper around the native WebSocket protocol, provides various features and benefits that would be difficult—to say the least—or impossible to implement in a small team. Since SignalR and the underlying protocol is open source,[3] you can implement the clients in any language—they do not have to be written in C# or .NET. SignalR clients work across a plethora of languages, platforms, and runtimes, including Android, iOS, and of course the web browsers.

SignalR works differently from just a native implementation of WebSocket-based data transfer, in that it supports remote-procedure calls. You can define the methods between the server and clients, and both parties can make calls, pass parameters, and receive response—*typically as another event*. A common behavior can be

- Server exposes a method Connect(username) method that connects an incoming client to the server.

- Server exposes another method JoinRoom(roomId), and this method adds the current connection—caller—to the list of the clients connected to a specific channel.

- Client exposes a method MessageReceived(roomId, message) that is called by the server to transmit a new message—which can be an update, a message, or an event.

- Server exposes a method LeaveRoom(roomId) that can be used by the clients to remove themselves from the rooms that they no longer need to receive updates for.

In the list above, I intentionally avoided the function signatures to focus on the intention and not the complication of the function. The method names indicate that this is a chat application or updates application where users can connect to the rooms and

---

[2] The official documentation for SignalR can be found at: `https://dotnet.microsoft.com/en-us/apps/aspnet/signalr`

[3] You can read about the protocol and its implementation on GitHub: `https://github.com/dotnet/aspnetcore/blob/main/src/SignalR/docs/specs/HubProtocol.md`

leave the rooms when needed. The users will receive the messages and process them—based on the room, either show them on the UI or keep them in the store to render when the user opens the channel for the room. If you see through the layer of realtime, this is an example of remote procedure calls where server and client both are making calls on the remote machine and triggering a function with some parameters.

The major advantage of using SignalR is that Microsoft offers pre-built hosting services for SignalR Hubs on Microsoft Azure. So, if you see your application being throttled due to the infrastructure limitations, you can always migrate to the Azure instances for SignalR which provide not only improved performance but are also highly available and geo-replicated for better performance across the globe.

Remote Calls with gRPC

gRPC[4] is a protocol designed and developed by Google for remote procedure calls across remote data centers and remote apps. While SignalR also supports remote procedure calls, gRPC is yet another protocol that offers speed, performance, and cross-language support to develop the RPC frameworks. SignalR and gRPC are both supported in ASP.NET Core and the development experience for both is equivalent, even though the development approach and the deployment of both are different. One of the major benefits of gRPC is that you can generate the clients from the protobuf[5] files. While SignalR uses the methods and functions defined in .NET (on the backend) and the JavaScript (or similar) client-side technologies,[6] replicating similar behavior in other languages—such as Kotlin, for example—would be a complex task if an existing community package is not available.

One benefit of gRPC is the performance as it works over HTTP/2, meaning it can multiplex multiple calls through one single connection—avoiding extra resource consumption. GRPC generates fully async/await-compliant code that can be used to

---

[4] Learn more about the platform on `https://grpc.io/`

[5] gRPC uses Protocol Buffers to define the communication standards, the structures of data, and their relationship between each other. Server and client use this structure to communicate and transfer the data between each other. Read more about Protocol Buffers here: `https://protobuf.dev/`

[6] .NET provides out-of-box support for JavaScript, Java, and Swift as client-side runtimes and languages, read more here: `https://learn.microsoft.com/en-us/aspnet/core/signalr/client-features`

run the methods and calls asynchronously without blocking the caller. ASP.NET Core supports gRPC out of box and thus you can create a new gRPC service with ASP.NET Core just by creating a proto file. Figure 9-2 shows an ASP.NET Core project that has a proto file and a project configuration file enabling gRPC:

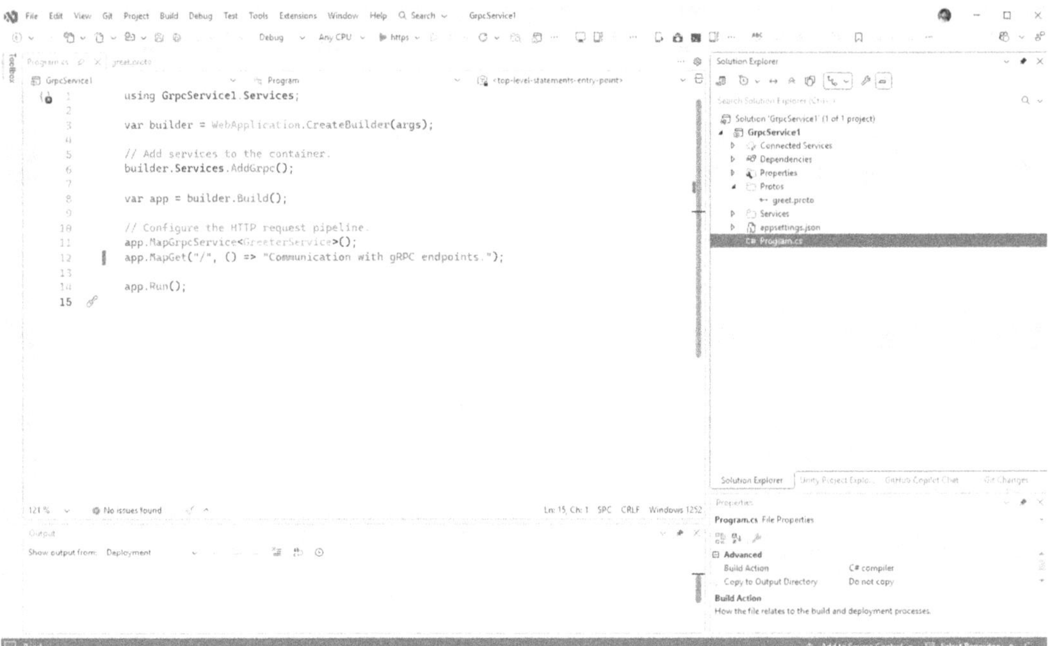

Figure 9-2. *A gRPC-supporting ASP.NET Core project that configures gRPC to read all the local proto files and generates a service hosted in ASP.NET Core instance*

One big challenge with gRPC is the debugging element of the content. Unlike JSON or XML, gRPC data is binary and is not human-readable. That said, gRPC is a well-tested suite of platform, so I would trust Google to ensure the basic functionality works as expected.

Hosting Infrastructure Practices

Real-time apps and the servers consume a lot of resources on the infrastructure side. The biggest challenge comes from the scale perspective. The scalability of the server resources is very complex. One of the reasons is that the clients and connections are tied to the server-instance. Redis is used to scale out the instances but that requires sticky sessions. The more clients you have, the higher resources you require and ultimately that requires a big infrastructure investment.

To learn more on how to scale the SignalR service, read the documentation on Microsoft Learn.[7]

For scalability, Redis is not the only provider, various other platforms are also possible. NCache is one example. Instead of just scaling the service based on a caching layer, it is better to plan how to allow the connections to come, how long should the client maintain the stale connection before the server closes the connection, and also, what should your sharding policy be. Should all the customers connect to one central server in EU? Or, can you make the customers connect to different regional servers? Azure SignalR service manages this behavior in that the service manages the scale automatically and balances the connection—in a non-sticky-manner—growth. Lastly, today, it makes sense for teams to hand out things they are not building for business. If you are already managing an infrastructure, perhaps continue maintaining and managing your servers in your own data centers. But if you are not in a data center business—let someone who knows how to do it, do it.

In the next chapter, we will tie all this together by exploring the security considerations for .NET projects and custom solutions built and developed on top of .NET platforms.

Further Reading

SignalR framework is the default real-time framework for .NET and .NET applications, but gRPC is also taking a huge chunk of consumers from the .NET platform. The main reason is that gRPC clients are available across platforms (whereas SignalR is mainly limited to either C#/.NET or JavaScript). Another reason is that gRPC is extremely fast because of Protocol Buffers. If you would like to explore the gRPC platform, check out the documentation for that: `https://grpc.io/docs/guides/`.

It is a good moment to build a gRPC project and do a "hello world." Use this tutorial to create the service and learn about the development experience for gRPC with ASP. NET Core: `https://learn.microsoft.com/en-us/aspnet/core/tutorials/grpc/grpc-start?view=aspnetcore-10.0&tabs=visual-studio`.

---

[7] `https://learn.microsoft.com/en-us/aspnet/core/signalr/scale`

CHAPTER 10

Adding Security

Security is like a fine fractal. You can zoom over it at any scale. It is applicable to business practices, and code, and infrastructure.

In this chapter, we focus on connecting the existing frameworks and platforms available in the .NET framework. The application of security across the .NET applications is so vast that instead of a single chapter, this is explored in chapters ahead in the book.

For me, the topic of Security is as important and vital as the intention of our software. The amount of focus and importance we give to the Security of our software-development life cycle truly shows how seriously we take our products. This is why, I do not consider Security as an aftermath, or a QA's job, or "we will observe the behavior in production." Security has to be the second nature of your Engineers, Product Managers, Testers, all the way down to the single lines of code that you write, the products and libraries you use, CI/CD processes that you use, and the final product you ship.

As already mentioned, Security is not just checking for vulnerabilities in the software code that you wrote but it goes beyond that single method. Security should be considered throughout the software development life cycle, and lessons learned in the later stages must be used to update the processes in the earlier state, as shown in the Figure 10-1.

© Afzaal Ahmad Zeeshan 2026
A. A. Zeeshan, *Building Mission-Critical Applications with .NET 10 and C# 14*,
https://doi.org/10.1007/979-8-8688-2347-3_10

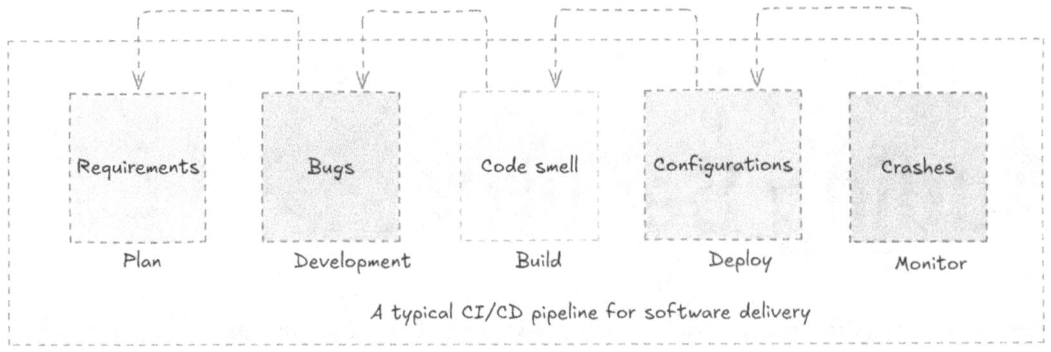

Figure 10-1. *The shift-left approach to making your software stable should have security practices to bring lessons learned (the easy way or the hard way) to improve the earlier processes*

Security—as also used in terms like DevSecOps—is a term that is being used for compliance, code smells, infrastructure security, static and dynamic analysis of the code and application, to ensure the application is reliable even at 1 am. For you and your customer. To achieve this mastery and control over the delivery and execution of your app, you do not just add security as a "sidecar."[1]

- **Development**: Your development environment should not only focus on the productivity toolset but security toolset as well. Validate each and every package and dependency that you use. Luckily for .NET engineers, most of the packages and runtime binaries are provided by Microsoft so we have to depend less on external/third-party products. I am not saying that Microsoft's products cannot be hacked, but the redundancies to avoid this are massive.

- **Delivery**: Software is extremely prone to a supply-chain attack. A very recent supply-chain attack (called Shai-Hulud, yes, that Shai-Hulud, search for Shai-Hulud NPM Worm in September 2025) has taken big projects by surprise and demonstrated that supply-chain attack is

---

[1] Sidecar, even though not a native Kubernetes concept, but is heavily used with Kubernetes and containerized environment to offload non-business-critical tasks a secondary process that collects telemetry, resource consumption, applies certain rules for inward and outward traffic. Common examples include Istio (`https://istio.io/`). In this note, I am not using the term to mention this sidecar but a general sidecar aspect where you throw responsibilities over the fence and don't care when fire starts.

not just a common thing among indie projects but massive ones too. Your CI/CD should not just validate that the code in your application works and functions as expected but also ensure that the build scripts being used are also not infected. If you are using external scripts, validating their SHA-checksum is a good practice. Before delivering the software, this is also a good moment to validate the licenses being used in your project. Open-Source projects give a lot of benefits to the Engineers; they speed up your development but can put a "Stop" on your deployment because the license does not allow you to.

- **Deployment**: Check if you are even allowed to make the deployment based on the practices used in the application. Is your infrastructure configured well? Do you have the right certificates and keys/secrets in place to enable the communication? Are you launching on a cold boot, or is your instance warm enough for the traffic?

- **Detection**: Continuous security should be the next thing in the DevOps culture, but wait, it already is with DevSecOps. Gone are the days when the development was the only thing done by the Engineers. You are expected, and you must feel responsible for the availability and reliability of your services. The reliability is a cross between the experience of your customers and the value to your business.

This does not mean I am an advocate for Zero-Everything[2] culture. The biggest challenge I have with this approach is, no matter how much you secure your application, there will always be a central point of failure. You make your infrastructure password-less, and then an attacker gains access to it via master password.

---

[2] Zero trust architecture is a key contributor to the deployment of successful and secure applications. I highly recommend that you read the concepts shared for a Zero trust architecture. Many vendors have their own flavor of a Zero trust architecture to support their customers in maintaining security. Read more here: `https://learn.microsoft.com/en-us/security/zero-trust/zero-trust-overview`

Master Passwords

I worked with a client who allowed certain operations on their production infrastructure from within the corporate network only, deployed behind a virtual private network (VPN). The system does not allow password-based authentication because passwords can be compromised so they use Vault (again, not the HashiCorp Vault, but Vault in the general term), which is secured behind a cryptographically generated master password as shown in Figure 10-2. Note that, master keys cannot be ignored. While we want to keep the system restricted and avoid using user accounts and persons to have totalitarian control over the infrastructure. We do need to make sure that we are not locked out of our systems. Platforms and frameworks solve this problem differently, for example, it could be possible to have a master password or key that requires at least three or more authorized people to approve an action before it can go through.

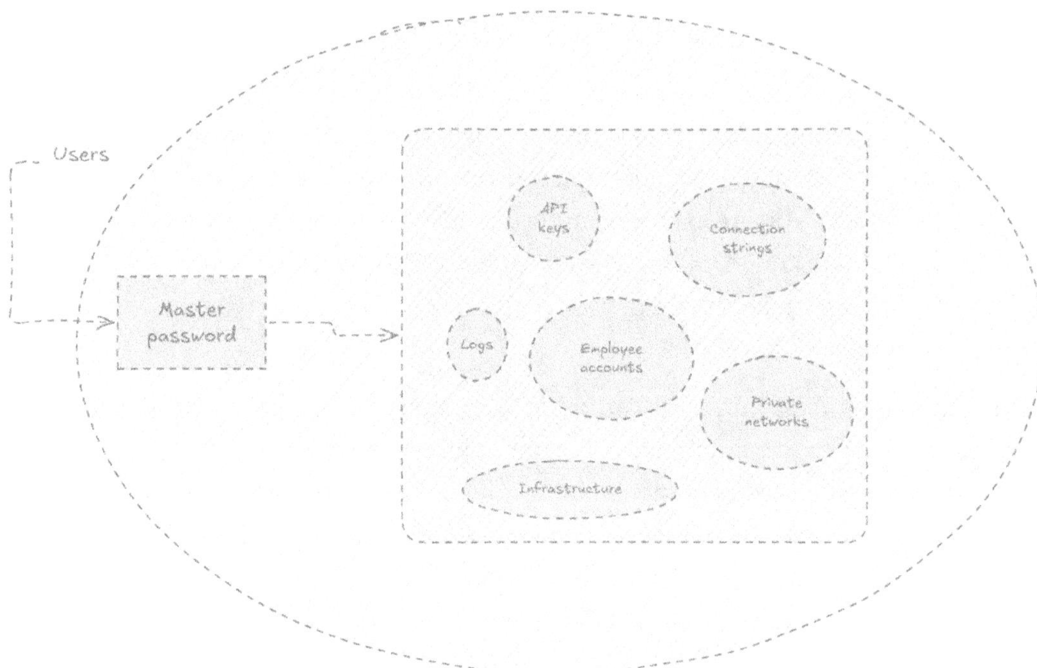

Figure 10-2.   While the master password is not needed for infrastructure to operate or for your apps to connect to the databases, the master password often gives you an entry through the main door. Once you are inside, the "zero trust" policy becomes weaker and the attacker can use the tools to break further in. Imagine a thief on the road, they have no idea what kind of security you have inside the house. Once they are inside, they can use the right tool to break further in to gain access to the sensitive areas and regions of your house because they now have access to this

Now, do I need to say how this approach reduced their attack surface by a large factor, but made this one single attack vector Achilles' heel? If the attacker believes that your honey pot is worth their while, they will come for it.

That is why I recommend "Secure by Design." In Secure by Design, you are not taking a leap of faith by just locking the doors to prevent entry, but you are also planning for what happens when someone does enter the enclave.

We will revisit Security and its application in depth in the later sections of the book. In this part, we focused on defining the platforms, the service-layers, and how to control the flow of data, the events, and how to provide real-time services to the customers. The security is a very important crucial glue that connects different components. It is incorrect to think that security slows the system, instead, it provides room to innovate in each space and center.

Further Reading

Security is a vast topic and must be reviewed frequently, start here: `https://learn. microsoft.com/en-us/security/`.

Security is applied differently to different frameworks. In the .NET space, almost every platform has its own dedicated section for the security. For ASP.NET Core, start here: `https://learn.microsoft.com/en-us/aspnet/core/security/?view=aspnetco re-10.0`. For WPF, start here: `https://learn.microsoft.com/en-us/dotnet/desktop/ wpf/security-wpf`. Each framework and platform has its own challenges, and must be configured and fine-tuned accordingly.

CHAPTER 11

Defining Contracts and APIs

Your customers do not just purchase a binary or executable, or an API endpoint from you or your organization. They purchase a service. Whether that is an Android application, an HTTP service, or a Desktop application. As you work on the service that your customers want to build a relationship with you for, you must keep in mind that these relationships do break often—while not at the first bad instance, but a repeat violation does lead to a churned customer.

In this chapter, we will learn how to document our services, APIs, apps, and contracts for external customers. While the OpenAPI specifications can be used by internal teams and ourselves, the primary goal is to communicate the services to other customers. These customers can be paying customers of enterprises, or can be tools that can automate the services.

Okay, so you are ready with your best-so-far product, after taking your best approach to doing the development and release. It is important to highlight what this Product is.

Engineers—myself included—think that their products are to be used by fellow Engineers only. Which is not true; your Engineers are the ones that review and provide direct technical feedback to you. Who the consumers are is not clear and defined— unless it is defined and you are building something for someone specific and then that is for that person or team or organization.

A lot of times, your products are used by non-technical people. Think of customer support, receptionists, data analytics—not every data person is a fan of Excel, and more. A good design of the software requires some attention to be paid to the end user's concerns and needs. Think of software documentation. Without proper documentation, software cannot be developed, tested, distributed, downloaded, consumed, or updated. Good documentation highlights

© Afzaal Ahmad Zeeshan 2026
A. A. Zeeshan, *Building Mission-Critical Applications with .NET 10 and C# 14*,
https://doi.org/10.1007/979-8-8688-2347-3_11

- **Development**: What are the requirements for the software.

- **Deployment**: How to run the application, and how to observe the application for misbehavior.

- **Discovery**: Find detailed information about the architecture of the system, how different components come together—such as the APIs, interfaces, and which models go where.

- **Delivery**: How can the consumers get access to the software, how to get the updates to the software, and more importantly, how to request support.

The documentation not only guides the consumers, it also guides the 6-month future you on why you named your controller, `HandleAccountCreationPingController`.[1] I don't remember why I named my controller that.

.NET offers XML-based documentation for our projects, called XMLDoc.[2] You can define the contracts that are present in your architecture, app, and classes.

Using XMLDoc

XMLDoc is an XML container for the documentation that is added to the source code by the Engineers. This is also available in other languages, for example, JavaDoc is a good example of using XML-based documentation to express the structure of the Java project. XMLDoc in .NET or C# apps is created using triple-slash comments or comments. The XMLDoc requires the commentary to be provided in a `<summary></summary>` element (as shown in Figure 11-1). This makes sure that general comments are not picked up and translated into an XMLDoc.

---

[1] Actually, I do. This is a name I used in a serverless function where the scope of this controller was to handle signups and send email notification via SendGrid. The controller was meant to be a temporary handler until an internal service was created, but hey, nothing is as permanent as a temporary fix. Right?

[2] Read the XMLDoc documentation here: `https://learn.microsoft.com/en-us/dotnet/csharp/language-reference/xmldoc/`.

```csharp
/// <summary>
/// This endpoint issues the account deletion token.
/// </summary>
/// <param name="email">The email of the user account to generate the token for.</param>
/// <returns>The deletion token.</returns>
[HttpGet("deletion")]
0 references
public async Task<string> GetDeletionTokenAsync(string email)
{
    var user = await accountService.GetAccountAsync(email);

    if (user == null)
    {
        return string.Empty;
    }

    return user.DeletionToken;
}
```

Figure 11-1. *The triple-slash comments in C# allow you to author documentation that can be read and added to your OpenAPI specifications. This helps generate the updated documentation on the OpenAPI specifications right from the source code*

XMLDocs can be generated as project documentation, downloaded as an XML file and then loaded and parsed into tooling or CI pipelines, such as for showing the support comments in the IDE tooling.

If you do use XMLDoc, you can use external tools such as Doxygen[3] to generate the website for the documentation based on the XML output.

Swagger and API Documentation

While the entire project documentation should have a similar look and feel, very often, you do not publish the entire project. You expose the project as a product to be consumed by external partners or customers. If you are using API as a medium to provide the services—which, to be honest, is like 70% of the web; I don't need to show a statistic for this, you get it. For APIs, Swagger (formerly known as Swashbuckle, and now known as OpenAPI) allows you to document your API and enable your customers to interact with the service.

---

[3] Check out the open source Doxygen project here: https://github.com/doxygen/doxygen

Swagger documentation is simple website (as shown in Figure 11-2) with all the endpoints of your API grouped together into products or tags which can be used to create categories. Your users can hit the endpoints directly from the UI. The documentation gives an interactive edition to your documents where the customers are practically experimenting with the services.

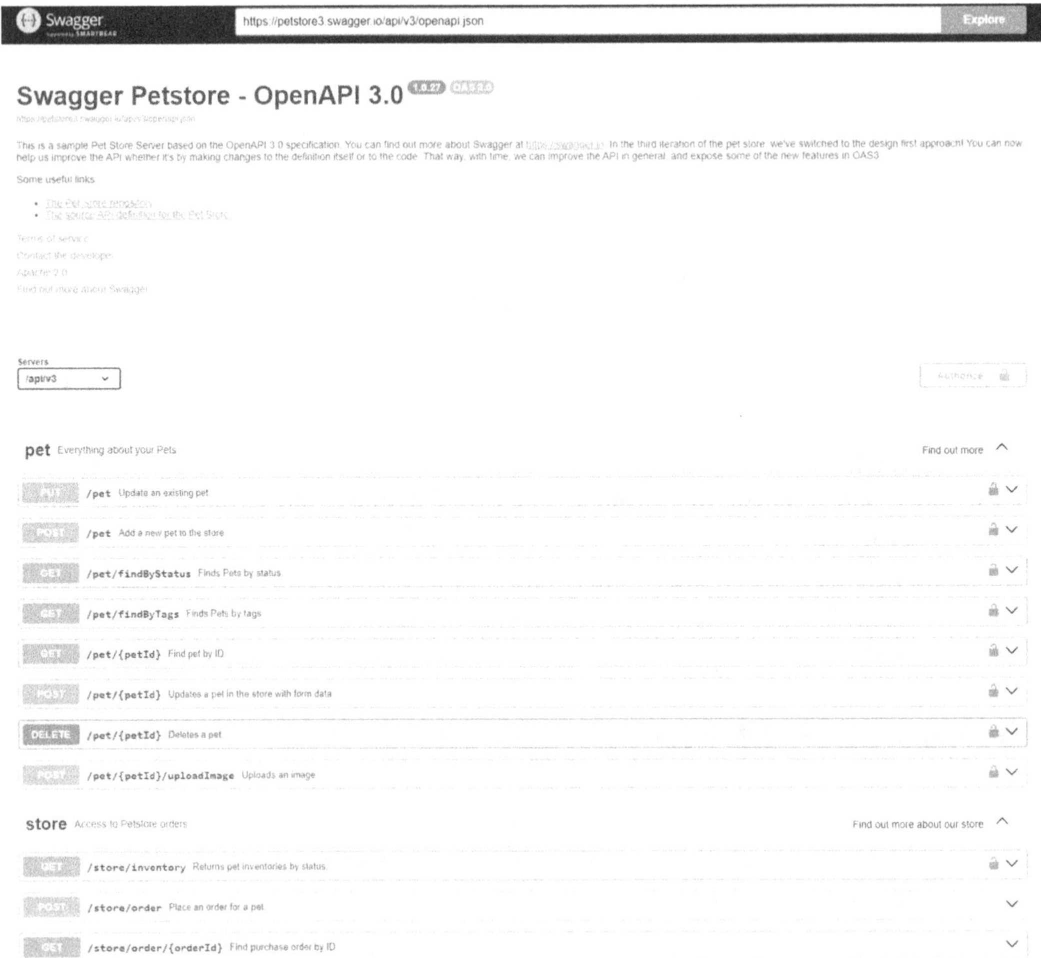

Figure 11-2. The petstore endpoint demonstrating the Swagger/OpenAPI documentation. This dashboard is available at https://petstore3.swagger.io

Today, if your APIs do not have an OpenAPI experience it feels incomplete. Developers do not have enough time to go through your APIs, skim through pages and pages of references, just to see if your product will help them or not. In today's market, developers and their decisions are very important in purchasing a product. A lot of developer-first companies invest heavily in ensuring that their documentations and references are easier for the developers to read, access, try out, and gain an opinion on.

Automating API Documentation

If you have an API, automating the generation of API documentation is as easy as adding an extra step to the build pipeline. In .NET, it is as simple as

- Including a Swagger package or using the native support for OpenAPI.[4] .NET 10[5] includes built-in support by calling `builder.Services.AddOpenApi();` and then `app.MapOpenApi()`.

- Generate the documentation for the OpenAPI specification to render in a UI or pass to external platforms.

- Enable the XMLDoc document generation to support the native OpenAPI specification content.

- Use the Swagger UI to show the documentation to your customers— don't worry, you can limit it to the development environments as well.

The native OpenAPI NuGet package was added in .NET 9, so it is new, and I believe the reason to add the native OpenAPI package was like adding System.Text.Json[6] to provide reference-compliant support out of the box.

API Documentation As a Contract

Postman is a good example of demonstrating the API as a product but also showcasing how to use the API to perform actions. For example, a travel agent can offer their

---

[4] `https://www.nuget.org/packages/Microsoft.AspNetCore.OpenApi/`

[5] `https://learn.microsoft.com/en-us/aspnet/core/fundamentals/openapi/overview?view=aspnetcore-10.0`

[6] Read about the differences between both the packages: `https://learn.microsoft.com/en-us/dotnet/standard/serialization/system-text-json/migrate-from-newtonsoft?pivots=dotnet-9-0`

ticketing API in a Postman collection to highlight how to perform the endpoint calls to make a booking on the system.

Postman provides CLI to run the tests on the endpoints and ensure they work as expected. The Newman CLI can validate from the basic HTTP incorrect verbs to inconsistent request or response bodies. Newman CLI can run in the CI/CD pipelines to ensure that any new change does not contribute a bug or a problem in the contract. If there are any regression issues, you can validate and fix them before the changes make their way to production and cause issues.

Respect the Contract

The contract is the central agreement between two parties; *team members, business partners, customers and providers, etc.*

It is important not to break the contract. If you are breaking the contract, know that there will be damages. The contracts start from the development phase and end up on the long-term client relationship. The requirements document that arrives from your product manager or the team is the start of this contract. The requirements that were agreed upon is the start of the business operation and the technical aspect of the solution that you need to build. If you are building something that does not really contribute to customer's business, then that is a wasted effort. As a developer, you write the code that meets the expected criteria for the final product. The tester makes sure that you meet the contract requirements before approving the changes. On the ending side, your customer or the client holds you accountable. If you break a contract, they will show that by either not paying you or no longer extending the contract payment.

Modern software systems have a "Status"[7] page that shows if the service is up or if there is an incident. If you continue to break the contract and provide a poor quality of service, your customers will leave you and move on to your competitors. Interestingly, mostly customers do not leave because your app's primary theme is purple or maroon, but, they leave if they are unable to use it or if the system is down most of the time. When you are providing the service to critical service providers—such as financial service providers, or healthcare providers, etc., you are required to agree to a service-level agreement (SLA) that defines the amount of service disruption that you are allowed for an amount of time.

---

[7] If you're looking to adding a Status page to your solution, check out this on Atlassian's website: `http://atlassian.com/software/statuspage`.

We do not need to repeat that building a software is not just for yourself—unless you do build software for yourself, in that case, enjoy! The software is built for others to use, and you have a contract to keep.

.NET supports the development flow of apps from the early stages to the complex growth of the applications. In this part we learned about the frameworks provided and supported by .NET, and we also learned how to install the templates to support the development process.

In the next part, and starting with the next chapter, let's start building and bundling the source code to prepare the software for deployment and delivery.

Further Reading

In .NET 10, Microsoft has included OpenAPI support natively and this helps make it easier to generate OpenAPI specification from your APIs. Consider reading the material on Microsoft's website: `https://learn.microsoft.com/en-us/aspnet/core/fundamentals/openapi/overview?view=aspnetcore-10.0`

The best tool to use with OpenAPI specification for automation is Postman (`https://www.postman.com/`), and if you have never used Postman or have never authored an API, I highly encourage you to give Postman a look and try to load the Petstore API (`https://petstore3.swagger.io/`) in Postman.

PART III

Software Quality

CHAPTER 12

Building for Testability

As we shift-left most of our practices in an SDLC, we need to involve our testing teams and testers on the most-left table as well. Building an application that does not break is half the picture. Your responsibility is to write the application in a way that enables testers to validate changes in the business processes and requirements, without having to ask you to change the structure of the application.

In this chapter, we learn about the reasons for why we should keep application testability in mind when we are developing the applications.

Take a few seconds and think of the testing platforms or runtimes available for your framework or language. Is it more than 1? Do you know them all? Now pick one that you believe will outlast an apocalypse. If you have answer, then you have not yet tried it fully on all sorts of messy web apps. I mean, today with the help of AI, even the most stable frameworks are unable to provide a flaky-free test suite. The reason is because most applications are built for usage and not for testing. For a really long time, we've always had manual testers who would mimic the behavior of a customer or end user and provide feedback.

- The manual tester would perform the same actions that a customer would perform but would also try to provide incorrect inputs to try to break the application.

- Manual tests collect all the parameters where the application breaks and provides this information back to the team.

- The Engineers fix the application and resend it back for another review.

- Testers (also called QA, for quality assurance) would give it another go and if they identify that the bugs are fixed—meaning the customer would be able to operate the software and get their job done—would tag the code ready for release, or whatever the next step is.

© Afzaal Ahmad Zeeshan 2026
A. A. Zeeshan, *Building Mission-Critical Applications with .NET 10 and C# 14,*
https://doi.org/10.1007/979-8-8688-2347-3_12

The biggest challenge with this approach is scalability. The only way for your testing team to run two of these workflows in parallel is by having two QA. There was no way evading that. A lot of times you would need to run the manual tasks yourself and there is no escape. One of the ways in which this was resolved was by writing automation scripts. Robot framework, UiPath, etc. And similar tools were created to assist this approach to automate the manual tasks. Now, instead of having a manual tester sit at the screen and run the tasks one-by-one, the automation script would take over the program—such as an application, a web browser, or other process—and perform the actions. On the web browsers, these would be the HTML DOM and the DOM events to interact with and execute operations, and for the web applications it was usually an accessibility layer that is used to capture the UI elements and then perform operations or validations on them.

Well, one problem solved. Another one pops up. The problem is that while the automation software takes care of your job, you cannot use the system. A decade ago, for example, the UiPath scripts or ROBOT automation scripts would be run on secondary screens where the ROBOT would start the browsers, or app windows, and click all over the screen, selected dropdowns, input values to forms, click buttons, and perform all sorts of actions. But, you cannot perform the same automation on two apps on the same machine. So, we saw how to scale the manual tester, but how do we scale the screens?

Two choices:

- Use rented screens.

- Use headless apps.

When you use rented screens—okay, okay, fine—cloud-hosted screens, you can run as many manual operations with these automated jobs as you want and you do not have to take care of the screens for the long term. If your budget allows, you can run hundreds or thousands of jobs on these screens, and they scale as your demand requires and then you can scale them down when you no longer need them. That works, but then the bill comes due. And the bill in the long run is more than those hundreds of screens. The benefits of the cloud-hosted screens or devices are

- You can have screens and devices or any resolution, color space, or orientation.

- You do not need to manage and set up the screens and the devices.

- The service provider has an API that you use to request a device and then run your program on the instance available.

- You do not just get a screen; you get a fully managed instance of a computer.

- You get not just one operating system, but you can also change the operating system to accommodate customers from different operating systems and ensure the app behaves as expected.

The scaled-up version of the screens and devices is good, but it is like throwing money at the problem and hoping it goes away. To solve a problem without throwing money at it, you attempt to engineer it. Luckily, you do not need to engineer it yourself, amazing Engineers have already done that.

That is where you attempt to run the programs headless, where your apps run in-memory without exposing a user-interface. When there is no user-interface, the process runs headless, it performs everything but instead of providing a visual output and expecting an interaction on the visual screen it handles input programmatically.

Most web browsers provide a headless approach to running them, especially for the testing purposes. While this solves the problem of scale and enables teams and organizations to get their work done, it does mean that your apps need to be different. They must be designed and properly developed to work in such a scenario. A lot of times, these headless programs do not behave the same way that a UI-driven app would.

Bot Limitations

While the application and the headless browser have their own limitations, the bots that we use to run the programs, Playwright, etc., all have their own limitations as well. How you interact with the HTML DOM, how you handle the events, how you make the interaction feel natural, or how you pass parameters to the server to let it know that this request is coming from a bot. This way, you prevent the server from blocking the requests.

Bots do not know the difference between "Continue" text on the account management section or the checkout session. If you tell a program to find the text Continue and click the button next to it, they will find the first one and click it. APIs return a list of elements that match a pattern, but how do you know which is the right one? A lot of ways to solve this problem is by using non-text selectors, such as XPath, or CSS selectors, etc. They all have their own limitations.

So, how do you solve this problem then? In short, instead of relying on your testing framework to find and identify what they need to do, your application needs to expose certain details that the framework will use to perform the operations, access the data and state, and then assert if the web application is behaving as expected. The simplest way to do this in the web applications is by using the `data-`[1] attributes. When you create an input field, you can attach a `data-` attribute such as `data-register-email-input` and then your testing framework can read the HTML DOM and find if this field exists. If it does, it knows "exactly" which field it has and what to do with it. In your CI/CD, if you have the framework set to launch the headless browser and run the script that reads the HTML document—your website—and then looks for the hooks that it expects, the test is performed quickly.

But we know the quick is a keyword only found in the theory. What happens when you execute the command, "`npx playwright test`"?

The concepts of testability go beyond just a single change in the application. There are patterns that you should use to make sure your application can be tested properly. These patterns are like a "hook" that your application gives to the hosting environment. On the development environment, for example, you can run the application with mocked resources, while on production, you use the live resources. One of such examples is decoupling the code from the resources so that your services do not rely on hardwired systems, but they use abstractions. Dependency injection (`https://learn.microsoft.com/en-us/dotnet/core/extensions/dependency-injection/overview`) in .NET allows us to modify the resources based on the runtime environment.

- On the development environment, your services connect to local database systems and services.

- On the testing or staging environments, your services either connect to a mocked instance of the services such as databases, or they connect to a test version of the resources.

- On the production, they connect to the live services.

---

[1] The data- attributes enable you to add extra attributes and fields to the HTML document. The web browsers do not know how to read or process these fields, and they can be custom attributes that are just useful for your processes. Read more on this here: `https://developer.mozilla.org/en-US/docs/Web/HTML/How_to/Use_data_attributes`

Further Reading

For testing, one of the books that I recommend highly is Effective Software Testing by Mauricio Aniche. While the book uses Java as the language and runtime, the concepts Mauricio teaches can be applied to other languages, and very notably to C# and .NET Core.

The .NET guide for testing provides a good starting point to talk about the strategies for testing. Read about the available testing packages and which packages to use based on your framework and app archetype: `https://learn.microsoft.com/en-us/dotnet/core/testing/`.

CHAPTER 13

The Wild West

You've involved your best testers, architects, and engineers to write, validate, and publish the best-possible service. But it did not meet expectations. At times it did not serve enough requests as you expected and for some cases it straight-out crashed. Why is it that even the best written and tested services and products do crash?

Why is it, that your SDLC and CICD pipelines were all green and indicating how successful the testing suites were, but your infrastructure is yellow, orange, or worse: red?

This is what I like to call, "The Wild West." This is the real testing grounds for your applications. Where everything out there is ready to get you.

In this chapter, we will learn about the practices that are used to break your system or abuse it. The bad actors do not use the same unit tests that your development teams use. They use state-of-the-art ways of breaking your applications.

Be careful what you test for. Your responsibility as an Engineer is to make sure that you put your best foot ahead, and for your organization to put their best food forward in from of the customer. Many things will go wrong. Before we start the chapter, let's get one thing out. You can never test your app for everything, every edge case, and make sure that your software will not get blown to kingdom come. It will. The best strategy is not to aim to have your app 100% fully tested and validated—not only is that impossible but it wastes a lot of time as you wait to reach perfection. The best strategy is to prepare for the worst. And that is what we will focus on in this chapter.

Our applications run in the wild west. They are always being attacked by malicious actors. The more mission-critical and impactful your business, the more attackers it will likely attract. To an attacker, your application or hard rocked infrastructure is like a puzzle. They want to solve it. They do not care if they get money out of it, because they are getting fun out of it. A lot of attackers are not motivated by a political gain—even though they do exist—but they do so because they find these protocols, architectures, security, and privacy practices as a challenge for themselves. White hat and gray hat

© Afzaal Ahmad Zeeshan 2026
A. A. Zeeshan, *Building Mission-Critical Applications with .NET 10 and C# 14*,
https://doi.org/10.1007/979-8-8688-2347-3_13

hackers fall within the category of "somewhat" safe space. The organizations that have mature Engineering cultures are more prone to these cyberattacks and malicious hijacks of their products and software.

Infrastructure Validation

Your applications may be ready, but is your infrastructure ready? The testing strategy must include the infrastructure as well. That is why we have Infrastructure as Code. We need to trust our infrastructure based on our requirements. If we are deploying the ASP. NET Core application, we need to know that our infrastructure is ready to accept the artifact and run it. A notable way to do this is with Terraform,[1] where you configure all the resources and then you make the deployment. Your IT staff does not need to create new secrets and tokens for each new deployment, but your IT staff must delete/remove secrets, tokens, identifiers for the resources that are deleted.

If you are looking into access management, CyberArk[2] is a good provider that helps you automate access management. For solutions on Azure, the Entra ID and basic Active Directory provide good amount of control over who does what. You do not require fancy tools and products, simple LDAP would do the trick to ensure that the right people have access to the right tools. Since we are talking about security, and risk management, this is the right time to open the manual and learn what is available on the platforms that you are using. Every cloud provider has good security practices enabled and right tools for you to (1) ensure bad actors stay out, (2) your application gets access to the resources that you intend it to, (3) you are notified of bad activity as soon as it is detected, (4) you have the right buttons to press to enter lockdown mode, and (5) you can run the applications in strict security mode once a bad actor has been identified and the application is flushing out the bad actors.

---

[1] Check out this documentation for an example case of automating the deployment to Azure App Service with Terraform and generating the resources: `https://learn.microsoft.com/en-us/azure/app-service/provision-resource-terraform?tabs=linux`

[2] Learn more here: `https://www.cyberark.com/`

Bad days happen everywhere—Azure servers go down,[3] AWS faces DDoS,[4] Google Cloud faces outages,[5] and Cloudflare DoS'd itself with React components.[6] There are no bad coders, just learning experiences. So when things go south, make sure your pencils are sharp as there would be a lot of notes and writing to maintain the knowledge to avoid the hiccups from happening again in the future.

Nothing Is Permanent

I am guilty of making a mistake of trusting the domain name to be a permanent thing in my control. I had a domain applied to an Azure App Service via CNAME (as it was a subdomain). I used the service for a while and then removed the application. For anonymity, let's use generated values here:

- My domain: something.com

- My subdomain: app.something.com

The application on Azure App Service was connected to the app.something.com subdomain and not to the something.com (via an A record). On Azure, when you deploy a new instance, they provide you with a randomly generated URL or you can use the name of your app there, so I called it "my-something-app." Azure-generated link was "my-something-app.azurewebsites.net." I added a CNAME to the app.something.com to "my-something-app.azurewebsites.net."

All went fine for a while and I used the application, but then I decided to remove the application. At that point, Azure would just remove the resources and allow anyone else to create their own applications with previously used app names. The structure of the application layout is visualized in Figure 13-1 (the technicality of the architecture is simplified for the sake of argument).

---

[3] Azure faces degraded performance based on a cable fault in the Red Sea, read here: `https://www.bbc.com/news/articles/c3rvx470yg8o`.

[4] AWS was DDoS with a 2.3 Tbps: `https://www.a10networks.com/blog/aws-hit-by-largest-reported-ddos-attack-of-2-3-tbps/`

[5] Google Cloud issued statement after a massive outage took chunk of internet down with the GCP: `https://www.cnbc.com/2025/06/16/google-cloud-outage-apology.html`

[6] Cloudflare's report on the incident: `https://blog.cloudflare.com/deep-dive-into-cloudflares-sept-12-dashboard-and-api-outage/`. Also note that this instance was an internal bug that caused the service to go down.

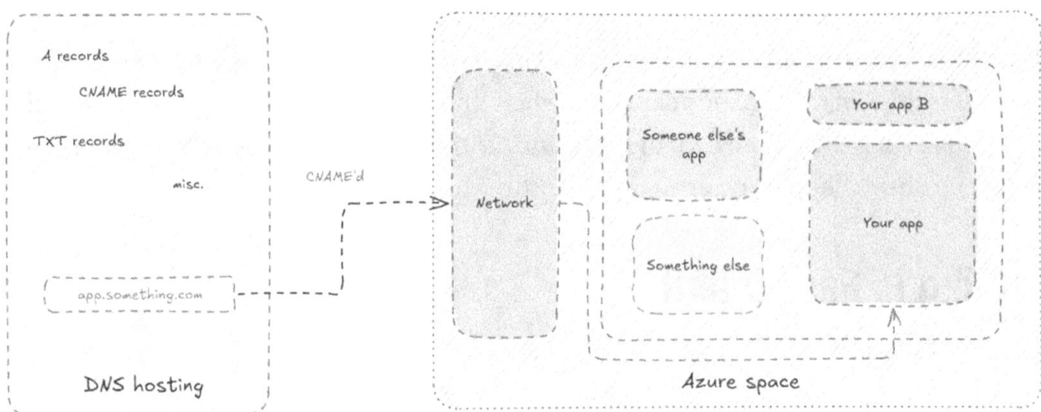

Figure 13-1. *The initial structure of the application points the domain with a CNAME record to the Azure infrastructure. Microsoft Azure manages the redirects indirectly to point to the right resource that belongs to you. Your application receives the request and provides a response back*

A few months later, I received a notification that Google Search Console has a new owner. I was shocked as the domain was still in my control and there was no way I had added a new owner; I would know if I did that. I ignored[7] that warning as a mistake on systems because I still had the domain and I could still see the listing in the Google Search Console. Over the course of the next few weeks, I received various emails from Google Search Console indicating that there was a traffic movement on my website, there were some issues with merchant listing, product snippets, etc. That is when I visited the website linked in the Google Search Console and found out that it was indeed the "app.something.com" hosting a completely different website. It was a website that contained references to products being sold on eCommerce websites, with user accounts, registrations, and cart management. All being run while the domain was still in my control.

---

[7] As a security person, this is the one word you must never do.

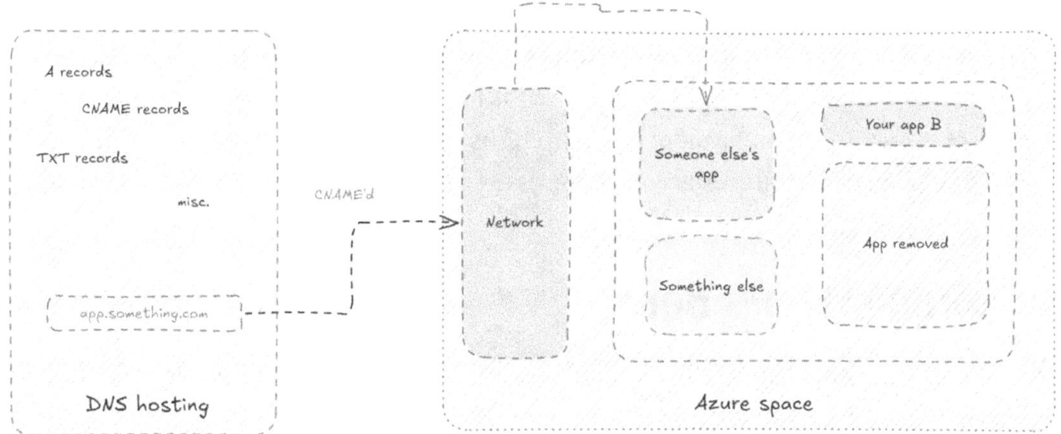

Figure 13-2. *The web app resource was removed from the Azure infrastructure, however, the DNS records were not removed. When someone visits the website, they are given the address for Azure's infrastructure. By now, a malicious actor (or someone by mistake?) has created a new resource and has linked to your domain. That is because Azure still has the records for the domain being linked to Azure infrastructure. This way, the domain still remains in your control but someone else is able to host their resources using your domain*

Here is what went wrong:

1. I removed the application from the infrastructure but did not clear the stale/obsolete DNS records.

2. Someone created a new app on Azure and used the name that I had used in the past—I had made some announcements for this app so perhaps they got the name from there.

3. When this site was created, and there was an existing record in my DNS to approve the CNAME linking between app.something.com to my-something-app.azurewebsites.net, the requests directly went to Azure resource. For a CNAME to work, you do not need to map the same CNAME in the Azure resource; DNS redirects the traffic.

That is how in this instance the user was able to use my domain (as shown in Figure 13-2), build a website on it, and then generate traffic and apply SEO practices. Too bad on my part, but boy did I learn how the DNS works!

Luckily, now Azure ensures that as you delete the resource which has a custom domain name applied to it, it cannot be deleted until you remove the DNS records to ensure such a scenario does not happen. That is a learning and we apply this approach to other components of our system as well. This is an approach that works and provides growth to our security cultures across businesses and industries.

How Do Versions Help?

Growth happens outside the comfort zone, but an application functions well within a versioned zone. Given a scenario:

- A mobile application

- A web-based API

- A database engine

- A hosting server (let's just say, it's Linux-based)

In which situation, do you think it would function "as expected"?

1. The versions of the OS, database engine are known, and the configuration is performed as per the manual with the defaults removed, and the API server is version-locked to ensure the request/response structures are respected, and the mobile-application validates the API version before making requests or transferring the user data.

2. You go YOLO.

I guess we do not need to address this, the list was rhetorical. The only sensible way to handle the uncertainty is by agreeing on some common details, such as the versions of the servers, the APIs, mobile applications. The versions provide us with a safe space to operate in by knowing what is present and what is not present.

We did our best, we gave our little red riding hood a mobile phone to call us when they encounter an animal. But luckily, they did not have to use the mobile phone to make the call. But wait... Did they not call because there was no danger or because they were in danger and something did happen? Do you still remember Murphy's law? It dictates that when something can go wrong, it will go wrong. So, in this case, if we had given the phone to someone else along the road to make a call and notify us on the status for Little Red Riding, how would that go? Let's check that in the next chapter.

Further Reading

When it comes to versioning your software, I highly recommend using the semantic versioning as it communicates all the life cycle events of a program, project, and a system. The semantic versioning is framework and runtime agnostic, and can be used for any deployment model. Read more about the semantic versioning on the official website: `https://semver.org/`.

The DNS instance that I highlighted was a very long time ago and Microsoft Azure has addressed this loophole by enforcing that all resources should remove the DNS connections when they are being deleted. Read this resource for the Dangling DNS on Microsoft Azure's website: `https://learn.microsoft.com/en-us/azure/security/fundamentals/subdomain-takeover`.

CHAPTER 14

Third-Party Testing Suites

It's time to catch a breath. We just escaped a lot of bandits in the last chapter. Right? If anything, we know that in order to survive we all need to work together. In your Microsoft tech stack, you do not have to depend only on the testing suites and frameworks provided by Microsoft. A lot of interesting testing strategies are available—open source, paid, or freemium—to use in your projects. My favorite, xUnit (`https://xunit.net`), is an open-source project.

The testing strategies also depend on the project and deliverable that you are aiming for. An API will be tested differently, from a Desktop application, which will be different from a mobile application.

In this chapter, we will focus on

- Third-party testing platforms that give you more controls and features to write the tests and run them

- Open source and free testing platforms, and also managed software systems that run complex tests on your applications

Testing the application is the easiest task in the software-development approach. Writing tests that work is the hardest thing. No wonder, engineers leave it to the last step in the software-development life cycle. Accrual of technical debt, inconsistencies in the system architecture, side effects across the domains of business, a massive blast radius are all an outcome of poorly tested and validated software that goes unchecked in the CI/CD. The most experienced software engineers are also prone to contributing bugs to the system, beyond a certain threshold of the repository size and complexity.

Food for thought: why do majority of scale-ups face the challenge of tech debt, bad coding practices, or slow launch times? If the founding Engineers were extremely experienced in the technology, why is it that juniors are being asked to fix the bugs? IMHO, if the problem can be resolved by a hackathon run by ten junior engineers, it was the carelessness of a senior engineer. It may not be a carelessness and rather a choice to focus on speed against stability of the system.

© Afzaal Ahmad Zeeshan 2026
A. A. Zeeshan, *Building Mission-Critical Applications with .NET 10 and C# 14,*
https://doi.org/10.1007/979-8-8688-2347-3_14

If you are not in the business of writing software tools—build tools, compilers, deployment package managers—it is best to leave the work of building and updating these tools to the best. For .NET, luckily, Microsoft advances the standards of technology to keep up-to-date with the modern requirements. That does not mean you only have to rely on Microsoft's tech stack. NuGet contains various packages and services that you can use and import to your projects.

Also, testing here does not mean 2 + 2 = 4. It means validating your software against all sorts of problems and concerns that may arise during build, deployment, consumption, and observation. The more critical the stability requirement, the more collection and telemetry of the data is required. A typical F1 race car could generate upward of terabyte of data per race.[1] While from a viewer's perspective, the data from the cameras and audios would be enough. The team is not just focusing on the visuals—as much as they are important. They also want to get the data from various sensors to understand how the car does an apex, information about engine, brakes, and other performance of the car. Using this data they are then able to optimize their systems based on the real-world conditions to "win."

If you in for a "win," you should follow the same. While you do not need to build a testing team that looks at everything, you can collaborate with others who are building this.

Bet on Open Source

The first and foremost option for everyone should be to focus on the Community-driven Open-Source initiatives for testing and security. A few notable ones include

- Aikido

- GitLab

- Security:

  - OWASP (Zap)

- Load testing:

  - JMeter

---

[1] Read more here: `https://www.racecar-engineering.com/articles/how-data-works-in-formula-1/`

- K6

- Locust

   – Snyk

The order of these packages is not preference-based sorting. You can use either one that provides a good integration with your apps, your repositories, and the license requirements. GitLab users can use built-in security and testing suites. GitLab Auto DevOps[2] is one of my favorite features on GitLab that quickly enables all dimensions of the app testing and validation before deployment. Of course, that is not complete and it does not know what your application is all about. You would need to customize that behavior a little bit to make it work.

Open-Source packages always start at the free tier and provide complete solutions for other open-source projects. That is a good way to start and then expand the contract for when the demand grows of your project becomes commercial.

If I must recommend one of the services from above, it is OWASP. You should run OWASP (ZAP) on your applications, especially web applications, to identify common security problems before you launch the application. I've run this on my applications locally

---

Note   If you do not fully own the code or you are working with an employer, get legal permission in written before running these scripts and tools on your employer's applications. It is not always allowed or legal to perform these actions on software or products that are not fully owned by you.

Apache JMeter is another example of a tool that helps you identify if your application will work under stress. K6 is another example. You must run these applications to ensure that your final product is ready to take in the load and stress that your customers will put it under. If you are planning for 1 million transactions per second, run a test that is equivalent. However, do remember that your production environment will have a different configuration and the user behavior will be different as well. Load testing tools will prepare you for the worst, not avoid it.

---

[2] Learn more about the support for all the SDLC practices and how GitLab Auto DevOps supports them for various languages here: `https://docs.gitlab.com/topics/autodevops/#currently-supported-languages`

Freemium Scalability

Freemium projects for the developers have a low-barrier to entry. Snyk, GitLab, etc. all allow you to start for free and then scale once your requirements grow beyond a point. JFrog[3] is a prime example of such a suite, they allow you to start free but is a very limited suite for advanced use case and they ask you to purchase a contract. While their products are all very polished, and contain a wide range of tests that they put your application to.

JFrog is one example of where you can scale as you grow. For mobile applications, or web applications, you can run the regression tests for functionality or performance of the web apps with BrowserStack.[4] Other important notable mentions include

- Firebase Test Lab (`https://firebase.google.com/docs/test-lab`)

- SauceLabs (`https://saucelabs.com/solutions/scalable-test-automation`)

I use freemium solutions all the time, and I've seen a lot of professional teams use freemium solutions professionally as well, of course, given the license permission.

Flakiness

This is the good moment for us to address the biggest bane in the testing experience. The flakiness of a test—or the uncertainty of the app behavior. There are many books that specialize in testing strategies and patterns, and I am not going to give you a Testing 101 in this section. However, I would definitely like to mention that a common problem that I have seen for a flaky test is the unknown behavior of the program. The unknowns in a program can come from anything:

- A failed query on the database that is not properly processed for the outcomes

- The network outage or degradation that takes more time for the documents to populate before the next test step

---

[3] Visit their website here: `https://jfrog.com/`

[4] Visit their website here: `https://www.browserstack.com/`

- The server-side changes on the pages that are not addressed by the
  test scripts

- Use of software patterns interchangeably; async/await with synchronous code

- Misconfigured launch of the tests or different testing environments; such
  as screen resolutions, user account information, or a randomly generated
  database

If your program has unknowns, you are more likely to face flakiness of the test
cases. There is no silver bullet to avoid flakiness of your test suites. Open any open
source testing framework's GitHub repository and you will find a few dozen issues or
threads talking about how their test cases are flaky—they pass sometimes and they fail
sometimes. If your test cases pass "sometimes," their failure has nothing to do with your
test codes but with the flakiness.

A few common approaches to solve the flakiness of the test suites are

- Mock whenever possible. If you are running unit tests, mock the parameters. If you are running integration tests, mock external resources such
  as databases or cache services.

- Insteadofusingliveorsharedresources,usededicatedinstances.Theycanbein-
  memory systems.

- Avoid complex patterns, and keep the test steps sequential and procedural; avoid branching, complex code flows as context switching requires
  synchronization and that may lead to inconsistent behavior.

- Do not run the tests in parallel if they use the same resources, or depend
  on either one of the other tests.

If you review the test pyramid, flakiness appears the more you go away from the
unit testing. That is because the further you go from the unit tests, the more services
and components you need to test in one go—UI interactions, database interactions,
data processing, etc. In .NET, you can use any package to reduce the flakiness by doing
these three

- Ensure that no tests use the same resource at the same time. If you have
  to run the tests in parallel, always avoid racing conditions and data share.

If your tests must use the same resource (database, UI, cache, network, framework, etc.), run them in sequence.

- If you are using asynchronous patterns in your code, ensure that the final execution happens sequentially. Meaning, you must await an operation before continuing ahead. If you are launching multiple asynchronous operations, await them all before you proceed to the next step.

- Always wait for the resource to be fully loaded. If an input field is not yet ready to receive an input, your test suite may fail. Also, setting timeouts, your test suite should not wait for minutes (yes, minutes, we're not even thinking of hours) before a resource is ready.

- Consider the retry approach, sometimes, it is a very basic problem in the service (such as a busy resource server, or a network error, or a resource not ready) and in these cases, attempting to retry—up to a maximum of three times—is a good strategy to ensure your test cases have a good chance at passing.

- When a test fails, hiding failure is a bad strategy. You must announce the tests that are failing, and you must announce them in a very loud manner. Flakiness can often point out a changing contract on the website that your test was not configured for, or flakiness can point out when resource consumption plans need to be modified, such as if more time is needed to run the test.

- Implement a cleanup strategy for your test cases. This is important if your tests' data is not needed in other test cases, as it may pollute the overall environment. If your tests rely on a database, consider using an in-memory emulated version (such as SQLite), but if the features are not available then consider creating a new database for each end-to-end test suite (this can be done very easily, for example, with GitLab PostgreSQL[5] service)

If you keep your test systems isolated and well contained, the flakiness is rare. And, honestly, flakiness is an often-seen behavior. Sometimes you do your best, and the network goes out and your test cases fail.

---

[5] Learn about the PostgreSQL service here: `https://docs.gitlab.com/ci/services/postgres/`

Further Reading

The biggest challenge in testing (manual or automated) is the flakiness of a test. Tests can be flaky for so many reasons, including changes in the infrastructure, changes in the applications, the code, and the third-party resources. Any change in the inputs or outputs or the behavior would cause your tests and test scripts to fail. There is no single way to avoid flakiness. Read about the flakiness of tests, and how to fix or avoid them: `https://www.browserstack.com/test-reporting-and-analytics/features/test-reporting/what-is-flaky-test`.

Building resilient applications takes a lot of effort in the architectural readiness. An elastic infrastructure that responds to the changes cannot be rigid in its technical specification. Microsoft's guidelines on reliability for your application provide a good starting point for backend and front-end apps and beyond: `https://learn.microsoft.com/en-us/azure/well-architected/reliability/design-patterns`.

CHAPTER 15

Question Yourself!

After a while, all the tests, validation, security start to become bells and whistles. These bells and whistles look really nice on the theoretical aspect of SDLC; the requirements. In the trenches, aim for speed. In the last decades, we've had multiple manifestos that focus on making our Engineering teams "agile."

While stability is the most important aspect of a platform, when stability leaves the rooms and your application turns to fire, you would wish you had the emergency pipelines ready before the damage became permanent. At that moment, you question if the extra linter was important.

In the last few chapters, we've listed a few third-party service providers, native Microsoft platforms to make sure that your application is ready for the production experience. Do you remember any of those? Let's start asking questions now.

Imagine you have a customer support engineer screaming down your throat that the latest feature you contributed has just brought down an entire site of the customer and the customer is very angry. You spend a few minutes and identify that the latest feature uses an SQL query that does not use indexed column, while indexed columns for the same behavior exist in the database. This SQL query leads to degraded performance across the platform and thus causes your customer to experience a downtime. You want to quickly update the SQL query to use the indexed column instead of the non-indexed column to speed up the performance. The customer support engineer asks for an ETA, and you say, 25 minutes. CSE says, customer cannot wait another 5-minute window as they're losing a lot of money and customers. You say, well, it's the pipelines and the quickest we can deploy a patch is 25 minutes.

Disclaimer: this is a mention of a hypothetical scenario, but I've seen similar scenarios happen in real life.

In the later part of the book, we will take a closer look at incidents and how to handle the incidents. For now, when you need speed, you need to give up some of the security and safety. In a moment like this, you must question yourself: is my linter more important or is the customer more important? When you ask this one question you get a response to what you must do.

Pipelines

A safe bet strategy for the release of an application is having a different and separate branch in your Git—or the other version control system. A typical repository has at least

- **A release branch**: This branch is used to deploy to the live environment.

- **A main branch (also known as the development branch)**: This branch maintains the up-to-date code for the project repository.

- **A staging branch**: This branch is used to make deployments to the testing or staging environment, also known as the QA environments.

Other branches are always created, either by the infrastructure or developers themselves. For the branches created by the developers, you can utilize some of the practices of GitOps to create an environment to test that specific feature before enabling it to be added to the mainstream branch. For infrastructure, on the other hand, we follow a very different approach. Note that the branches owned and maintained by the infrastructure are not just to publish new features. It is actually used to patch the bugs, firefight, and resolve incidents across the platform. Think of plumbing. When your toilet or shower is clogged, you're not going to have the feeling of a warm bath, but you're going to be prepared with the right gadgets and tools to make sure you quickly resolve the problem without making the problem worse. The infrastructure teams—or the Ops team, for the DevOps friends here—have only focus, to make sure the platform is available for the customers to use. At this moment, the warm towel is not only wasting time but is not needed at all. Similarly, when you are building the pipeline to quickly resolve a problem on the production, you do not need to check if your code has the perfect code structure, and if the brackets have closing brackets on the same column a few rows down, or if the quotations are consistent across your code.

These infrastructure branches are like "emergency exits" or the "break glass." They exist in the buildings but are not used regularly and for scenarios of "just because." They are to be used in panic situations where you see a danger. Just like every day, where you take the door to leave the building but use emergency exits when the situation is not normal. You should use the regular 25-minute CI/CD, but when there is a danger, you have to use the 2-minute window to perform a quick patch or a hotfix to put the fire out.

Further Reading

If you prefer to fix the bugs in later stages of software development life cycle, read this guide that calculates the costs of incidents based on the engineers that you need to involve: `https://leaddev.com/software-quality/the-hidden-costs-of-tech-support`.

PART IV

Bundling Source Code Together

CHAPTER 16

The MSBuild

The MSBuild[1] is an open sourced build platform for .NET and is used in Visual Studio. The MSBuild platform is used by the `dotnet build` CLI command. The purpose of the MSBuild is to orchestrate all the necessary steps for your project to be built and be consumed. While MSBuild is the backbone of the build pipeline, we use the hooks and levers to operate the underlying platform.

The build pipeline starts with the build platform, the build platform ensures that the software is prepared in the sequence that makes sure everything is bundled together and then delivered.

In this chapter, our focus is on the introduction of MSBuild software without going hands-on, but the objective is to help you get comfortable with MSBuild.

MSBuild is a mature build orchestrator platform, which has been tested for the harshest environments in Microsoft's own repositories and projects and various projects owned and run by communities and large enterprises across the globe. Various Fortune organizations use .NET, and ultimately MSBuild for the building and bundling of their applications for their customers. MSBuild is used to configure entire solutions[2] and projects and any dependencies that they might have.

MSBuild uses an XML file format to define the projects, and the resources that they contain. These resources can be the files or folders to compile, dependencies to resolve, and output directories to use to generate the outputs into.

---

[1] MSBuild is available on GitHub: `https://github.com/dotnet/msbuild`

[2] Solution is a term used by Visual Studio. Solution is a container for one or more projects. A C# console application is a project within a Solution. A Solution can work with only one project, but can help manage and optimize the dependencies across multiple projects, including external ones.

© Afzaal Ahmad Zeeshan 2026
A. A. Zeeshan, *Building Mission-Critical Applications with .NET 10 and C# 14*,
https://doi.org/10.1007/979-8-8688-2347-3_16

Tip   For in-depth explanation of the MSBuild, read this guide that explains each step that MSBuild process takes to evaluate and build the files and also how the build process identifies which targets and platforms to build for: `https://learn. microsoft.com/en-us/visualstudio/msbuild/build-process-over view?view=visualstudio`. Majority of the .NET platforms do not fully use the MSBuild, and there is no reason to do so. The `dotnet` CLI offers a complete suite of executables that you need to interact with and operate the MSBuild platform. The `dotnet` CLI offers

- Ability to create new projects or add new projects to an existing solution created by the `dotnet` CLI. The CLI also exposes the Solution tasks to manage your Solutions created in Visual Studio.

- Add dependencies or remove the dependencies from the project as the needs of a business change. This command also adds new records to the project (**.csproj**) file.

- Resolve all the dependencies to download their corresponding libraries and packages—either from NuGet or from other package management repositories.

  - Manage the packages from NuGet, or add references to local projects.

- Build the project, compiling all the required files and linking necessary dependencies together to generate an output file.

- Run the necessary tests, prepare the environment for the tests and pass any parameters and arguments to the underlying testing or orchestration framework.

- Publish the project, based on the target platforms, set framework, and the type of release—self-contained or framework-dependent.

- Developer experience toolkits: Including, but not limited to, hot reload with the `dotnet watch` command.

- dotnet CLI also offers a tools command that brings together the entire .NET ecosystem of tooling and frameworks to assist your development workflows. Entity Framework Core, for example, uses the dotnet ef tool to generate migrations and apply them.

Since you are able to perform these actions directly from the (much simpler) dotnet interface, interacting directly with the MSBuild makes very little sense. Plus, MSBuild is maintained now for the feature parity across Visual Studio and Visual Studio Code. And, for new projects, using the dotnet CLI is recommended.

That said, MSBuild is a rather powerful framework that allows you to create tasks, run conditional branches, and store the variables. For a quick review of the power of MSBuild and how it offers you to customize the build experience and execution order, check out this Microsoft Learn documentation page: https://learn.microsoft.com/en-gb/visualstudio/msbuild/walkthrough-creating-an-msbuild-project-file-from-scratch?view=vs-2022.

If you should take away one thing from the chapter, it is that MSBuild is a piece of software that you do not touch directly, but you use it every time you bundle, build, and deliver a software to your customers or to the artifacts repositories.

Further Reading

Microsoft is actively developing MSBuild, and has invested a lot in ensuring the platform remains ahead of the market and provides cutting edge efficiency, performance, and features. Check out the roadmap and changes to MSBuild that Microsoft has contributed in the last few years: https://learn.microsoft.com/en-us/visualstudio/msbuild/whats-new-msbuild-17-0?view=visualstudio.

You can download and set up MSBuild on your Windows platform when you download and install Visual Studio IDE (https://visualstudio.microsoft.com/downloads/). In this book, we will not touch the MSBuild scripts and files, because that is beyond the scope, but it is useful for you to see how the build scripts and files are written and how you can configure the platform to extend the existing features. Read this getting started guide as a reading material before you move to the next chapter: https://learn.microsoft.com/en-us/visualstudio/msbuild/walkthrough-using-msbuild?view=visualstudio.

CHAPTER 17

Build Patterns

Unless your applications are developed using an interpreted programming language—JavaScript, Python, Ruby, etc.—they need to be built. This is the case for .NET framework languages, including C#. You cannot test the behavioral changes in your program unless you build the application and run it (*let's put SAST to the side for a minute*).

In this chapter, we will learn about

- Deployment models that are supported in .NET platform and how to configure them in our project

- How to configure the projects to build on CI platforms and servers

- The benefits of parallel builds and when we should consider building in sequence

.NET engineers are not lucky to run their changes quickly without having to rebuild the applications. Whether you are running your application on your own machine or you are building the application in a regular build server, or as part of the CI/CD pipeline. You need to optimize not only the application but also the dependencies, the script, and use any options or flags to minimize the time.

Two scenarios:

- You are running the application on your development machine.

- You are building the entire solution on a CI server to prepare an artifact for delivery and deployment.

In the first scenario, you need quick feedback, and you need to be able to iterate on the changes that you are making or the changes that got added to the central repository since your last pull. When you are running the applications on the local machine, you need to keep the resource consumption low—you cannot simply run the entire platform on your own machine. Every team should be able to deploy their own service and get a mock service or a replicated system that fills in for the other teams to provide the "system."

© Afzaal Ahmad Zeeshan 2026
A. A. Zeeshan, *Building Mission-Critical Applications with .NET 10 and C# 14*,
https://doi.org/10.1007/979-8-8688-2347-3_17

For the continuous integration, or the build systems, you are not looking for a response or feedback within a few minutes—but also not tens of minutes. A good number for an average sized team should be less than ten minutes, including the build scripts, dependency management, test scripts, and any linters to ensure the best practices are applied.

Both the environments have different and unique use cases, but what remains unchanged is the deployment model. The customer expects their software, whether you publish it from your own machine or you publish it from a complex build server from a cloud infrastructure.

Self-Contained

.NET is a cross-platform solution, and thus runs on any operating system. The challenges come from the fact that not every customer will always have the .NET runtime installed on their system. This is more important for tools, and CLI-driven software, or embedded apps. The self-contained applications are compiled to native executables and contain the runtime and other dependencies needed to run the program and offer the services.

You can configure the self-contained deployment during the publishing process. On the publish window (see Figure 17-1), you can configure not just the deployment mode but also if you would like to trim the code, optimize or change the runtime for deployment, etc.

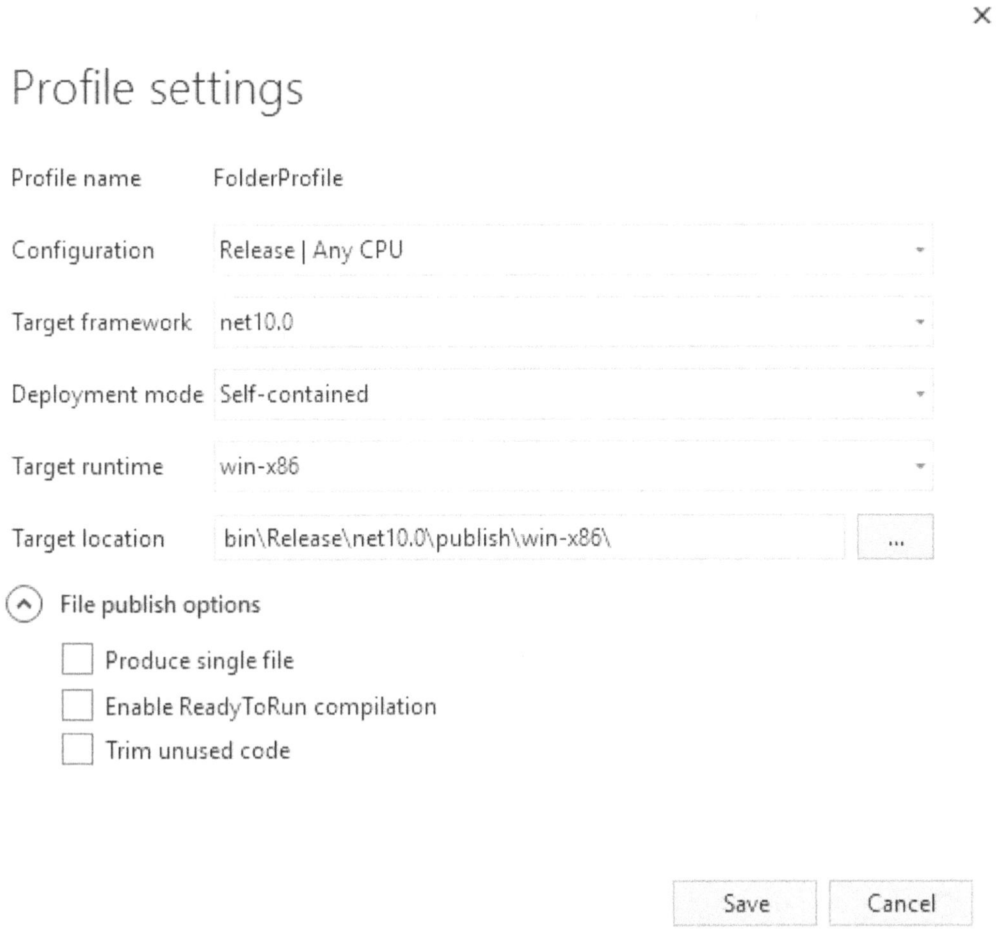

Profile settings

Profile name   FolderProfile

Configuration   Release | Any CPU

Target framework   net10.0

Deployment mode   Self-contained

Target runtime   win-x86

Target location   bin\Release\net10.0\publish\win-x86\   ...

File publish options

☐ Produce single file
☐ Enable ReadyToRun compilation
☐ Trim unused code

Save   Cancel

***Figure 17-1.** The publish profile window on Visual Studio shows more settings and options that we can use to configure how the project is built and prepared for deployment. The key attributes to look at are the Configuration, Target Framework, Deployment Mode, and Target runtime*

The configuration of the project will allow you to prepare the application to run on different targets.

The best benefit you get when using the self-contained application is that you can bundle the required dependencies into the final artifact and copy it as many times as needed to redeploy. You do not need to validate the environment. If you would need to use one situation for self-contained, it would be when you are using disposable environments, such as virtual machines, embedded devices such as IoT devices, and cannot rely on having a runtime available. This is also an example of using the application in CI/CD servers, where every time your application is started, it is started on a new environment. When we publish the project with these settings, we will receive an output, as shown in Figure 17-2.

Name	Date modified	Type	Size
clretwrc.dll	2/19/2026 7:11 PM	Application extension	311 KB
clrgc.dll	2/19/2026 7:11 PM	Application extension	433 KB
clrjit.dll	2/19/2026 7:11 PM	Application extension	1,672 KB
ConsoleApp1.deps.json	3/15/2026 2:44 AM	JSON File	28 KB
ConsoleApp1.dll	3/15/2026 2:44 AM	Application extension	5 KB
ConsoleApp1.exe	3/15/2026 2:44 AM	Application	129 KB
ConsoleApp1.pdb	3/15/2026 2:44 AM	Program Debug Database	11 KB
ConsoleApp1.runtimeconfig.json	3/15/2026 2:44 AM	JSON File	1 KB
coreclr.dll	2/19/2026 7:12 PM	Application extension	3,699 KB
createdump.exe	2/19/2026 7:11 PM	Application	59 KB
hostfxr.dll	2/19/2026 7:21 PM	Application extension	306 KB
hostpolicy.dll	2/19/2026 7:21 PM	Application extension	309 KB
Microsoft.CSharp.dll	2/19/2026 7:39 PM	Application extension	907 KB
Microsoft.DiaSymReader.Native.x86.dll	4/28/2024 1:23 AM	Application extension	1,890 KB
Microsoft.VisualBasic.Core.dll	2/19/2026 7:39 PM	Application extension	1,131 KB
Microsoft.VisualBasic.dll	2/19/2026 7:26 PM	Application extension	18 KB
Microsoft.Win32.Primitives.dll	2/19/2026 7:22 PM	Application extension	16 KB
Microsoft.Win32.Registry.dll	2/19/2026 7:39 PM	Application extension	107 KB
mscordaccore.dll	2/19/2026 7:10 PM	Application extension	1,205 KB
mscordaccore_x86_x86_10.0.426.12010.dll	2/19/2026 7:10 PM	Application extension	1,205 KB
mscordbi.dll	2/19/2026 7:10 PM	Application extension	1,158 KB
mscorlib.dll	2/19/2026 7:27 PM	Application extension	59 KB
mscorrc.dll	2/19/2026 7:11 PM	Application extension	132 KB
msquic.dll	10/24/2025 4:45 PM	Application extension	589 KB
netstandard.dll	2/19/2026 7:27 PM	Application extension	99 KB
System.AppContext.dll	2/19/2026 7:26 PM	Application extension	16 KB

Figure 17-2. *The outputs generated are verbose but important, as they contain the runtime libraries and files that are needed to run the application on the target platform*

Keep in mind that since your application is self-contained, it will access the framework that is shipped with it (or perhaps the client device does not have a .NET framework installation) and that would lead to runtime problems or app start-up issues if the version is mismatched. If you need flexibility of deployment and don't want to bother with the versions of the target or .NET framework, you should use the Framework-Dependent option.

Framework-Dependent

When you are deploying your applications to the environments with the .NET framework installed, half the job is already done. The other half of the job is more difficult. Most of the times these are your own environments, for example, the server environments for your web applications. They can also be the environments by your clients and customers.

If they are environments for your customers, you need to validate which .NET runtime version is available before launching the application. It is very easy to tell that the customer does not have the right .NET runtime available. For critical customers and applications, you need to validate the runtime yourself. A very simple way to do this is

```
$ dotnet --list-runtimes
```

This lists all the runtimes that are available for your application to use. The output of this process highlights if the runtime is available, or if you need to go the extra mile to install the runtime on the environment.

If your application requires the SDK availability, you can check for the available SDK versions on the machine as well.

```
$ dotnet --list-sdks
```

When an SDK is installed, it is shipped with the runtime. The runtime is smaller in size, but can run the applications on the environments. However, runtime cannot build the source code for the applications.

The framework dependent deployment makes the use of framework runtime availability, and thus, the application artifact output is much smaller in size because it does not need to contain the framework runtime. This gives the teams a lot of advantage:

1. Smaller build times, because you do not need to copy the runtime resources for the environment.

2. Smaller artifact size, same benefit, the runtime is not copied over to the output.

3. If the framework is made available, your apps do not need to make the environment ready for the deployment. The environment variables can be shared across the apps and deployments.

4. Your application can be updated without updating the framework, and vice versa.

In short, the best benefit you get by using the framework-dependent application is that you can deploy the same application on other platforms, without having to rebuild or package the runtime along with it. If you decide to use the .NET framework's framework-dependent deployment, you will receive a much smaller output, as shown in Figure 17-3.

Name	Date modified	Type	Size
ConsoleApp1.deps.json	3/15/2026 2:46 AM	JSON File	1 KB
ConsoleApp1.dll	3/15/2026 2:44 AM	Application extension	5 KB
ConsoleApp1.exe	3/15/2026 2:44 AM	Application	129 KB
ConsoleApp1.pdb	3/15/2026 2:44 AM	Program Debug Database	11 KB
ConsoleApp1.runtimeconfig.json	3/15/2026 2:46 AM	JSON File	1 KB

Figure 17-3. *The output artifacts are much simpler, shorter, and do not contain the runtime/framework libraries. The output artifacts expect the framework and runtime to be available on the client*

Multilanguage Solutions

Alright, so far we have explored the build patterns for the offline approach. Where you build and run the application directly on your own machine. But, what happens when you have to build the application on a remote machine for a different architecture deployment?

The different languages give you a benefit:

- The projects are built separately—no point in mixing F# and C# in a single project.

- Your builds can run in parallel, and thus save you time.

- You can version-lock the different projects and work

Each project uses its own language and exposes an artifact that can be used by other projects. In the example shown in Figure 17-4, a C# project uses libraries that are written in other (.NET) languages.

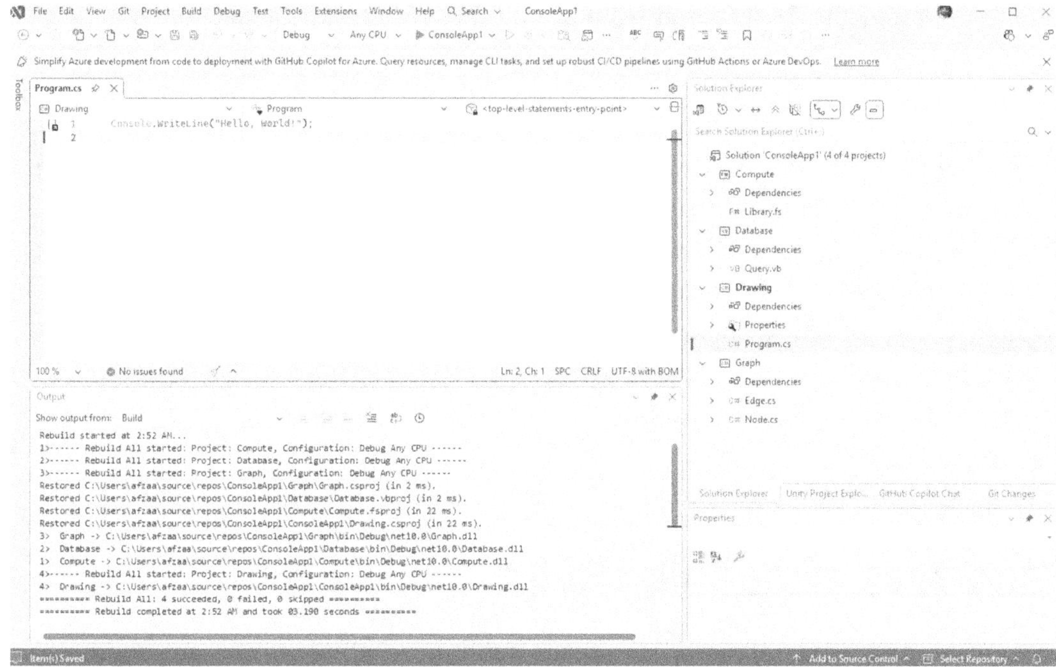

Figure 17-4. *The C# project Drawing uses the other projects in the solution and links to the DLL file that is generated. In the output, it shows that the project is built in a sequence to provide the artifacts to the Drawing project*

The applications are broader than just a C# project, they can be used to reshare a project code across all other projects in your organization.

And, now, this leads us to the CI servers and CI/CD pipelines.

Building in the CI Server

When you are developing the applications, you are also downloading and configuring the dependencies. The CI servers—unless owned and configured by your organization just like your development machines—do not have access to the dependencies, runtimes, environment variables, user accounts, access controls, or external services. In order to build the application, you need to replicate the environment. Two things are most important when building your application in a CI server:

1. Providing all the necessary dependencies and resources that are needed for the application—preferably, only the code that was changed—to build.

2. Minimizing the open-ended processes to save the time it takes to complete the process. On CI environments, you need to quickly move from one step to another without missing a check or step.

In .NET code, the `dotnet build` runs the dependencies restore and then compiles the sources. If your application has hundreds of dependencies, it will take a long time for the .NET CLI to prepare the project for the next step: building the source. Once the dependencies have been managed, the next step is indeed to build and compile the project. .NET 10 and the C# compilers have improved the performance massively, but it is not going to bring the build time down to 2% of the actual time. A big contributor to a high build time is the size of the solution or the project. The bigger your size, the more time it would take.

Parallel vs. Sequential Builds

It is very important to note that when you are building multiple projects and some of them depend on others, you would be triggering a recursive build for these. This problem is evident in larger projects, or monolith projects that reuse the same folder across multiple teams that work in their own roadmaps and pipelines but reuse the core components as the backbone.

Further Reading

We explored the deployment options (framework-dependent, or self-contained), when you publish the packages, .NET generates a lot of output for when the source code is built. One topic we very briefly touched was the trimming of the code. When you publish the project, the unused code can be trimmed from the outputs so that the artifacts are smaller in size. The compiler can make mistakes when deciding on the code to be trimmed and the patterns that are to be trimmed. Read this guide to learn how to write the code that does not misbehave because of trimmed code and structures: `https://learn.microsoft.com/en-us/dotnet/core/deploying/trimming/trimming-concepts`.

The .NET distribution packaging is an interesting structure of the package: `https://learn.microsoft.com/en-us/dotnet/core/distribution-packaging`. The structure makes it easier to deploy your application on multiple platforms. If you are publishing your applications on different platforms, check out how .NET lays out the bundle.

CHAPTER 18

The Basic Build

Every .NET application goes through a build phase. Regardless of the archetype or deployment environment chosen, you need to compile your source into an executable. The entry point for a build[1] expects the input artifacts and produces an output artifact. There are lots of complexities that can be added for a custom flavor of a build, which we will skip in this chapter.

The goal of this chapter is to teach you about a basic build, and to help you get onboarded to extend the existing build scripts to suit your own needs.

You can revisit this chapter when you write your own build scripts in a CI/CD or DevOps pipeline.

For a C# or a .NET application—of any sorts—there are generally three steps needed:

1. Prepare the dependencies for the project to use, or the ones that the project depends on.

2. Compile the sources and build the project together.

3. Generate an artifact as an output for other processes to use.

Typically, and especially in a CI/CD pipeline, a lot of other processes are added and for a very fair reason. These include, but are not limited to

- Conducting the tests on the source code

- Performing linting and code styling

- Running security scanning and validation

- Checking if any necessary steps are missing; such as documentation

---

[1] The dotnet build command is a simple one-step executable that takes your current folder as the Solution/Project folder and attempts to generate the output as expected by your project configuration. Read more about the dotnet build command here: `https://learn.microsoft.com/en-us/dotnet/core/tools/dotnet-build`.

© Afzaal Ahmad Zeeshan 2026
A. A. Zeeshan, *Building Mission-Critical Applications with .NET 10 and C# 14,*
https://doi.org/10.1007/979-8-8688-2347-3_18

They are all important, and honestly, I recommend them all. However, they are not what make a build procedure a build procedure. The bare minimum of running a build is as simple as performing a

```
$ dotnet build
```

This script does three things.

#1 Restore Dependencies

In .NET, the dependencies are mainly managed as DLL packages and are downloaded and imported from the NuGet package management system. There are two sources from which you can import the dependencies:

- The default source for the NuGet

- A custom feed for the sources

The default source for the NuGet is preconfigured as part of the SDK, and points to the official feed for the NuGet repository. The default NuGet repository contains several thousands of the packages.

When your .NET project is being built, the package restoration process imports all the dependencies based on their versions and adds them to the project—also the NuGet cache.[2] The packages downloaded are versioned, and the version is controlled by the project file.

If you decide to configure custom NuGet repository, you can do so by specifying which feeds to use.

```
<packageSources>
    <add key="nuget.org" value="https://api.nuget.org/v3/index.json"
protocolVersion="3" />
</packageSources>
```

You can add a key for your custom resource here, and NuGet would use this repository when fetching the dependencies. You can intermix the NuGet feeds and .NET

---

[2] NuGet packages can be added to the cache, global, or temporary folders. Read more in the official documentation: https://learn.microsoft.com/en-us/nuget/consume-packages/managing-the-global-packages-and-cache-folders.

would import the dependencies for you. To reiterate, the best way to keep your internal sources secure is by deploying these packages on the internal NuGet repository.

#2 Compile the Sources

With the dependencies now out of the way, and ready to be used, the next step is to use the compilers to build the project. C# uses the Roslyn compiler platform, and it is also open source. The Roslyn compiler platform does a really great job at compiling the projects and very fast.

The dotnet build command can also run the Roslyn platform's code analyzers as part of the code building process to provide feedback on the static analysis.

#3 Generate Artifacts

Now that the project has been built, it is time to publish the output artifacts. The output is controlled in the project file as well—even though you can always provide flags and options to the CLI. The .NET CLI can generate the outputs that have an executable path, or not. A library project, for example, does not have an executable code in them. The library projects provide code and services to other code that can be executed.

The OutputType field of the project can be used to control whether the output would be executable or not:

```
<PropertyGroup>
  <OutputType>Exe</OutputType>
</PropertyGroup>
```

The output of this build procedure would be an executable. To launch the application, you would run the file that has the .exe executable. The output folder also contains the .dll file that contains the project code, but you would use the .exe file to launch the process. When you run the dotnet build command on a .NET console project, the following output is generated:

```
Mode                LastWriteTime              Length Name
----                -------------              ------ ----
-a----         10/1/2025    7:20 PM               425 PlatformApp.deps.json
dw-a----       10/1/2025    7:20 PM              4608 PlatformApp.dll
-a----         10/1/2025    7:20 PM            150016 PlatformApp.exe
-a----         10/1/2025    7:20 PM             10536 PlatformApp.pdb
-a----         10/1/2025    7:20 PM               268 PlatformApp.runtimeconfig.json
```

The important files are **PlatformApp.dll**, **PlatformApp.exe**, and **PlatformApp. pdb**. The .exe file runs your application and the .pdb file contains the debug symbols. You cannot debug your application if the debug symbols have been stripped. The .dll contains the code for your application and will run just fine with the dotnet CLI; however, the practice is to use .exe file. Here is the output when I use the .dll file in the terminal:

```
PS C:\> dotnet .\PlatformApp.dll
Hello, World!
```

This is the same result that you would see if you ran the .exe file.

This step only generates an output that you can test and validate the functionality of the application. To get the final output artifacts that you can publish the application, you will use the dotnet publish command.

On a CI server, you would create a script that automates the execution of these steps so that you receive an output artifact after each push to the version control. I use Azure DevOps, and the build pipeline shown (in Figure 18-1) belongs to the Azure DevOps, but you can use GitHub or GitLab or other build automation platforms to write the same steps and scripts.

```
   master ∨        api    / azure-pipelines.yml *

 6   trigger:
 7     branches:
 8       include:
 9         - master
10     tags:
11       exclude:
12         - '*'
13   pool:
14     vmImage: 'windows-latest'
15
16   variables:
17     buildConfiguration: 'Release'
18
19   steps:
     Settings
20   - task: UseDotNet@2
21     inputs:
22       packageType: 'sdk'
23       version: '10.x'
24
     Settings
25   - task: DotNetCoreCLI@2
26     displayName: 'Restore dependencies'
27     inputs:
28       command: 'restore'
29
     Settings
30   - task: DotNetCoreCLI@2
31     displayName: 'Build the project'
32     inputs:
33       command: 'build'
34       arguments: '--configuration $(buildConfiguration)'
35
     Settings
36   - task: DotNetCoreCLI@2
37     displayName: 'Tests (with Code Coverage)'
38     inputs:
39       command: test
40       projects: '**/*Tests/*.csproj'
41       arguments: '--configuration $(buildConfiguration) --collect "Code coverage"'
42
     Settings
43   - task: DotNetCoreCLI@2
44     displayName: 'Publish artifacts'
45     inputs:
46       command: publish
47       publishWebProjects: True
48       arguments: '--configuration $(BuildConfiguration) --output $(Build.ArtifactStagingDirectory)'
49       zipAfterPublish: True
50
     Settings
51   - task: PublishPipelineArtifact@1
52     displayName: 'Upload artifacts'
53     inputs:
54       targetPath: '$(Build.ArtifactStagingDirectory)'
55       artifactName: 'sentential-master'
56
```

Figure 18-1. *A simple .NET build pipeline running on Windows. The build pipeline prepares and restores all the dependencies, builds the project, conducts the tests, and then publishes the artifacts for deployment*

If you are using GitHub, check out the Actions for .NET projects (`https://docs.github.com/en/actions/tutorials/build-and-test-code/net`), and for GitLab, check out the CI/CD templates (`https://docs.gitlab.com/ci/examples/#cicd-templates`) to configure and setup a pipeline for your .NET project. All in all, the simplest flow of the build works from gathering the dependencies together, running the compiler to build an output and then packaging them into a deployable format. Note that the testing stage can run before the building stage (if your project can be interpreted) or after the project has been built (especially when you need to test the built artifact itself).

Further Reading

The .NET platform is supported by all major DevOps platforms, and CI/CD and build platforms. GitHub, GitLab, TeamCity, Jenkins, and even your own custom development and building platforms can be converted into CI servers. Learn how Microsoft provides support for .NET builds on GitHub: `https://learn.microsoft.com/en-us/dotnet/devops/github-actions-overview`. As already mentioned in the chapter, my preference is to use Azure DevOps—primarily as it allows me to create repositories that are structured around projects and not have groups structured around projects.

CHAPTER 19

Managing Dependencies

For starters, the .NET platform is the largest dependency that you have in your projects. While the .NET platform provides everything to develop and deploy your applications, products, and services, most of the time you need to use a third-party service or product to develop and deploy your applications. This includes, but is not limited to, development frameworks or packages, deployment services and scripts, observability and telemetry tools, database connection providers, and more. All of these are an important part of your artifact that is generated during the DevOps pipeline.

In this chapter, we will learn how to find and add the dependencies to our projects, how to manage our internal dependencies, and how to optimize the package and artifact size that includes the dependencies.

We can get two things clear before we enter the chapter.

1. The default package manager for the .NET ecosystem is NuGet.

2. dotnet restore is an implicit command that is run for various dotnet CLI operations and the command manages the dependencies for the projects.

While .NET is an SDK or a runtime that you can install, a lot of packages and dependencies you must download and set up for your project. The default runtime for .NET contains various libraries that come shipped with the installation and you can use them out of the box (check out the list here: `https://learn.microsoft.com/en-us/dotnet/standard/runtime-libraries-overview`). A few examples would be the System. IO for working with file system on a device. But for most packages, you need to add a package dependency and then download it before you can use it in your code. A few examples of this would be the Microsoft.Data.Sqlite, Entity Framework Core, or caching services. The extensions (`https://github.com/dotnet/extensions`) are available to bring the industry-tested and battle-ready features to your applications without having to reinvent the wheel.

© Afzaal Ahmad Zeeshan 2026
A. A. Zeeshan, *Building Mission-Critical Applications with .NET 10 and C# 14*,
https://doi.org/10.1007/979-8-8688-2347-3_19

Believe it or not, the biggest bloatware in your applications comes from the dependencies. The .NET framework is the primary dependency, but the external dependencies that you depend upon also take up the final artifact size.

- The dependencies impact the overall artifact size that is generated at the end of the CI/CD pipeline process.

- If a dependency is not available, or a version of the dependency is not available, it would need to be built for the application to use. This also contributes directly to the build time.

- The dependencies also need to be copied, if they are coming from an external server or a cache resource.

- Often, dependencies come with a license or certificate and that must be copied together with the application in order for the application to launch and use the dependencies.

This is why it is often recommended to minimize the dependency count. The very bare minimum dependencies that enable your application to operate must be included in the software bill of materials. A good example of managing this list and minimizing its impact on our operations is by using a software bill of materials (`https://www.cisa.gov/sbom`). The software BOM helps you and your security/risk management teams track project dependencies and create plans for migrations, maintenance, upgrades, and deprecation.

Third-Party Dependencies

One of the reasons that I always use .NET framework for my applications is because the framework comes packed with almost everything that I would need to build, iterate on, and update my applications. From web application frameworks, mobile applications, database management, performance optimizations, security, user management, everything, Microsoft and the community has contributed a lot of packages for the community to use. The open source projects have also contributed to the development of the new dimensions. The MAUI framework came from the Xamarin project, which was an application of Mono framework to run C# on non-Windows environments. Today, we take that for granted.

NuGet is the home—or at least the first step—for the package discovery. Every unique challenge that you face has a package available for you to use.

Private Dependencies

Not every dependency or a package will be publicly available. A lot of libraries, packages, and dependencies would be available as a private installation. A very easy way to handle this is to just copy and paste the `.dll` file to the outputs without having to manage it via NuGet.

The private dependencies is also an approach used by enterprises to keep their packages, source code, dependencies, and properties private and on their own premises or within their own organizational accounts. The challenge of private dependencies is that they are your own responsibility. If your private repositories are down, then your applications will not be able to deploy or launch on the infrastructure. Another challenge is, you cannot really get any help on them from partners or community because they are private. And last, but not least, your teams consider this a private thing and not plan for a future for the repository. When your application depends on a project that must always be in a perfect state, you need to be cynical. You need to be mindful that perhaps what you are doing is the not the right thing, but a wheel reinvention. For various use cases, never reinvent the wheel, and never create private projects that are easily available from the community.

- Security

- Encryption

- User management

- Database pooling

- Thread management

- Privacy controls

And much more, where the impact is too massive. You must never, for example, create your own password hashing algorithms. Your algorithm will fail and that would lead to a major problem with compliance. Similarly, database or connection pooling may sound as simple as just maintaining a list of connections, but it is much more complicated. The security practices, such as SQL Injection prevention, the cross-site scripting or anti forgery, they seem very simple concepts; however, these areas require continuous research and an iterative approach to minimizing the risk.

Further Reading

The biggest challenge that most platforms face is the lack of community support, or the dependencies. .NET does not face that, and has a lot of packages either directly developed and provided by Microsoft, the .NET team, or third-party packages. The open source and community packages are also a lot. Check out the NuGet website for the statistics: `https://www.nuget.org/stats`.

CHAPTER 20

Artifacts Caching

One of the biggest blockers or friction points in speedy delivery to market is the extended build times. For every compiled runtime, the biggest challenge is reducing the build time for the project. In Software Engineering, the first attempt to improving performance is by putting something in a cache—HashSet, Dictionary, or the traditional in-memory approach to speed up the looks up and avoid re-computation. If we spend a lot of our build time on rebuilding sources that have not changed, we are simply wasting time for nothing. In such scenarios, it is best to cache the artifacts and reuse them.

Important: Go programming language was designed to have a very fast build process. The performance boost in the build comes from how Go manages and handles dependencies. Check out the Go at Google (`https://go.dev/talks/2012/splash.article`) and read this Stack Overflow thread (`https://stackoverflow.com/a/2976675`).

Azure DevOps platform offers a central caching platform for all the internal and external dependencies. In this chapter, you will learn about artifact caching in Azure DevOps, but similar concepts apply to other similar platforms—including GitHub, GitLab, or third-party platforms such as JFrog, etc.

In the last chapter, we explored the dependencies. Dependencies provide important features to our applications but are also a cause of bloating in the application. The more dependencies that you add, the more bloated it becomes. If the dependencies are internal—such as a monolith—the biggest problem is the added build time for each dependency.

There is a very easy way for us to skip this iteration of the build every time we modify something.

1. Orchestrate the team set up around a business activity that the team fully owns. We already mentioned Conway's law in this book, which is very important for the team structure for efficient software production.

© Afzaal Ahmad Zeeshan 2026
A. A. Zeeshan, *Building Mission-Critical Applications with .NET 10 and C# 14*,
https://doi.org/10.1007/979-8-8688-2347-3_20

2. The dependencies of these teams must follow the organizational dependency pattern. Meaning, if your organization has internal database teams (compared to outsourced databases, or cloud-hosted database teams), the database team should be responsible for the "data layer." The SDKs, APIs, controls, everything must be owned and managed by the database team, where the consuming teams should only be responsible for connecting to and consuming the services. The changes in the end-products may not depend on the data layer; and publishing new versions of data or application must be done independently.

3. Your teams must follow a strict contract for the dependency management. Meaning, if your team is using version 4 of the database provider, then version 4.2 must not break anything in the application.

Any caching system requires a "key" to check if a resource exists for the current look up or if an operation needs to be executed to get the resource. In our case, "version-2.0" is a valid key to identify the 2.0 version for our application or system. If our cache system has a resource for "version-2.0" then instead of rebuilding the system, we just deploy the artifacts generated for the operation "version-2.0." If the version does not exist, then we have no choice but to build or rebuild everything. The build procedure is a recursive approach. When you are rebuilding the "version-2.0," you also need to validate internal dependencies to make sure they are built as well. Your "version-2.0" may depend on "serializer-1.9," "parser-5.5," and "logger-8.3." Your build script will validate if these dependencies are available. If they are, they will be copied/linked as a process, and the project "version-2.0" will be built. However, if one of these is not built then your build script will start the build process for one of these. And, recursively, it will continue until the entire subtree (our project as the root, with dependencies and their dependencies as branches and leaves) is built and ready to be linked. A simpler scenario of this flow is demonstrated in Figure 20-1.

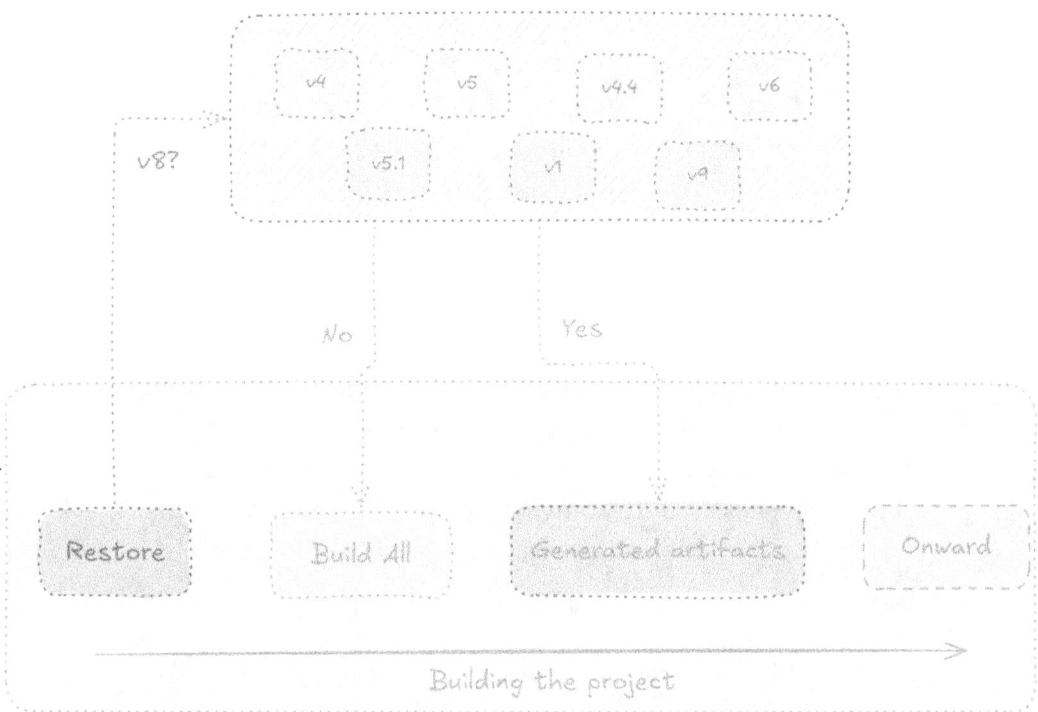

Figure 20-1. *In a build pipeline, the projects and their dependencies are built or downloaded as they are made available. If your dependencies are available through a feed, the pipeline can import directly from the channels. If a version is not found, then a new version of the dependency is attempted to be built to be used in the project*

In NuGet, luckily, most dependencies are available ready-to-import. So, our build times do not have to face a big challenge when importing the libraries from NuGet environments. Large dependencies do take a long time to download and import in the system.

Remember: There is always only a little in which caching can help you.

The major players, Azure DevOps, GitLab, GitHub, etc., all offer caching services. They offer caching not just for the dependencies but also for your source code. If you use tags in your Git version control, your build pipeline can skip the steps and return the already-built resource to the next phases of deployment. This is most important when you are using internal dependencies. Your teams may be working on their own roadmaps, and thus, a change in one team's source code or repository may require a rebuild for other teams. To avoid having to rebuild every repository for every change, cache the repositories and the outputs.

One biggest challenger in this domain is the notorious "**Copy Always**" value in the "**Copy to Output Directory**" field. If you use this, Visual Studio will always (re)build your projects, even if there are no changes. To avoid the unnecessary build, use "**Copy If Newer**" value instead. Visual Studio will (re)build your projects when it detects that a change has been made in the files and not always.

Invalidating Cache

Cached artifacts give us that extra speed that we are looking for to launch fast and avoid extra build times. However, that extra speed comes with a big challenge. If your built resource is faulty and you need to replace it, then you need to invalidate the cache key to make sure future references for the resource do not point to the invalid artifact.

- Cache miss is a very expensive operation in a high velocity environment.

- Invalidating a cache needs to be fast to avoid misconfigured or faulty resource propagation.

- Cache systems come with basic arithmetic built-in, and instead of invalidating the cache you can perform an increment operation to provide a latest resource; instead of "version-2.1" your cache sees a latest resource "version-2.2" or "version-2.1.1" available and provides it as a resource. The challenge with this is that you can no longer read by the key directly, you need to read the value for the live resource ("version-2.1.1") in this case and then fetch the resource for that.

In all fairness, caching your built outputs has a very big advantage. It does come with a big cost:

1. Costs of the storage

2. Cost of infrastructure complexity—considering the cache operations

3. Cost of the cache operations and monitoring

The cost pays for itself in quick feedback to developers, avoiding duplicate build times, recursive builds, avoid CPU cycles being wasted for computation of versions and dependency graphs, and most importantly, keeping the right dependencies always available by their "keys" for the infrastructure to use and (re)deploy.

If you are using Azure DevOps, you can use the internal Azure DevOps's provided Azure Artifacts that hosts your internal (or external) dependencies and packages. The packages can be from any language and package management platform (NuGet, npm, PyPi, and others are all supported). To learn how to use the Azure Artifacts for your projects, read this guide: `https://learn.microsoft.com/en-us/azure/devops/artifacts/start-using-azure-artifacts?view=azure-devops`. Figure 20-2 shows an internal feeds channel created for the packages where you can publish your packages and have them shared across all of your internal webapps.

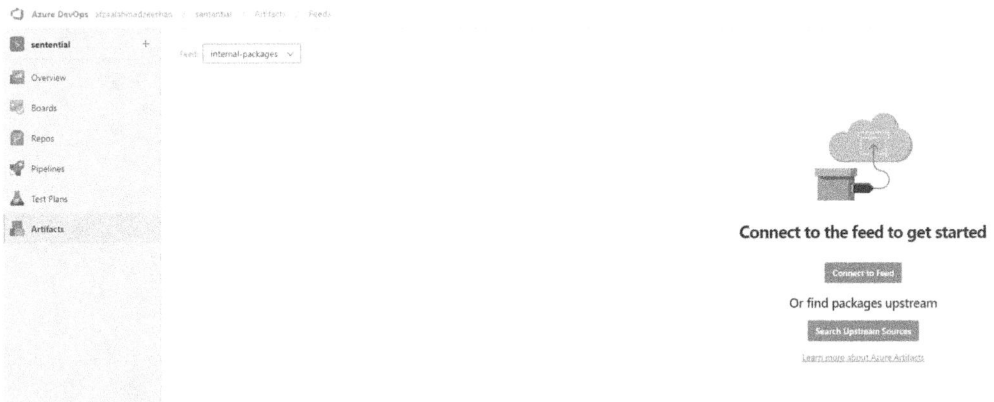

Figure 20-2. *The internal artifacts storage can not only keep your packages and dependencies secure but also speed up the build pipelines by caching the outputs of versioned build stages*

The Azure Artifacts is not an unlimited service, and it comes with its own limitations, but you can use the best practices to simplify the process and make sure your web applications can get benefits from the platform and not be blocked by it. Read about it here: `https://learn.microsoft.com/en-us/azure/devops/artifacts/concepts/best-practices?view=azure-devops`.

Since we use dependencies in almost all of our projects, it also exposes us to malicious and bad actors. In the next chapter, we will learn how to prevent the most common of the attacks to keep our software, our repositories, and our customers safe.

CHAPTER 21

Supply-Chain Security

With the greatest packages comes the sneakiest malware. The biggest risk that your software is exposed to in the modern software development life cycle is the supply-chain attack. It is sophisticated, simple, zero-cost, but very dangerous in its attack. While it may not attack your software directly, depending on your industry, this attack may use your software as an attack surface for the victim that they are interested in.

Generally, supply-chain attacks happen on libraries or packages that are developed in the open source or community-led environments. It is still possible to see instances of supply-chain attacks in Inner Source projects. Also, contrary to popular belief, not every supply-chain attack originates from a malicious external actor. Supply-chain attacks can be accompanied by a socially engineered attack.

Not a week goes by without the news feed being filled by small- and medium-sized supply-chain attacks on some of the biggest packages. Compared to other types of attack, such as DDoS, or ransomware, where the intention is to bring down the operations of the organization to prevent them from offering the services. The goal of supply-chain attack is to attack the weaker components of your software supply-chain and either attack your organization or use it as a puppet in a larger attack against other organizations.

First, the supply-chain for the software. What is it actually? The supply-chain is the entire operational procedure that your IT or infrastructure team uses to take the software's source code from your developers and brings it to the customers. Just like a real-world supply-chain of retail, grocery, or clothing stores, where the prepared materials are collected from the vendors and then supplied all the way to the customers, wherever they are. The software supply-chain works in the same way, but digitally. The supply-chain is demonstrated in Figure 21-1 as a simplified version:

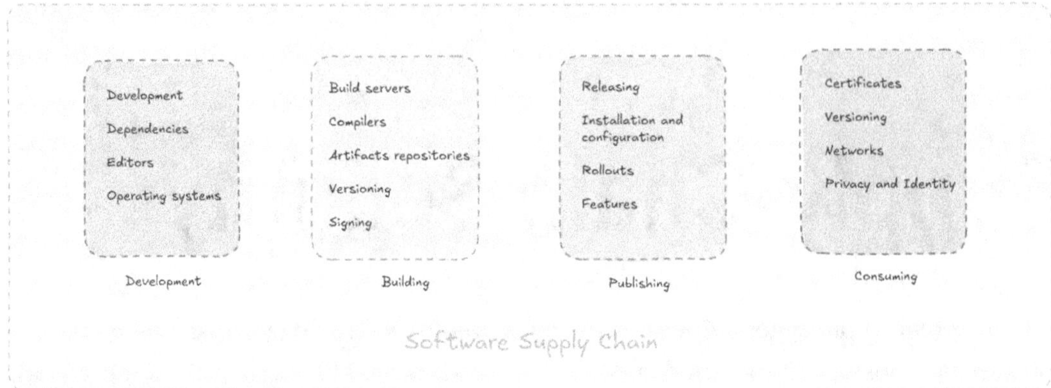

Figure 21-1. *The supply-chain is a reflection of the industry practices for producing and consuming, where the supply-chain makes sure that the produced goods are consumed in a safer manner*

The source code lives in the version control, the build script compiles and tests it for quality, the bundler then prepares it for delivery, and finally, the software is served to the customers. Two core components that are a byproduct of the supply-chain (again, taking from the real-world concept of supply-chain):

- The automation of the product delivery

- The collection of receipts with the software bill of materials

You use the two together to ensure that the product is of good quality and vetted. In some manners, the software supply-chain is a mirror of a DevOps practice applied in an organization where you automate the pipeline and bring both the ends (producers, consumers) closer.

Before we dive into the software world, let's take an example of a grocery store serving fresh bread to the customers—the real-world supply-chain management.[1] What does the grocery store need to consider validating the quality of the bread? It is certainly not just the looks of the bread. The supply-chain procedures in the software development resemble the software development life cycle. The planning, requirements gathering, and the continuous feedback aside, let's focus on the development, quality control, and delivery of the product to the customer.

---

[1] Read more about the incident management procedures here: `https://www.ibm.com/think/topics/supply-chain-management`.

Development

The development and building phase is where the supply-chain attacks attempt to sneak into the entire pipeline. The common challengers include

- Exploited dependencies and libraries—including from the package management platforms

- Exploited build platforms, CI scripts, or CI servers, including and mainly exploited and vulnerable VMs used to build the applications

When you are developing the product, you will need to secure not just the framework but also the development machines. You can isolate your build servers, but if your developers download all sorts of malware on their devices, or if a broken or faulty dependency injects a worm in your environment, the worm will very easily replicate itself.

Prepare your applications for a thorough security scan during the commit and push on the build environments but also on the development machines. A lot of organizations attempt to do this by locking the systems down; and that is not enough, social engineering is possible with a fully locked down system. You must run a thorough scan of the development environments, build servers, build dependencies, code contributed, the identity of the contributor—very important for open source projects—and, last, but definitely not least, the infrastructure resources that you are using to build the project. A lot of DevOps platforms offer the scans out of the box, such as GitLab, GitHub, Azure DevOps, but you can also use platforms such as Aikido,[2] Snyk,[3] etc., which are some platforms that can scan the contributions.

Building and testing the application is an important part of development, because it should primarily be a responsibility of the developer to make sure that their software does what it is expected to do. Manual QAs (quality assurance) and automation engineers can write the scripts that test the application behavior in an aftermath, but by that time, it is already too late. If you must take away one thing from this paragraph, it is that you must shift-left (that is to do more work before you push the code to the next stage). This includes testing the code. While it is required to conduct tests in the

---

[2] Read about the supply-chain security on Aikido's website: `https://www.aikido.dev/glossary/software-supply-chain-security`.

[3] Check out the contents for the supply-chain attack on Snyk's website: `https://snyk.io/articles/software-supply-chain-security/`

build stage, and validate and verify the artifact binary hash, the client certificates on the infrastructure, it is better to test the application during the development process. The tests conducted in development phase are cheaper (even though they may take longer time to run, more engineer hours, etc.).

Quality Control

This is a rather safe zone and it is rather difficult for a supply-chain attack to enter the pipeline at this stage. But it is not impossible. The supply-chain attempts can happen at this stage, for example, an exploited build dependency can contribute the exploit to your applications as well. An exploited build, for example, can add malicious code to your build outputs that may or may not further contribute the exploits to other builds or products.

Snyk, for example, will be the most suitable platform applicable at this stage of the software development life cycle. You would validate not just the changes contributed but how they behave. Using the dynamic analysis (DAST), you can review the performance and quality of the code as it is executing. The quality control aspects apply to building, packaging, deploying, and running states. You need to make sure that the software is safe, that the user is protected from any man-in-the-middle attacks, any expired certificates are updated before their expiry date, the dependencies are all updated, and security patches are applied. The job of a quality assurance person in a tech space is not to just make sure that a button pressed performs an action. It must also validate if the action is safe, if the data collected and generated is safe and protected, and that the bad actors are kept at bay.

Delivery

The most notable problems are identified in the delivery or deployment phase of the software development life cycle. This comes in various factors:

- The dependency hijacks[4] are a leading cause for delivery problems, where a well-known dependency is spoofed and a developer is misled into using it. An example of this is where a well-known internal dependency is listed on a public package manager and the software starts to use the publicly listed—probably malicious— dependency and gets exploited.

- Man-in-the-middle attacks, although easily avoidable, but very strong and powerful if proper security is not enforced. If your applications do not use security, such as TLS security with HTTPS, your application content and communication can be very easily read, altered, and exploited.

- Checksum-less software are prone to be downloaded from malicious websites and leads to client platform being compromised. If you are releasing your software that can be downloaded and installed from the "internet," consider providing a checksum[5] with your application binary. Your customers can then validate if they downloaded the right binary or if the binary was compromised—during the transport. And, this does happen, sometimes the binary was just corrupted on the network and it had nothing to do with a malicious user.

If your user downloads your application, and faces damagers—user privacy issues, data loss, misrepresentation, financial loss, etc.—they would certainly legally challenge you. Even though the problem was not caused by your application and it was caused because your application was mutated on the way to your customer; your customer does not have a way to validate that. It is your responsibility to provide a way to validate that the product is "in fact" yours. A retail, for example, provides a receipt to the customer when they make a purchase and this purchase has the information about the products that were purchased at the grocery store visit. The retail store can challenge back if

---

[4] Read this OWASP report on the dependency-related problems and vulnerabilities: `https://owasp.org/www-project-top-10-ci-cd-security-risks/` `CICD-SEC-03-Dependency-Chain-Abuse`.

[5] Read why a checksum is important, and why you must always consider sharing a checksum with your software: `https://linuxsecurity.com/features/what-are-checksums-why-should-you-be-using-them`. Your checksum doesn't have to use quantum cryptography to be produced, just a way to validate that malicious users cannot produce the same results.

the receipt does not contain the product that caused the damage. For example, if your customer claims that they got sick because of the cheese they used with the bread, you can check if they purchased the cheese at your retail store or not.

While in the software world we do not have to worry about a return being rerouted to our warehouses, we do have to worry about the license procurement or license invalidation in case we have issued a refund to our customer. A license that should be invalidated, but is not, can be abused by the customers to resell your product and claim their money back.

Writing the code for the software is part of the software life cycle, and this part feeds into the next part, which is the infrastructure that runs and manages your software in production. In the next part, we will now turn our attention toward the infrastructure aspects of our architecture and learn how to build smooth and automated pipelines that deliver and deploy your mature and tested software. In the next chapter, we will start by first introducing the link and relation between DevOps and the infrastructure for our applications.

Further Reading

We discussed that we should shift left to improve the quality of the software, while that is one metric, another metric is the cost of bugs in production. If your supply-chain does not do due-diligence, then the production operations are going to be more expensive. Read this guide that discusses the costs element of production bugs: `https://testomat.io/blog/software-bug-cost/`.

The shift-left strategy has often been used to explain the testing of the software. While that is true, as shown in this IBM post: `https://www.ibm.com/think/topics/shift-left-testing`, I believe shift left is not just for testing and making sure that your software works. It is also to share feedback, to provide information to your development team on software chokepoints, bottlenecks, quality loss, and more. If you're trying to understand how your application behaves in production (on the right-side of the chain), check out this blog post to learn how to improve the performance and system of your application: `https://www.crowdstrike.com/en-us/cybersecurity-101/cloud-security/shift-left-security/`.

PART V

Going Live

CHAPTER 22

DevOps and Infrastructure

Your application is as resilient and available as the underlying infrastructure. You cannot have a 99.9999% available application on an infrastructure that is available 99.99% of the time.

DevOps is a manifesto—*I cannot stress this enough*. DevOps is not a framework or "do this" approach, it is a manifesto that encourages collaboration between developers and the operations teams to run a "service." If there is one thing that you can observe by implementing DevOps principles, it is speed and agility. The ability of your development team to flexibly ship services and products to the market will gain a plus point when they work in collaboration with the operations team/infrastructure team, compared to if they take best-guess shots.

In this chapter, we will learn about

- Uptime and downtime, and why a downtime occurs

- The infrastructure, resources, and explore how to prepare your software for deployment

This also ties back to the first paragraph here; your developers would be aware of the availability of the underlying system and thus they will not be shooting for the stars—you must go for the Moon before you go for Mars.

You may close your eyes—hey, hey, not yet, continue reading—and imagine what DevOps may look like. DevOps is a flow, like water, of your source code to a compiled state in which it provides services to the customers. DevOps is the function that mutates the input and provides an output. And using the same concept, DevOps pipelines must not have side effects or depend on the external state of the infrastructure to produce different results. If you are not using the automation and continuous harmony offered by the DevOps manifesto and workflows for your applications as well as the infrastructure resources, then you are not really using DevOps. DevOps was never really implemented by organizations; it was part of the DevOps manifesto that worked for them that they

© Afzaal Ahmad Zeeshan 2026
A. A. Zeeshan, *Building Mission-Critical Applications with .NET 10 and C# 14*,
https://doi.org/10.1007/979-8-8688-2347-3_22

used and then gave up and moved on. DevOps, SREs, Platform Engineering, they are not the name for the same thing, and they each have their own advantages and disadvantages. For .NET projects, DevOps has two important values:

- A unique approach to building the products and delivering them

- Automation of the infrastructure and resources

In the chapters ahead, we will explore how tooling can be used to automate and speed up the delivery of the products and provide important feedback to the developers to optimize the source code and the infrastructure or use the infrastructure as a "wave" and ride it.

Uptime vs. Downtime

The balance between Developers and Engineers (for the uninitiated: infrastructure Engineers) is the same as the balance between Uptime and Downtime. At a service level, we can run multiple updates and configurational changes to get our latest software and product live without any impact on the customers or the end users. But behind all the abstractions, there is no way for a process to be updated when it is running. You need to reboot, restart, or relaunch the process or the system to update it to the latest version. Figure 22-1 shows a simpler process where you update an existing application, and as a result, you encounter a downtime in your application.

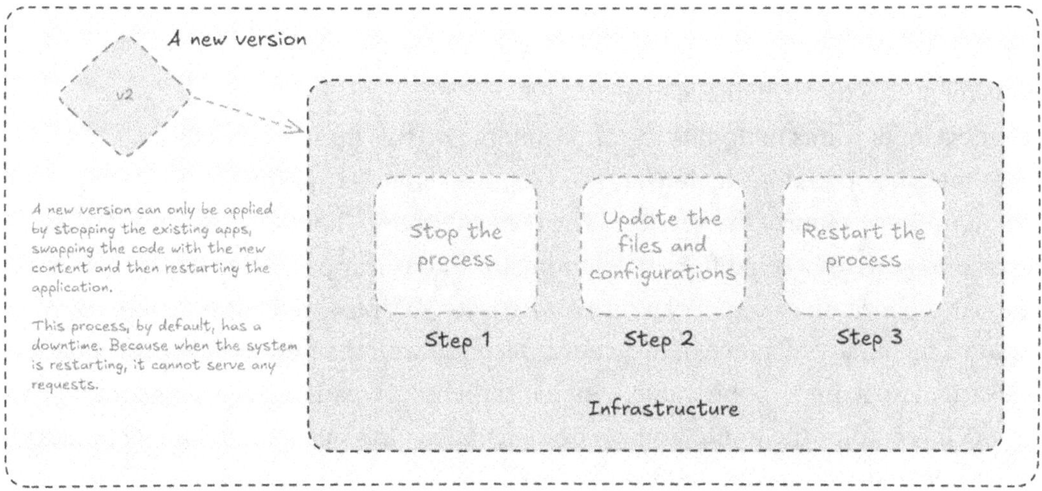

Figure 22-1. *The default update process for any application resource would lead to a downtime. The downtime does not have to be days, but it can be a few minutes. The downtime, thus, is a byproduct of releasing a new version*

Modern application architectures enable a seamless update because

- Every system is deployed at least a few times across the clusters; to make it elastic, available, and resilient to fault.

- The deployments strategies on various cloud providers enable creating an extra process to make the new deployment to.

- The process and app with the older deployment continues to serve new requests until the new process is ready to accept new requests.

- Once the new application is warm, traffic is routed to the new application that has new configuration and code.

Information: In this context, cold vs. warm means the state of the dependencies and readiness of the application. In .NET, or even Java apps, an application starts with a cold boot where the dependencies and the stack are not ready to accept the first request. This is why the first HTTP request or command execution takes a long time. After a while, once the dependencies are ready and the application is "warm" then the requests are handled properly with no delay. After a service downtime, the initial few requests are always slow. To make the downtime, or the zero downtime, non-existent, the throughput, latency, response time, all need to remain the same and this blue/green deployment[1] is a way to achieve this.

A developer wants to update the application, and this update comes with a downtime. The operations team wants to keep the services running and they want to focus on the uptime of the services. The concept of zero downtime is a result of an abstraction used between different components and web apps used to deploy a service. Figure 22-2 shows an example of Azure App Service's Deployment Slots, where you prepare a secondary instance of the web application with the newer and latest code and warm it up to receive the traffic. When instance #2 is ready to receive the traffic, the network layer swaps the traffic from go from instance #1 to instance #2 and it happens in an invisible[2] manner to your end users.

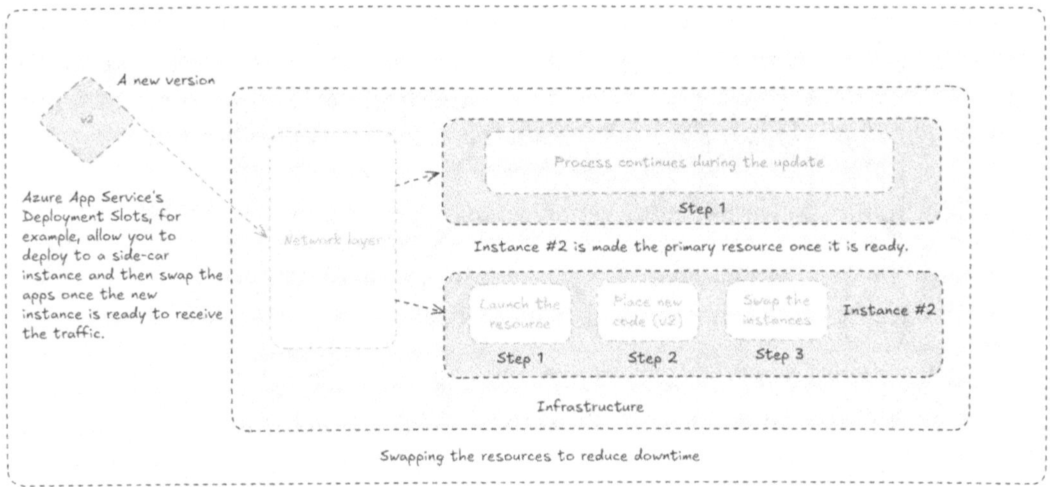

Figure 22-2. *The zero-downtime release is an architectural pattern where you use multiple resources to conduct a single release. This does mean that while there is a downtime internally in the app instances, the overall system remains online*

---

[1] Read more about blue/green deployments here: `https://codefresh.io/learn/software-deployment/what-is-blue-green-deployment/`.

[2] This will be invisible provided that you are not using in-proc or sticky sessions, where the user information is stored within the process itself and when a process dies the user session is removed. Read about sticky sessions, and how or why to use or avoid them: `https://traefik.io/glossary/what-are-sticky-sessions`.

When these two forces come together, we have DevOps. And the approach is always to find the right fit and the balance between when to say no and when to say hello. When you say no, you are making a conscious choice between selecting who your customer and end user is and who you are adding to the backlog.

Infrastructure Management

The advent of cloud platforms has made the infrastructure management very simple. There is nothing to manage. You just set up a pipeline and release to production. YOLO.

No, not really. The infrastructure has changed from what it used to be. The major change is that you are not responsible for managing the provisioning and maintenance of the infrastructure; however, you are responsible for setting up the resources on the platform. Take Azure App Service, the underlying "platform" is managed by Microsoft Azure. Your only responsibility is to have the resource allocated in your subscription and configured for the runtime version that your application needs; such as a .NET version, Java runtime, or Node.js version.

Note   In the next chapter, we will explore how to automate the delivery and changes to the infrastructure, regardless of the level.

If your applications are released continuously, your infrastructure must be ready to accept the changes any time of the day, even weekends. The major benefit of cloud platforms over the legacy hosting service providers is that you do not need to create tickets to make a change in your infrastructure or allocate an extra resource. The cloud platforms enable you to scale the infrastructure as needed, and then scale it down when less resources are needed. This is known as the "elasticity" of the cloud platform. Today, with millions of dollars invested in the infrastructure, "elasticity" is no longer a public cloud concept. The elasticity of the infrastructure platform means that your platform grows as the demand grows, so it is not a rigid hardcoded configuration to grow to a certain size and then turn belly up. Which will not be an efficient approach to running and managing the infrastructure, especially when your application is ready to go flying with a continuous deployment.

The biggest mistake in infrastructure provisioning is

- Wrong number of hosting resources allocated; either too many or too few. One is bad for your customers, and the other is bad for your wallet.

- Experimenting with the non-LTS features that may not be available in the long term. Pivoting for the sake of experimentation is good, but it does take away from your capacity of building business.

- Relying on LTS versions of the software and frameworks for too long, and missing the deadline to updating your infrastructure to newer versions that support updates and patches in case of a security vulnerability.

  - From a security perspective, this is the biggest risk. Many times, critical infrastructure is deployed on a legacy system that does not receive security updates and patches, which leads to exploited systems and data leaks.

  - WannaCry was an example of such an infrastructure. The impact was more than hundreds of thousands of devices that were all held for ransom, impacting the most critical systems—healthcare, National Health Service (NHS), to be precise. Read more about WannaCry here (`https://www.cloudflare.com/en-gb/learning/security/ransomware/wannacry-ransomware/`) and honestly, it could've been avoided by just upgrading your infrastructure once a year. The costs for upgrades pay off for themselves.

  - Another interesting aspect of WannaCry was that it was not developed by the hackers in the dark web. It was developed by the US National Security Agency (NSA), EternalBlue (`https://www.hypr.com/security-encyclopedia/eternalblue`), and was released in public when the NSA itself was compromised. If NSA can be compromised, you should have a reason to do the basic due diligence.

- Not taking the limitations of the cloud platform into account when designing your architecture and infrastructure.

The availability of the applications depends entirely on the availability of your infrastructure. The moment your infrastructure goes down, the application goes down. There is no recovery for your applications if the infrastructure is down. The efforts and effectiveness of the development teams are tuned down to zero if the effectiveness and reliability of the infrastructure is compromised. This situation is already a very bad experience for your customers, or their customers. And what is worse than having your infrastructure down? Having your developers pointing fingers at the infrastructure teams as if they are "them" vs. "us" who sabotaged our applications.

DevOps aims to solve this by turning the entire pipeline into a jigsaw puzzle. The puzzle then offers the gauges and knobs for your teams to turn and twist to optimize the service. DevOps, just a manifesto, nurtures a culture of working together, blameless incident management, optimizing the system by reviewing the pros and cons of each approach on the development or operations side, and finally, ensuring every mistake made is a lesson learned for the business.

Lastly, it is also important for you to remember some of the values for the uptime or availability nines (9s), some values are shown in the Table 22-1.

Table 22-1. *A grid about the uptime target for the apps and how they respond to the possible downtime for them on a daily, weekly, or yearly basis.*

Uptime%	Daily downtime	Weekly downtime	Yearly downtime	Notes
95%	~1.5 hours	~8 hours	~18 days	Only for POCs and MVPs
99%	~14 minutes	~1.5 hours	~3 days	For non-critical applications
99.9%	~1.5 minute	~10 minutes	~8.5 hours	For critical applications
99.99%	~8 seconds	~1 minute	~1 hour	For mission-critical applications, where every minute matters.
99.9999%	~1/100th of a second	~Half a second	~30 seconds	When your application provides services to other critical platforms.
100%	None	None	None	You must not be targeting for this, as it does not exist.

If you'd like to play with the numbers and learn what different values mean for your business and your targets must be, check out this website uptime (`https://uptime.is/`) to learn more.

If you study the table above, you'll realize that the downtime seconds (or minutes in a few cases) move from daily to yearly targets. An application in development can be down for a few hours as your developers debug it, but for critical applications, the entire year must not encounter more than a few minutes or an hour in downtime. For more critical platforms that are then used by other critical service providers—healthcare, etc.—the entirety of the downtime must be almost negligible.

Remember: Unless you are a platform provider, such as an infrastructure company, your infrastructure is not what you are selling to your customers. Netflix, for example, does not sell their cloud or microservices, they sell their streaming platform for end users to watch content on. Microsoft, or Amazon, on the other hand, do have a platform-selling business. If you are also in platform-selling business, then the availability of your infrastructure is important, but if you are selling a service, or a product, then the availability of your product is important. If your product is naturally "available" to your customers, then they would not care if your infrastructure faced downtime internally.

The funny thing about "negligible" is that it is not measurable, and thus, as an Engineer you cannot rely on something being negligible. It may be negligible, but for your customers it may not be. For this, you must always work on numbers and metrics as they are tangible and non-negligible. Just saying that your service is down for 30 seconds may be negligible for you but not for a business that loses thousands of dollars in those 30 seconds, especially during their business time. This is where you get a service-level agreement with your customers to have a "tangible" binding between your business and your customers, and when the problems should actually be non-negligible. We will revisit this topic in the "Observing Apps" section and study how you can observe the applications, how they are operating, and providing this feedback to the customers to **(1)** notify them when something is going wrong on your side and **(2)** provide them with a clear metric about your service's performance.

In the next chapter, let's take a look at how to automate the provisioning of the infrastructure and all the resources, and also how to make sure that our infrastructure stays the same using Infrastructure as Code.

CHAPTER 23

Infrastructure As Code

Infrastructure as Code—or as I specified a notion of "Everything as Code" in my last book *DevSecOps for .NET Core*[1]—is not a new concept, but heavily used concept today in Engineering. I believe we are overdoing the concept of X-as-Code. And due to the overuse, it is not well understood—*just like technical debt*. As our applications mature toward cloud native or agile applications, shouldn't our infrastructure be given the same growth? Why do we have .NET 8 apps running on Ubuntu 22.04 or a legacy version of CentOS, or almost-end-of-support Windows Server? Why are you still using the default credentials? No, no, just because the process lives on the server and is behind a VPN does not merit default credentials.

Infrastructure as Code (also abbreviated as IaC) is not the end goal, it is the journey. It is a journey that allows a company—or a team of Engineers—to help their infrastructure grow into a mature platform that enables the growth of their applications. IaC is not a yes-or-no, IaC is not "entire stack." IaC is a choice for the tools, configurations, that give your operations teams control over the behavior of infrastructure while automating mundane tasks to free up your Engineering resources to "think" about business challenges.

With all the fancy and shiny tools, infrastructure is still an uncharted territory for many developers. They are either not allowed anywhere near infrastructure, or they do not consider it an important skill for their own development and growth. Both are wrong.

Terraforming the Unknown

Terraform has been the de facto for infrastructure deployments on (hybrid) cloud environments. While the configuration management comes from Ansible, or Puppet, or

---

[1] Check out the chapter here: `https://link.springer.com/chapter/10.1007/978-1-4842-5850-7_4`.

© Afzaal Ahmad Zeeshan 2026
A. A. Zeeshan, *Building Mission-Critical Applications with .NET 10 and C# 14*,
https://doi.org/10.1007/979-8-8688-2347-3_23

Chef, the infrastructure deployment needs a different approach. Once your teams start using Terraform (`https://developer.hashicorp.com/terraform`), or Infrastructure as Code tools, such as Azure Bicep (`https://learn.microsoft.com/en-us/azure/azure-resource-manager/bicep/overview?tabs=bicep`), or even a framework that is language agnostic, you will never go back. Infrastructure as Code in the hands of the Engineers is just like a match in the hands of a monkey. They will set everything on fire.

- They will set fire to the old ticket-based infrastructure upgrade or maintenance approach.

- They will set fire to the silos that exist in your Development and Operations and add an automation to it.

- They will set fire to the lazy, boresome, and slow runbooks, and turn them into automation, scripts—such as Kubernetes Operators.

- They will set your wallets on fire as well.

If you're not a fan of Terraform, look at Pulumi,[2] Pulumi is a scriptable Infrastructure as Code platform. Instead of having to learn any domain-specific language to "write the resources" you just need to add, you use the language that you are already hands-on with. Pulumi offers you to use Python, C#, or JavaScript, or other languages[3] to write the infrastructure states and work on upgrading the infrastructure as GitOps[4] operations. The benefit of Pulumi is

- You only need to have a brain-model of what your infrastructure requires.

- You can use one of the main programming languages to write the infrastructure and have it deployed.

- You can apply the best practices of GitOps, and speed up the delivery and deployment of your infrastructure.

- You can perform "code" reviews on the infrastructure changes to avoid any unnecessary changes.

---

[2] Visit the website here: `https://www.pulumi.com/`

[3] Check out the latest langauges supported on Pulumi platform here on their website: `https://www.pulumi.com/product/infrastructure-as-code/`

[4] Read more about GitOps on GitLab: `https://about.gitlab.com/topics/gitops/`

- GitOps ensures that the infrastructure is always in the state that you need it to be in.

- Pulumi computes the result and generates the infrastructure for you, and since it is written in your own languages, it does support conditional generation of the infrastructure, or conditional state and configuration.

- It is open source.[5]

Read more: If you would like to see some examples, I'll highly encourage you to visit Terraform or Pulumi, or other IaC tools on their GitHub or their website to learn how you can use the platforms. Those websites would have the latest and up-to-date examples, compared to the ones that I would provide here in this book, which may not be the latest by the time this book gets published in a few weeks.

Going Beyond the Infrastructure

Although the platforms enable the configuration and management of the underlying infrastructure resources, they are not limited just to the virtual machines and database engines. These IaC platforms also enable you to go one step beyond and configure the applications and their state as well.

A good example is configuring the container image to be used in the latest release. Since the IaC files can be templated,[6] the variables can be controlled and modified based on what we need our infrastructure to contain. The benefits of this approach are

- The infrastructure resources remain the same but the application changes or gets updated.

- You version control the changes and can verify who made a change to the application or the packages.

---

[5] I've added "open source" as the last benefit here, because, today, honestly, just being an open source platform is not enough. Licenses change all the time. And to be fair, I am not saying that Pulumi is not open source or would change, who knows, but be mindful that once your infrastructure is deployed with a specific tool, moving around would be difficult.

[6] Read more on how we can configure IaC with Terraform to deploy Azure Container Instances: `https://learn.microsoft.com/en-us/azure/container-instances/container-instances-quickstart-terraform`

- You can roll back the changes if you encounter a hiccup on the production.

The challenges, just like any other automation are

- You need to have a human review the changes, or the machines would make mistakes.

- The images need to be rebuilt and deployed. You cannot make changes to the currently running instances.

- Redeployment is not always fast, or cheap.

As Engineers, we can solve these problems too. Ability to modify the configuration or the behavior of the runtime in production is possible and is never a blocker because of infrastructure or application framework. Feature flags, toggles, remote configuration can be used to control and modify the behavior of the application. One thing to remember, when you change the configuration of the application, in a majority of the cases, it has to reload or restart. And that is the best case, your application gets some breathing time to restart and prepare itself to capture the requests.

I cannot stress enough, how time alone can show so many bugs and breaking points of your application. More than a decade ago, I worked with a company who would perform tests on their application overnight. The tests were not just unit tests, in fact, they were all sorts of tests; including and most especially stress and load tests. The stress tests would expose all sorts of cracks in the architecture of the software.

- Memory leaks

- Communication gaps

- Latency degradation

- Backlog filling

- Request dropping

- Application crashing

And many other problems show up when your application runs for more than a few hours. Often times, it happens because when you are debugging the application, you run a "fresh copy" of the application. The fresh copy of the application uses the latest configuration and there are little to no side effects in the system. When the application continues to run for a few hours, or days, the "internal state" of the application changes. This leads to several unknown behaviors, that lead to bugs, misleading results, crashes, resource consumption, etc.

So, while you can control the configurations and features remotely, the opportunity that you receive by restarting and swapping the components is that they start fresh. The benefit of using containers—Docker-based or using other runtimes—is that your infrastructure is immutable. Once your application is packaged, you do not need to provide any additional configuration files or resources for the application to boot up. After you have conducted rigorous testing on the source code as well as the binary, you can be sure that every deployment will result in the same service; *external services ignored.*

Infrastructure Lockdown

All in all, Infrastructure as Code offers you the ability to lock down the entire infrastructure from any mutations, changes, or unwanted deployments. Every configuration, every resource, and every application is deployed as per the configuration that you write. You can use Kubernetes, Terraform, Bicep, or other infrastructure-dependent deployment tools to get the same results. Cloud-specific providers give more control over your infrastructure and services to your infrastructure teams, while cloud-agnostic providers give you more flexibility to make deployments based on certain conditions. For example, the conditional deployments[7] in Terraform can be used to either deploy your services to private cloud or to the public cloud.

To wrap, the biggest challenge comes from the fact that the more complex your architecture becomes, the more complicated it gets to make changes or add flexibility to the system. We talked about performing container deployments with a resource manager, but how would you change or deploy just the container application without changing the entire infrastructure stack? How would you perform blue/green deployments when the containerized deployment is attached with your infrastructure? For this, we can say that with great power comes great complexity and with that we need to have a dedicated team of infrastructure Engineers who not only write the complex

---

[7] Even though the conditional statements as basic, they can be used with other state providers in Terraform to make complex decisions. Read more about the conditional deployments in Terraform here: `https://spacelift.io/blog/terraform-conditionals`.

scripts but also manage them. It becomes evident that while Infrastructure as Code is focusing on "stability," it does so by taking away some of the "speed" that your teams may be looking for. Your developers need "speed." The speed is the currency of innovation.

Now, in the next chapter, let's take a process to prepare the software from the development machine all the way to the production environment.

CHAPTER 24

Development Machine to Production

Let's put the peanut-butter and jelly together to make a sandwich. All the jigsaw pieces come together to make a puzzle. The best way to put it is "you are as strong as your weakest link." You can have the perfect infrastructure with elasticity, scalability, availability, and security, but if your build script is faulty, all that scalability and availability is for nothing. In this chapter, you will learn how to ensure every component of your DevOps pipeline is ready for the production.

Off the bat, all modern applications can use the standard Git flow approach to develop, test, deploy, and rollback the changes. For larger enterprises of organizations with legacy source code, you may need to customize the flow of the code from the developer's machine to the production environment.

You want to go from the most comfortable machine to the most capable machine for your applications. Which is, the development machine—where you have all the control over your framework, database, and configuration—all the way to the production machine—where you are in control, and have many restraints applied, and need a special SSH access to review what's happening in the system.

From the moment you press F5 to debug the application, to when the CI server finishes the deployment to the production environment, there are various steps where you can hook up some tests and checks to validate the quality of the application, and automate these checks.

Today, there are several Git flows in the market. The sole purpose of the Git flow is to help you with a suitable "branching strategy" in your version control to help you optimize the collaboration among your teams and speed up the delivery of your software to the market. A few notable examples are

- GitHub Flow (`https://docs.github.com/en/get-started/using-github/github-flow`)

- GitLab Flow (`https://about.gitlab.com/topics/version-control/what-is-gitlab-flow/`)

- GitFlow (`https://www.atlassian.com/git/tutorials/comparing-workflows/gitflow-workflow`)

The gist of a GitX Flow is that it enables

1. Better collaboration between different teams and departments

2. Improves the visibility of hierarchical initiatives and changes

3. Optimizes and speeds up the delivery of your software, while keeping your services live and available

4. Simplifies the access management and control over different features and roadmaps

5. Isolates the changes across your repository to minimize the conflicts

It does not matter which GitX[1] flow you choose to go with. Naturally, the version control hosting system's GitX flow should be preferred because it would come naturally. A lot of times I have seen the term "merge requests" pop up in a team that uses GitHub, and vice versa. That is natural, we as Engineers build a muscle memory of using terms to denote a procedure without realizing that the infrastructure or the team has changed.

For modern applications, a GitX flow helps speed things up, but for older applications, large or complex systems, or systems that have a regulatory requirement to perform certain actions before the code can enter the production environment you would need to customize the GitX flow. It is wrong to compare the deployment or delivery speed of an application that is not regulated, does not have to abide by the privacy restrictions, to an application that has strict regulations and requires manual checks.

Read more: This Stack Overflow Podcast with Shell Engineering Leaders on how they are improving the Engineering culture, one step at a time, is very interesting for

---

[1] By GitX Flow, I mean the GitHub Flow, GitLab Flow, etc. with the "X" being a placeholder for the platform that we are using or following. Important to note that you can use GitHub flow on GitLab, if your team prefers this.

anyone who likes to throw the term 10x around. 10x is not just about the results but the experience, the onboarding, and the speed with which you do development. How quickly you bring in feedback from end users? How quickly can you handle incidents? How more on top of audits and regulatory requirements are you? Listen to it here: `https://stackoverflow.blog/2023/10/25/forget-the-10x-engineer-it-s-about-building-a-10x-culture/`.

Let's not forget, for every new piece of code, the production environment is a wild west, or the far side of moon. While our application as a whole has seen that region hundreds of thousands of times, the new feature has just entered this new space after being pampered in the development of testing environment. In the next chapter, we will learn how to create situations for our features and releases to be prepared for this new region and make sure they can handle the stress and load.

Finally, how would you make your infrastructure teams aware of a breaking change in your source code? How would you communicate these to the customers? That is where your version numbers play a critical role. Every organization has their own strategy to version the applications, but the one that makes the most sense is the semantic versioning[2] (or SemVer for short). Semantic versioning uses major, minor, and a revision or patch version has a standard to communicate how the API or the SDK has evolved. The version 3.22.76 means that your major version is 3, minor version is 22, and the patch version is 76. In simplest terms

- You communicate each major change that will be impacting the client-side with a major version. Your clients would be prepared to accept any major changes, and only apply the major changes when they are ready to work extra to fix any build breaks.

- The minor versions of the software and the changes can continue to propagate as they guarantee to the client-side that these changes will not break the behavior of the applications. The behavior of the SDK, nor the client-side will change.

Microsoft follows an IP-style versioning—of course without the 255-max-size restriction—to communicate how an API or an SDK has been prepared for deployment, and whether a change will break the client apps or not.

---

[2] Read more about semantic versioning on the website: `https://semver.org/`

Important: I have seen many a time organizations using semantic versioning but forgetting the underlying semantics. If you increment the major version number, it denotes that something is going to break or a new feature that requires changing the existing code on the client side for it to work. If you are adding a new feature that does not require changes on the client-side to avoid breaking builds, or runtime crashes, do not bump up the major version and instead bump the minor version.

GitOps Pro Max

The biggest irk that I have with GitOps is the ability to spawn a new infrastructure for every new Git branch, just because someone made a new change or is working on a new feature. You will see this pattern appear in modern "startup" culture where your CTO or VP of Engineering wants to preview every change in an isolated environment and give everyone an opportunity to review each change or feature independently. These applications or the repositories can be

- Microservices and nanoservices

- Documentation repositories

- Sidecar'd[3] applications

- Service or proxy layer

While these applications are smaller in size and complexity, having a unique infrastructure does not warrant you to spawn a new "punystructure" for every new feature or change. Let's take example of two repositories:

1. A documentation project

2. A serverless backend for contact form

Looking at the documentation project, you have a few technical writers, who each are working on pages and push out the new pages on their own branches to avoid conflicts. Each writer expects a review from the other writers and the team lead to publish their page. Instead of running the flows in a sequential flow where you accept one change before moving on to the next one to maintain the history of changes in the

---

[3] The term sidecar'd in this context means mini apps that process non-functional aspects of your microservices, such as handling logs, or metrics, or certificates.

Git repository, you decide to deploy a self-hosted version of documentation website for each branch.

- Joshua publishes his branch "**doc/updated-pricing-page**" to **joshua-doc-updated-pricing-page.docs.hosting.domain**.

- Cindy publishes her branch "**fix/removed-all-typos-on-website**" to **cindy-fix-removed-all-typos-on-website.docs.hosting.domain**.

- And so on.

- So forth.

Each instance of the site has its own content that is deployed from the content of the branch. If the changes made by Cindy do not exist in the Git history for Joshua, Joshua's instance of the documentation website will not contain those typo fixtures. And that is fine. Joshua is not fixing the typos; he is updating the pricing page.

1. The website provides the updated content that Joshua worked on in his version of the update.

2. Website is not impacted by changes made by others, even style changes, or changes that Joshua did not consider when he started working on this project.

3. The website deploys the app just like Joshua wants and expects. These are his changes after all.

4. If Joshua's changes need extra resources, he can add those changes to this branch and have them reviewed. These resources are not shared between other branches or feature stories.

Joshua receives the response from other writers and the team lead and continues working. Cindy, on the other hand, has her own instance of the documentation store and the she is waiting for a review for the typos that she has fixed.

1. Cindy's changes come from her branch and only provision the resources that were configured in the original repository.

2. Cindy's Git history does not have Joshua's changes, so she does not have the updated pricing page. She did, however, fix the typos in the old pricing page as part of the project.

3. Cindy's project uses a new script to find common typos and log
    them during the build phase, and this is a new configuration
    added for this branch to test and get a review on, before making it
    a mandatory step on production website.

There is nothing wrong with this approach. Each change, feature, or an initiative gets its own infrastructure. Each change is isolated, and independent, and can be reviewed in their own cycle and be approved or suggested some changes before it can be accepted. The common challenges found in the Git flows exist here too:

- The changes are not shared across the branches. Joshua's changes are not visible in Cindy's branch and she cannot fix typos that Joshua would contribute in the updated pricing page. This could lead to rework.

- If branches deviate too much from each other, they will have to face the big bang conflict on their way back.

- Organizations are less interested in individual features or new components or initiatives, unless they work well together.

That is why, GitOps' approach to initiate the process of deploying the applications from the development machine and spawning an infrastructure for testing make sure the majority of the features share the common infrastructure to demonstrate their ability to work together. It would be better to get Cindy's work done on Joshua's page, otherwise, Cindy is working too early, or Joshua is working in isolation.

For development of the applications, the problem grows beyond just isolation. A serverless backend, for example, would need infrastructure resources such as databases, firewalls, or network resources. If your developers make changes to the database schema, you need a "new database" that is deployed specifically for this instance of the branch. This leads to

- Extra costs for the infrastructure. For no reason at all

- Take extra time to deploy a new infrastructure for each branch

If Nathan is contributing a new column "notes" to the contact form, and Sara is modifying an existing column, while John is removing a column, these three changes would require a different database that each has a table with the schema that their branch has defined. Again, when these branches come together, they will come back in a bang due to **(1)** the conflicts in the schema file and **(2)** database migrations need to be configured properly.

If you can, avoid using GitOps Pro Max, unless

1. It does not contribute heavily to the infrastructure provisioning.

2. It does not contribute to the infrastructure costs.

    a. You can compensate the extra time taken in code reviews here.

3. Your team has less than five members.

4. Your branches are never more than two leaves away from master.

    a. If your branches start to deviate more than two changes from the master, sync the repositories.

.NET framework provides many runtimes that can be supported by GitOps Pro Max, such as .NET for Serverless, and while it would be very easy to use a new infrastructure for every developer and every branch, it is not a smart move. So what should we do?

1. It is okay to provision the infrastructure for business objectives, and not individual initiatives. It is okay to provision a new environment to test an entire new build pipeline of your documentation, but it cannot be justified to add a typo validation script.

2. It is okay to give your teams the speed to get reviews and approvals quickly, and it is justified if the time it takes to provision new infrastructure and its cost is justifiable compared to the time it takes to manually test the system.

3. It is okay to let the teams do their own work in their own space, and break things as they continue the innovation, as long as they do not turn an internal repo into forks.

Each pipeline can point to an environment, and each environment can have its own configurations to make sure that the application behaves the way it is expected to. In the next chapter, we will focus on the environments and how the application gets promoted from one environment (e.g., development) to another environment (staging, production, etc.).

CHAPTER 25

Environments and Promotions

In a non-Euclidean space, the shortest path between two-points is not a straight line. The reality is very different from the world of theory. Software Engineering graduates learn how to write code and publish it, often building their applications on a streamlined DevOps pipeline that is a single script to build, test, and deploy the application—all in YOLO style. That is a good way to learn. In reality, that is not how you—should—perform your SDLC. You must always have check points and safe zones. These safe zones are responsible for ensuring your product is what you intend to ship.

Similarly, the safest path taken by code from development environment to production has at least three hops. Let's call this Zeeshan's suggestion. ;-)

Your development machine is an environment. You setup the environment, download and install build and compile tools, install the editors, install the runtime to launch the applications, provision the resources such as databases, cache systems, handle the network routing on your machine, to test the application on your own machine; by visiting localhost or 127.0.0.1. The environment is fully capable of running the application, and have everything ready to serve the requests, and in many cases can serve requests from external customers as well—such as by exposing on local network, by running behind a proxy server, or to connect and handle traffic via a remote service provider, like a cloud front door or ngrok, etc.

But this environment is not ready for our business customers. What happens when more than a few hundred customers connect with our development machine? In production, we have a few hundred thousand customers connected to our servers concurrently. Our development machine cannot handle that many connections. Very soon, we will start to experience customers dropping or the requests dropping, or our machine gasping for air as it runs at near 100% resource usage. That is where we

A. A. Zeeshan, *Building Mission-Critical Applications with .NET 10 and C# 14*,
https://doi.org/10.1007/979-8-8688-2347-3_25

have a production environment, which is much more resource heavy. The CPUs are production-ready, the RAM is equivalent to the storage size on your development machines—I've seen terabytes of RAM in some infrastructure regions.

Feature Behavior

Over the last few years, feature controls have been a part of non-enterprise systems as well. The reason is that handling features, new ones, or the ones that are time-bound, or the ones that are prone to breaking is difficult and rather complex. It is one thing to provide the infrastructure for your feature to work, and it is another to handle the production load on the features. When you test the application along with the new features, you are not running the full suite of the tests. The full suite of tests is not possible, because a vast spectrum of the tests is not even available to you. How a user interacts with the system is not limited to what your developers or testers imagine. What happens when your new application version was released with a new feature, but the feature configuration was not rolled out in the infrastructure.

Feature configuration is a way to modify the runtime behavior of your programs and control this switch from a remote server. A few good examples to use for feature handling include

- LaunchDarkly (`https://launchdarkly.com/`)

- Unleash (`https://github.com/Unleash/unleash`)

- Azure App Configuration (`https://learn.microsoft.com/en-us/azure/azure-app-configuration/manage-feature-flags?tabs=azure-portal`)

Read more about feature flags, the nature of the ecosystem, and the purpose of the project on the openfeature project (`https://openfeature.dev/`).

Various frameworks also provide feature flags as part of their solution, such as

- GitLab Feature Flags (`https://docs.gitlab.com/operations/feature_flags/`)

- Firebase Release Configs (`https://firebase.google.com/docs/remote-config`)

Important   Do not confuse the Feature Flags with a Release Strategy, where you release a feature to a percentage of your audience to ensure that the feature is ready for a global rollout. Once the feature is rolled out, the release strategy lapses.

Hop, Hop, Hop

Riddle me this, which of the following is faster time to market?

- Launch the application directly from the development machine using FTP, or a bundler, or integrated Git-based deployment, or Web Deploy.

- Deploy the application to a central test or staging environment, where a CRON job or a QA picks up the stable version of the application to deploy to the production environment.

- You push the changes to a central repository, which is then picked up by automation to test everything, every angle, and automatically deploy and deliver the software to your customers if it meets all the requirements and passes all validations.

Of course, the first option is the fastest. Depending on the size of your repository, your internet connection, you may be able to deploy a new version of the application in less than five minutes. It offers the ultimate speed of validating your changes on your machine and making them available to your customers right away. They do bring challenges:

- Your solutions are not tested enough. Just testing a happy flow does not work.

- Each time you deploy the service, your production encounters a downtime, because your server is swapping the instances.

- You cannot rollback the changes if the new version does not work.

- The responsibility to handle the versioning of the code is entirely up to you.

- Scaling this process from one person to two is infinitesimally difficult. You would think three to four times before going to five head count.

That is where the environments step in and help you prime your applications for the "next step." When your developer is ready to release the software, they push the changes to the central repository. At this point, the branch is in prime state to be tested and validated for any changes or state. The "dev branch" is ready for

- Test cases

- Integration validation

- Automated testing

- Conflict resolution

- Code review

The "dev branch" is not ready for

- Production release

- Regulatory checks

- QA/manual tests

The "dev branch" is the first hop from the "dev machine." The "dev branch" has the same version and copy of the source code as the development machine, but it does not live on the developer's machine. When your code moves to the branch, you can pull the changes again and continue working on it from another machine, if need be. The next hop is to integrate the code into a central branch, "main," "dev," or whatever you call it. The central branch is ready for

- Regression testing to ensure features were introduced, not bugs

- Code review(s)

The central branch is not ready for

- Production release

But the central branch is ready for regulatory checks, you must run validation to ensure data is not leaked, the application does not break, the application performs the business operations as expected. This makes the second hop for our code from the development machine. By now, our code has been validated to work in our feature space, but also within the central repository where the bleeding edge code lives, it has made its way into the repository but may have contributed bugs, degraded performance, etc. And this is where we allow the final hop before adding the code to the "release" or "production" branch. The release branch is ready for

- Production environment

The release branch is not ready for

- Modifications from developers

- Post-release changes "just because"

The release branch has the code that is vetted to have the required stability, availability, and quality levels met. The code that takes three hops, has answered the questions, whether the code is ready for the customer's request or not. This includes if the code would leak the user data, or whether this code would crash on an invalid input, or whether the code would fail when a misconfiguration is encountered. Every step requires a manual or automatic promotion of the code contribution to the next stage, where it is exposed to extra checks, validations, reviews, and tests. If and only if the conditions are met, the code is moved to the next stage. This helps keep the risk to a lower level, while enabling the code to have a speed-element to it. The code moves from one stage to another, not just to move but to go through the next phase. An example of this behavior can be seen in the carwash. When you enter a car wash tunnel, your car moves from one step of cleaning to the next one until it reaches the last stage of "clean car."

Environments in ASP.NET Core

While feature management does not require your application to be taken down and restarted to apply new configurations, and the updates also happen on the fly, there are ways and reasons when you need to mutate the configuration and rerun the application as a new instance. Changing the connection strings, the runtime version, dependencies, etc. all require that you rerun the application to propagate the changes down to every single method or service launched in the application and avoid any misconfigured cache repositories.

In ASP.NET Core, there is a special element for View generation, or to modify the program behavior on runtime. This `<environment />`[1] element (or a Tag Helper, to be technically correct) or the `IHostEnvironment`[2] class provides the information to your backend services or the View files to render one or the other block or run one block of conditional code or the other. The default boilerplate template contains a precise example of this, where you read either the bundled CSS when the environment is production, or the unbundled CSS when the environment is development. Out of box, ASP.NET Core provides three environments:

- Development

- Staging

- Production

These can be read on the runtime, to connect to the right services and prepare the right modules.

```
if (env.IsDevelopment()) {
    // verbose logging, test databases, etc.
}
```

.NET supports these environments for its `Startup` and `ConfigureServices` method variations.

That said, there is no rocket science behind this. It is just a fancy way to read an environment variable and run conditional code. Since this is just an environment variable, you can customize and read the Git branch as the environment, for example, **"feature/read-last-name"** and then you can read this value to perform different code execution.

```
if (env.EnvironmentName == "feature/read-last-name") {
    clients = await dbContext.Clients.FirstOrDefaultAsync(c => c.LastName
    == lastName);
}
```

---

[1] Read more about the <environment /> Tag Helper on the documentation: `https://learn.microsoft.com/en-us/aspnet/core/mvc/views/tag-helpers/built-in/environment-tag-helper`

[2] Read the reference for IHostEnvironment here: `https://learn.microsoft.com/en-us/dotnet/api/microsoft.extensions.hosting.ihostenvironment`

If the condition is not met, you can continue executing the previous code that exists in the repository. With this code, you can continue to run the tests and validate that the new changes or this new feature does not contribute bugs or faults in the system. The environments not only help you control the behavior of the application but also allow you to provide the right state of the application to test, validate, and promote when the application and the source code is ready for promotion. Figure 25-1 shows how code moves between environments and how each environment can have its own state of resources, configurations, and who it can be for.

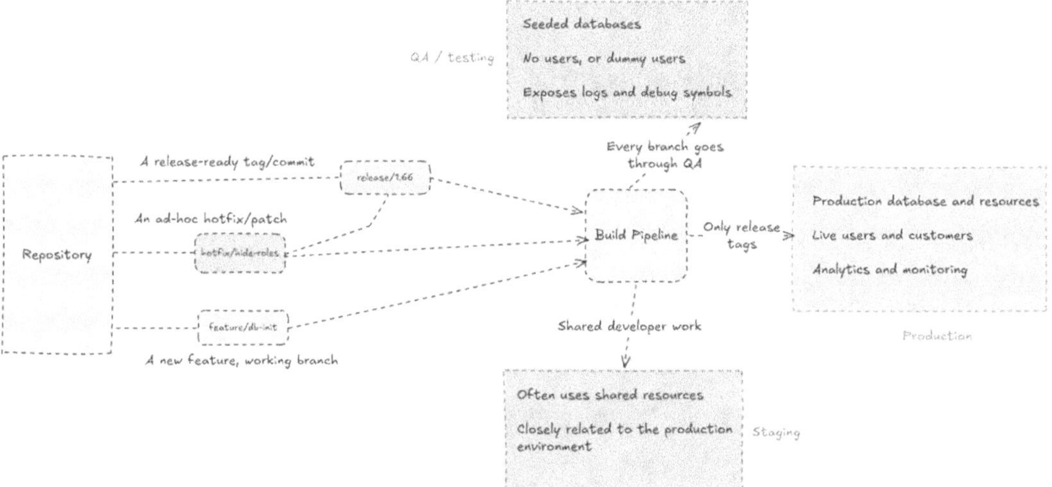

Figure 25-1. The environments allow your teams to perform actions that may or may not cause damage to the business operations or user data. Each developer can share the code that they write when it is mature enough, and also allow the security patches and hotfixes to move quickly in the production

However, note that this code would require an app restart to apply the changes and you cannot simply update the variables to apply the patch. If your code does not need to mutate on the fly, this approach is fine, but to apply the patch on runtime, or live, in real time, then this approach is not suitable as it brings a notable down time to your application. This also leads us to the three-hops. The feature branch is used by the code to make a jump to a central development branch. The goal of this development branch is to make sure all the ongoing and continuous work of developers and teams is conflict-free. In Git-based repositories, the biggest blocker is the conflict that teams need to evaluate, resolve, and then proceed. Making sure that your code is merged frequently and branches are kept short-lived, keeps the development healthy, fast, and stress-free.

This development branch then gets merged (pushed with on GitHub) to a staging or QA branch. The purpose of the staging or QA branch is to run rigorous testing to ensure the code is compliant, deliverable, and ready for deployment. This does not mean that the development branches or local branches should avoid testing and validation. You must definitely write the test cases on development; however, on the development environment, speed and agility of movement is needed. Then, the staging environment can be promoted to a release branch, or a release tag which, after further tests and validation, gets promoted to a production package. You can add more steps to get a more stable system at the cost of slower deployment, or remove a step to go faster but break things along the way.

In the next chapter, let's bring this all together to explore the distribution platforms that are available for us.

CHAPTER 26

Distributing Platforms

You cannot always publish the changes directly to the customers. Often, you wait until the customer requests for the updates. Various industries, platforms, and businesses use this approach. There is nothing wrong with letting the user continue with a specific version—even if that is one or two versions behind the current latest. One quick example is a shopping cart. While you need to ensure the latest version of payment gateway is running, but a shopping cart is nothing more than a container. It contains the list of all the items the user is interested in purchasing. I cannot stress enough how many times users leave a checkout experience just because their shopping cart list was inaccurate.

This is where distributing platforms come into effect. When your application is being used by customers—or customers of customers. You do not want to push updates without confirmation or a manual prompt to initiate the update procedure. Mobile stores, physical terminals, etc. are an example of where you should rely on a staging environment that requires users to manually initiate the update.

In this chapter, we will focus on the platforms that we can use to distribute our applications. While, most web applications are deployed directly on our platforms, the mobile or client-apps are often deployed and distributed through customers or partner's portals. You will learn how to prepare your application for deployment on third-party platforms.

You want to get the new version of your application in the hands of your customers, or their customers in two situations:

- When you launch a new feature that you want your customers to use

- When you fix a critical problem in your existing software

Theoretically, you write the software, publish the changes and the customers can download the latest version of your software. That is easy, for a web application, or a hosted service where you are in complete control. However, in scenarios where you are deploying your services to external or partner platforms, you do not have this flexibility.

And, you also lack this control when the software runs on the business premises of your customers. Such as a platform provider, if you are providing an appointment booking service to your customers, for their customers to make appointments on premises, then you lose the theoretical advantage to update the software on demand.

The marketplaces, such as Google's Play Store, or Apple's App Store, or even Microsoft's own Microsoft Store, all have their own procedures set in place that make it difficult for publishers to modify the approved software and application behavior without a revaluation. If the version 2.34 is approved on the stores, the version 2.35 or 3.0 needs to go through vigorous testing and quality control before it can be approved for user consumption or deployment. That is to make sure that the latest version does not add anything to the software that it does not advertise, promise, or declare as its intention. Your software on the marketplace also exposes the marketplace to trust breaches when it fails, or gets exploited. Mobile platforms have made it very easy for organizations to publish their applications, and update them regularly, with little to no friction. How, you must time the updates properly, or face delayed updates or patches to the software. In a typical flow, the latest changes would need around two days or a week to get approved and then propagate to the customers. If you have identified a bug, or a security vulnerability in your application you want to be able to quickly take action and update the application. If you take a few hours to fix the problem, and are waiting on the marketplace team to review the changes and it takes a few days, then your customers are exposed to the security vulnerability for a few days. This is not good.

1. Your customers have no idea what is happening; you are required to communicate the security vulnerability or incidents to the customers and partners, but the communication is less serious if the user has not been hit yet.

2. You do not want your customers or partners to panic, because you have already resolved the problem and you have a plan to tackle the challenge and provide a safer environment for your customer to use.

3. You want to give your teams the ability to move quickly, and update or control the application on their own, and not depend on external factors that are beyond their controls.

4. You are now being blocked by an external party, that has their own
    roadmap, SLAs, and priorities. Many times, the review times take
    longer on public holidays. Your business priorities are not their
    business priorities.

One way to take this back in your control is by using feature flags and only enabling
the features when everything is live and ready to be accessed. This means that the
features that you need to release on new year go live at least a few days, or even a week
before the launch date. During December, the marketplace teams are busy, on holidays,
and thus a 2-day wait time goes to a week or two weeks. If you do not have feature
controls, or time-bound UIs, then you get into these troubles where you cannot launch a
new product without having it reviewed by the marketplace teams.

Note   I am not suggesting hiding the code for any reasons, always share what
has been added to the application in the latest version so they can review it
and give them a way to test and validate the changes before they allow your
application to go live. The pattern here is not to hide anything but to publish it and
communicate it early and position your customer in the right place so they can see
the fireworks at the right time.

When you release the features beforehand, and put it behind a feature wall, your
customers do not have to wait for the approval on the marketplace, but they get the live
features disabled or enabled at the right time. The best applications for this are

- Release the new launches or discounts and make them visible in the
  application at the right time.

- Stop a discount, or feature, when the time runs out with one button
  click from the infrastructure, or based on the time on the user's or
  server's clock.

- Put the new features on the application and only enable them
  when the launch time arrives—think of launching a new season in
  your game, you can publish gigabytes of data beforehand for your
  customers to download and be ready for the next season.

This feature and the challenge is more infrastructure-focused, and less development-focused. The development changes only require that you keep the code behind a feature wall, and control the propagation through a switch on the infrastructure. If the switch is disabled, the code would never execute and the customer will take the other route. When the switch is enabled, the customer can start to use the new feature at the right time. If you detect a bug or a vulnerability in a feature, you can disable the feature to control the spread of the vulnerability and the exploit before it causes damages to your customers.

Customer-Owned Platforms

While partner owned platforms provide you with controls to either automatically deploy your products and services to the customers, the customer-owned platforms do not offer the same flexibility. Customer-owned platforms exist in the B2B2C domain, where your customers are licensed to redistribute your products or use your services to offer products or services to their customer. A coffee shop owner who sells coffee to their customer can be a good example here. The coffee shop owner purchases the front desk software from your business, and handles all the coffee orders, prints receipts, handles tips, manages the stock and inventory, table management, and more.

- Customers often update their systems when they close their shops. This may send a spike on your infrastructure to download the updates.

- Customers dislike and do not like when a change is pushed to their devices during working hours, as it causes delays in their business, makes their customers unhappy if they have already prepared the checkout cart.

Unfortunately, there is no .NET way to convince the partner to keep the software alive. You need to give control to the customers for the components that do not need to be updated because of a vulnerability—appointment booking front-end, inventory browsing, etc. Whereas the complex systems live either on your systems or can be updated on the fly without impacting the customer experience.

And this brings us to the wrap for this chapter, and this part. The next part will focus on monitoring your applications that are deployed to infrastructure. The objective is to learn about monitoring and expand our knowledge to observability and best practices.

In the next chapter, we will start with exploring how we can review and make our applications easier to understand, explore, monitor, and then observe.

PART VI

Observing Apps

CHAPTER 27

Understanding Your Apps

The source code provides one part of the map to understand how your application works and how your customer uses it. Think of the electromagnetic spectrum—the visual range is just a part of it. To best understand the entirety of the electromagnetic spectrum, different telescopes have been set up to study the natural phenomenon. In the same manner, to fully understand what is happening in the application environment, you need to use various tools and services to get the full picture.

In this chapter, we will take a naïve approach and look at monitoring, diagnostics, observability of our applications, and how important it is to prepare your applications for observability. In photography and videography, it is a common belief that a good end result is only possible when thoughtfulness is used in preparing the grounds for the shot. You cannot always get great results just in post-production. Similarly, an application that is developed as a black box will not be as observable as an application that opens up and provides enough hook to collect and instrument metrics and traces.

As I like to say, a full picture observation of an application is better than a thousand guestimates.

There are several levels at which you must understand the application. The closer you are to the source code, the better you understand the application. You understand why the application behaves the way it does, and you understand why certain extensions are installed, and why our CI/CD has an extra step to do some house chores. In a team of 15, most would understand where our database is and what tables are used for configuration. In different teams, this knowledge starts to fade away, and then across the departments, it is very difficult to know how this particular team manages their data and the source code. It is not easy to remember the release cadence of every team, the version or the version strategy used, the rate limiters, infrastructure resources, network or secrets, the patterns, you tell. These are the spectrums, where, on the one hand, you understand how "your" application works, vs. how "business" operates.

© Afzaal Ahmad Zeeshan 2026
A. A. Zeeshan, *Building Mission-Critical Applications with .NET 10 and C# 14,*
https://doi.org/10.1007/979-8-8688-2347-3_27

The challenge in the operations is not to understand but to observe the systems. A developer can make a change any time, thus "changing" what you understand. Today the application uses five database connections, and has a rate limiter of 500,000 requests per second, but next week the application starts to make 500,000 requests per second to one database and the same to the remaining 4 together. The stress on the database is bearable by the database, but now other teams are crying because their services are performing very bad and clients are seeing bad performance, or dropped requests, and thus lost business. It was important to "understand" the systems but in the bigger picture, understanding does not take you very far, and you must leave the "understand" cabin and join the "observe" cabin. The goal of the "observe" cabin is to, well, observe what is happening and then "trace"[1] the pattern back to the original source of the problem.

Your applications are created using different components, the basic ones are

1.   Compute resources; CPU, RAM, GPU, etc.

2.   Network; for connectivity

3.   Storage; for persistence

Different topologies of these components are put together to make your application work. The applications that are compute-intensive focus on specialized systems and architecture around compute-resources. The application that demands heavy bandwidth supports require a good topology of network to optimize the service delivery. And that is what you need to understand, compared to the language constructs used in the source code. A lot of applications go down in flames just because the code reviews focus too much on the lines of code written, but not the impact that they will have on the architecture of the entire service or the solution.

The architecture of your application is not just the diagrams but also the challenges of the structure that you have built. If your application uses multi-threaded data processing, you can be sure that the memory exhaustion is going to be a concern for you in your application. You can optimize it a little bit by using thread pools, reshare the resources, add extra memory, use thread management libraries, or use farms of devices that also offer their threads to use. As you patch the application, you start to build a heavyweight muscle in terms of memory management, but the next challenge comes in

---

[1] We will visit the topic of "tracing" in a later chapter in this section.

the shape of scalability. Thread-per-request models do not scale well and are a prime candidate for "throw money at problems" metaphor. Say, you do handle this by adding more servers, how do you synchronize the data or the processes?

To study the network behavior of your application, it is very important to understand the limitations of your network and the limitations of your application. Is latency a bottleneck caused by your application or network? Both. Think of the network pipeline as the water pipe. If you have a larger pipe, but less water, the output will be small. If you have more water, but the pipe is very small or tight, the behavior is different. The water will gush out fast but in small quantity. Stress and load-testing platforms are perfect to use in this scenario to understand and learn about the weak spots of your application. My personal favorite is k6,[2] and the main reason for this is that it offers a programmable interface to generate the traffic and detect the problematic patterns on the system. The integrated dashboard shows different behaviors of the system; CPU, latency, requests/second, etc. you can see what breaks and when exactly. It is important to note

- You must understand your application before the calamity falls.

- If you are in an incident, it is too late to understand. You need to react now.

- You are understanding "components" and not "code."

- You must think in terms of how different services bring the services up or take them down.

- The connectivity of services, where downtime in one means a collapse in another.

Performing a pre-mortem[3] is an example of understanding your application and being open to worst receptions. A pre-mortem is a hypothetical scenario, where the team members sit together and role-play the failure of the recently launched service—which at the time of this pre-mortem is still to be launched—and assess why the service failed. Pre-mortems are very simple:

1. You are the team reviewing why the service failed. The service has failed, it is not just performing bad, it is outright the worst product you shipped.

---

[2] Learn about k6 here: `https://k6.io/`

[3] Read more here: `https://www.atlassian.com/team-playbook/plays/pre-mortem`.

2. You are not trying to bring the service back. This is not incident response.

3. You are reading the logs, metrics, errors, stack traces, and other support material to identify why it failed and what could've been done to avoid it.

4. You note the biggest contributor for the failure, along with notable contributors for the failure.

    a. Some pre-mortem scenarios also talk about contributors that would not be a contributor.

    b. The goal is not to find a solution. The goal is to find the problems.

5. Now, with this information, you review the existing product to avoid such scenarios in the real world.

It is very difficult to think in future. Of course, the product that you are building, you love it so much. But the moment it gets released to the internet, it will be blasted with a lot of challenges, attacks, misinputs, and what not. And a pre-mortem helps you and your team take an extra moment to think what could go wrong and recheck and validate the application and the content before you press "Deploy".

Lastly, do not think of "Understanding" as a technical challenge. This is this as a gamified version of exploration. The source code is your temple, and you are finding the treasure. The treasure doesn't have to give you gold. It can give you an antidote to a plague, or a button to press to restart the system.

We discussed and laid the foundation for observing your apps. The goal is to look for new patterns where your application or system might break and not just rely on one monitor. In the next chapter, we will start expanding the topic of monitoring and observing your applications from the operations standpoint. We will also touch how to prepare our apps to be observed by the operations team.

Further Reading

From an operations standpoint, it is important to note whether your application is a microservice or a monolith. The monitoring and observability of the application or a system is unique for each platform, and each archetype of deployment has its own best practices to monitor a process. Check out this guide on Microsoft Learn platform to learn about the architectures of .NET apps: `https://learn.microsoft.com/en-us/dotnet/architecture/`.

The Diagnostics guide (`https://learn.microsoft.com/en-us/dotnet/core/diagnostics/`) is a good resource to learn about the best practices for logging, tracing, telemetry, and metrics collection. In the later chapters, we will learn about these concepts and how they each relate to (1) each other and (2) among the larger system at scale. If you have never debugged an application, it is a good time to take a look at what these concepts and constructs mean in the broader development and engineering terms.

I am building a community-driven load and stress-testing demo using k6, if you are interested in learning how to write scripts to automatically test your applications for performance under load and stress, check out my GitHub repository: `https://github.com/afzaal-ahmad-zeeshan/spring-k6-load`.

CHAPTER 28

Monitoring vs. Observing

Every enterprise has always had one or another type of monitoring. For ASP.NET, you can monitor your applications for the number of requests it receives, how many errors occur, the internal resource consumption—CPU, memory, network, I/O usage, etc. The monitoring tools enable your IT operations to check if the application is responding in the right amount of time or failing to meet its service-level agreement (SLA; a legal agreement between provider and consumer to ensure service availability).

Modern applications tend to go one-step ahead and focus on "observing" the applications. They do not only check if the response is on time. They also tend to check if the response is correct, they also check the paths a request takes and validate it against the business requirements—think of a different flow for the request and data flow for consumer that protected, such as children, etc. Observing the application provides higher fidelity information but also requires higher investment.

In this chapter, we will learn

- The differences between monitoring an application and observing an application

- Cardinality of a system, its purpose, and how to control it

- How to navigate the observability and monitoring landscape?

While Monitoring and Observability are often used interchangeably, they are identical just as DevOps and SRE are identical. They provide the same results but use a different approach and target a different audience. Just like DevOps, which resulted in a very fruitful process of building, testing, and delivering the software called "CI/CD," monitoring also exposes similar fruits. Organizations do not need[1] to implement the

---

[1] To be clear, I am in favor of organizations adopting a DevOps-mindset, but organizations do not change their cultures just because a book talks about it or an author recommends it. Organizations change their culture to gain benefits of Conway's law.

© Afzaal Ahmad Zeeshan 2026
A. A. Zeeshan, *Building Mission-Critical Applications with .NET 10 and C# 14*,
https://doi.org/10.1007/979-8-8688-2347-3_28

entire DevOps pipeline across their development practices. They can get most benefits of DevOps just by implementing a working and functional "CI/CD" pipeline. The CI/CD brings the "Dev" and "Ops" together but still leaves out the customers, business, stakeholders, while the on-call teams have one foot in.

Monitoring, in general, would be a way to monitor how your application is doing. There are several platforms available to monitor your application. Every hosting platform provides a tool that you use to monitor different metrics of your application. Each resource has different metrics and dimensions that you need to monitor its performance on.

On Microsoft Azure, monitoring is provided as an integrated service for all the resources but also as a solution for your infrastructure as a whole. Azure App Services, Azure Function, and other notable services such as Azure Storage, Azure Virtual Machines, all have integrated monitoring services that provide a basic view of the functionality and availability of the service (as shown in Figure 28-1).

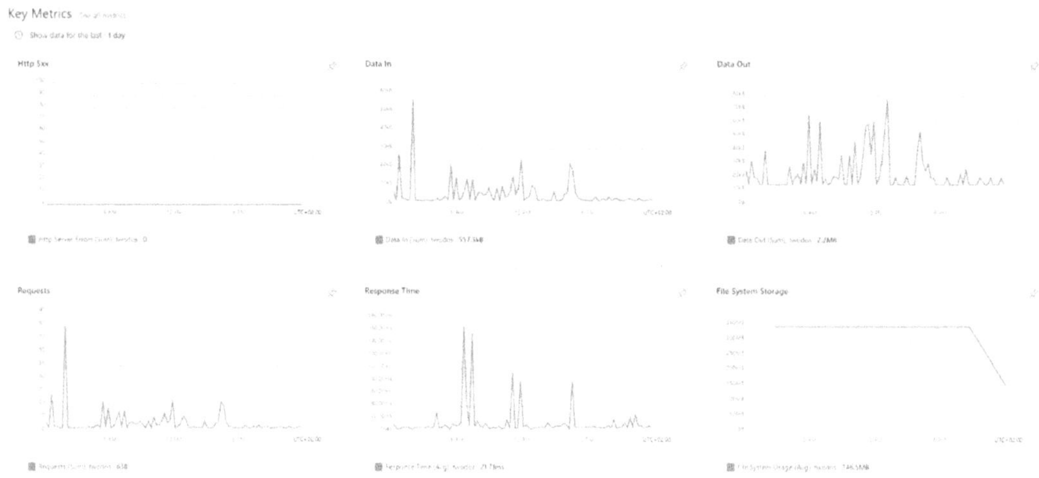

Figure 28-1. *Built-in and integrated monitor in an Azure App Service instance showing errors, network data, requests, and system stats*

If you only need to monitor the "usage" or "consumption" of the service, this monitoring grid gives you enough information. It even tells you when something goes down or when a significant change occurred in your service. You can change the timespan from one day to a few hours for fine-grained view or weekly or monthly views, as per your needs. And that, overall is the monitoring process to monitor how your application is behaving.

Start with Monitoring

The recommended way to start building an operational view of your systems is with monitoring dashboards. Monitoring simply means keeping all the vitals of your system in a check. Monitoring approach and patterns differ based on the type of resource:

- Web servers

- Databases

- Virtual machines

- Message brokers

- Networking

- Web applications

And many others. Every resource exposes a set of metrics that tells part of the story about its health. For example, for a web application, its ability to respond back to an HTTP request is crucial. At the very basic, it is important that a web application is able to respond back and not crash. For a web server, on the other hand, it is also important how many requests can it handle, what is the IOPS, is it crumbling under load, is it putting clients on wait, is it able to balance the load automatically? You always start with the simplest question and make your way to complex questions.

1. Simple: Does it work?

2. Complex: Can it keep it up?

If you look at the graph above, that graph tells you if the service works. It gives you a view to see the number of requests, network performance, and errors all in one place. It is important to note that "CPU usage" does not answer whether our application works. Even a broken application, or an app that does not start or break on requests consumes CPU and memory. The "works" part is communicated by the error responses (top-left). We need that chart to be at the low range.

Where it limits is whether the application will continue to serve.

Fun fact: unlike humans, note how the healthy computer systems have a very linear graph.

Enter Observability

Observability is a way to bring all these pieces together and then see what's missing. In production environments, it is rare that we fully know everything that would or could happen.[2] Monitoring tools work perfectly fine to tell you how much resources the applications are consuming. Until they don't. And since our monitoring dashboards and tools do not have the missing dimensions, it becomes very difficult to see what is happening and to identify the root cause. That is where observability steps in to give you more insights on what is happening in your systems and what you need to do.

While monitoring tells you to look at the CPU or memory consumption, observability enables you to study the patterns of CPU consumption based on your team's interactions. How does the CPU usage change when we release a new version? Which version spiked the CPU the most? Or what happens to the database cluster when we release a new version, or when we keep an existing version live for a few extra days? Observability is a long process of studying the behavior of your system and then collecting the useful insights and applying them across the platform—some to the development phases, while others to the operations.

Today, various open source and proprietary platforms offer observability solutions. Most notables include

- Grafana[3]

- Datadog[4]

- Chronosphere[5]

- Dynatrace[6]

---

[2] Recently, a major incident was encountered on AWS which "actually" brought down a big part of the internet, with various big providers and platforms down because they relied on AWS and expected AWS to be available. Read more about the story here: `https://www.theguardian.com/technology/2025/oct/20/amazon-web-services-aws-outage-hits-dozens-websites-apps`.

[3] Check out on Grafana's website: `https://grafana.com/products/cloud/application-observability`.

[4] Read the knowledgebase for Observability on Datadog's website: `https://www.datadoghq.com/knowledge-center/observability/`

[5] Chronosphere has open-source platform for observability: `https://chronosphere.io/platform/`

[6] Dynatrace focuses on infrastructure and application observability: `https://www.dynatrace.com/platform/infrastructure-observability`. I like to keep observability as a single unit, no silos, please.

Azure Monitor also has observability features and can be used if you have your infrastructure set up on Microsoft Azure.

As a scenario—based on a true story—you are releasing a new feature to the staging environment for testing and review. As you publish the application, you do follow the practice to put the untested and unreleased features behind a feature wall. The feature wall makes sure that the code is not run until it has been tested on the production. The feature wall prevents your production environment from blowing up—which, we are not yet deploying to. As your code reaches staging environment, you start to hear screams from the floor above. The checkout (for the lack of another) team is unable to connect to the database.

While the team is attempting to bring the staging environment back, they learn that the database was active but could not accept new clients. They also identified that the database started behaving this way after a recent feature drop was pushed to the staging environment. Rolling back the changes did solve the problem, but since the feature drop had the problematic sequence, they dug deeper. They identified that the new code was making connections to the database and reading a table that was not yet deployed—a missing migration, because the feature was not yet released and thus the database mutation was not applied—and the code was written to only work when the schema was ready. Which was never prepared. This caused the application to enter an infinite loop to continue to connect with the database, exhausting the connection pool resources and causing other services to go down.

The monitoring system was unable to see the problems beyond the database cluster. Monitoring system, and the alerts were going off in the wrong direction. The fingers were pointed toward the database cluster. A simple solution would be to increase the resources available to the database. Increase the IOPS, or memory, but that would only delay the inevitable. Observability practices help us look beyond—or in the past—where the changes in one system contribute impactful results in other systems. An incomplete code commits in the software repository contributed to the database systems being overwhelmed and causing service degradation across different systems.

Cardinality

As you study the entire system, different inputs and all the possible values, the problem space very quickly moves toward infinite space. It is no longer possible to study the behavior of one specific region from dozens, based on what one microservice is contributing to among hundreds of thousands of microservices. That is where cardinality comes into play.

Cardinality is the unique items that are available in your data set to give you a fine-grained overview of the system performance. Say, you have a basic record where you track the performance of each containerized service, you can read information such as

- Service ID

- Region

- Container Runtime Version

- Container Tag

- Application Version

And more, and each of these fields would have a set of values based on your infrastructure setup and code deployment frequency. Frequently releasing the application and if you update the container version each day, after a week you would have seven values in the container-tag record, that dimension would complement other values. Your application version may contain information about internal dependencies, and the service may be a long-running unique value, such as "users-service," or "checkout-service." Plotting the service across all these dimensions gives a good timeseries record of how the service responds to external and internal changes. External changes include the changes in the user demand, external resources, or outages, and the internal changes include new versions, container restarts, etc.

While increasing the system cardinality[7] may lead to good overview of all the gears in motion, it increases the load on your observability system and increases the blind spots for bugs and problems to creep into. You can increase the cardinality of the data by incorporating the hour of the day field to each record and then group the dimensions around it. Does it help?

- Yes: you may be able to understand how different times of day (e.g., 9 am peak) attempt to topple your infrastructure.

- No: if your application does not have peak and trough, extra data is just noise.

---

[7] Read how Grafana Mimir compacts the dimensions to provide "unlimited cardinality": `https://grafana.com/docs/mimir/latest/references/architecture/components/compactor/`

There is no perfect rule[8] for something to be part of your cardinality set, or be outside it, but just see what helps you get closer to identifying an opportunity for improvement and keep it, and what takes you farther away, remove it.

Continue with Monitoring

That said, just like an SRE is an Engineer, whereas DevOps is a cultural shift, the monitoring is often done on the operations-side whereas observability is not limited to operations only and includes Engineers as well.

Monitoring is good and good enough for us to know when something goes off. Especially for the cases where things go off repeatedly, we can rely on monitoring. In a later chapter, we will also take a look at the alerts and how they work for your applications. For the sake of scope, monitoring dashboards provide a more "needed" view of the applications. If your team owns the API of the product, your application can focus on the monitoring view for the API only and does not need to focus on the underlying services. It is interesting to have a dedicated dashboard for each team or product. Visualization tools such as Grafana enable you and your teams to build dashboards or group them together into a folder so that each team can focus on the important metrics to track the performance or problems in the application.

It is also important to note that observability is often ignored when your services are available and there are no problems/incidents in the service. For example, when your services show that the service is performing well, the SLOs are being met, there are no complaints from the customer, and your CI/CD pipelines are running fine, should you be finding dark alleyways where problem may be lurking or take this opportunity to work on new features?

In this scenario, the SREs practice enforces a concept called "error budget."[9] The error budget is the amount of quota that you can spend on mistakes. If your service is functioning fine, it can continue to operate and be updated by the teams on their own routine and as needed. When your application misbehaves or leads to unwanted behavior—errors, crashes, downtime—then your application starts to consume its error budget. If the service-level objective is the amount of time that your application needs to

---

[8] Continue reading about Cardinality here: `https://chronosphere.io/learn/what-is-high-cardinality/`

[9] Read more about error budget in the SRE book by Google: `https://sre.google/sre-book/embracing-risk/`

provide services without downtime, then the error budget is the time that it is allowed to be unavailable. In short, the error budget is the difference between 100% and the amount of uptime percentage. If your SLA commitment is 99%, the error budget is 1%. If your application has a downtime of more than 1%, then your application is overconsuming its allowed budget and care must be taken. The care can be

- Put the application in maintenance mode until the error budget quota refreshes.

- Put the application in maintenance mode until the end of contractual obligation.

- Delay the release of the new features until the existing features become stable and available.

- Revisit the SLOs and SLAs committed to, to review where the right investments need to be made.

I am not in favor of putting a block on the CI/CD without a thorough review of the commitments, contractual obligations to customers or regulatory bodies, and also, the solution that you are providing. SLAs are legal contracts between you and your customers; it is not an Engineering-thing. The SLIs and SLOs are Engineering-focused and must be set by the teams, developers, product managers, and departments. The SLA must be set based on the available SLAs of underlying services. This is why

1. You must never promise a 100% availability SLA.

2. You must never promise an SLA that is more than or equal to the underlying services.

    a. For example, 99.95% SLA on a 99.9% available service is a mistake.

As is a given, observability is a concept, just like DevOps. There is no one tool that you can install to add observability to your infrastructure or architecture. That said, there are certainly tools that allow you to apply the observability practices, like GitLab does for DevOps.

Further Reading

Observability is indeed a new concept, and it is being introduced in the tech stacks around the organizations. The main challenge of observability is the "too much" aspect where you start measuring on all dimensions and increase the costs for the infrastructure visibility. Read how you can optimize and minimize the costs for observability: `https://logz.io/blog/optimize-observability-spending-recap/`

Since observability is expensive, you can use the concepts and regions uncovered through observability to automate them via monitoring. For example, if observability uncovers that your cart checkout fails when the user is a guest, then you can apply a monitoring to measure the performance and progress of the sessions there. You do not need to use the expensive tools to "revalidate" that. In fact as we learned in this book, you must shift left to bring this concept to an earlier stage. Then validate that this behavior is controlled and patched to prevent such unwanted scenarios from happening. Can you think of other ways in which observability can be used to uncover uncharted regions of the software architecture to apply monitoring?

Last, but a very important collection of resources to learn about observability is the `https://thenewstack.io/introduction-to-observability/` website. The website contains several topics around Observability from technical and conceptual standpoints and provides examples from real-world applications of observability topics.

For a deep-dive and in-depth difference between monitoring and observability, read this guide: `https://blogs.helixops.ai/observability-vs-monitoring`. This guide goes well beyond the technical and conceptual knowledge and explains the history of observability and how it is gaining traction today.

CHAPTER 29

Traceability and Telemetry

Just like tracer bullets are used to track the projectiles in ammunition, you need some manner to trace the path a request takes within your system. While a simple MVC-patterned application provides a simple way to trace the requests (from controller-layer ending on the views), a complex system such as microservices does not have the same luxury of simple and easy tracing.

Collecting telemetry enables your operations systems to understand what is happening at the application level. Tracing the requests enables your development team to identify the performance bottlenecks for each individual request and study the lowest performing requests to improve the performance. Adding traceability to the telemetry collection enables you to study the application and improve it on different levels—code level, module level, service level, application level, or at the infrastructure level.

In this chapter, we will focus on

- What is a request trace and how can it help us debug the applications and systems in production environments?

- Adding the telemetry and instrumentation to our projects

Beyond a certain size and scale of the application, each request takes several hops from entering the system and exiting as a response. For each of the requests, two things are important:

- Being able to see how much time the request takes across each of the services (especially in a microservice-style environment or distributed services)

- Being able to see which service accesses the request after which service and how does this tail impact the overall system.

In this chapter, we will take a look at the two important concepts of telemetry and tracing of the requests.

A. A. Zeeshan, *Building Mission-Critical Applications with .NET 10 and C# 14*,
https://doi.org/10.1007/979-8-8688-2347-3_29

Important: If your application is a monolith and does not have layers over layers of dependencies or service layers, then you can skip this chapter because traceability usually steps in when your requests take multiple hops from one service to another, leaving behind some part of the context and then starting the execution in the next service. It is good to be prepared, but do not invest too much time to solve the problems of the future today.

While we often indicate how important debugging is, and how important a friend debugger is to a software engineer. The traceability (distributed tracing) from the observability is often different from debugging. Observability happens in background, while debugging interrupts the process to expose the state of the program, including variables or choices. Observability—logs, metrics, traces—on the other hand, does not rely on these, and checks the available telemetry sent via the program. The telemetry is then collected, processed, aggregated, and shown in a dashboard or a chart. This way, you can view the live states of the applications where debugging is not possible. For example, you cannot interrupt the production programs to debug the internals. For various reasons

- If you interrupt the processes on production, even to pause them, no requests will flow, and users will start to see a degraded experience.

- The program contains live user data, and exposes this information to any Engineer, just for the sake of testing could lead to massive fines and lost trust.

- To attach a debugger, your executable must contain the debug symbols, which are often heavy and bloated, making your production apps slower. So, even if you do not attach a debugger, the entire time your app runs on the production it consumes more resources—for no reason at all.

Traceability

Let's put more focus on tracing the requests, since we are in a spaghetti-situation with our services. The traceability of our applications and services is the ability to track how each request navigates in our system and reaches a final stage. Traceability is possible in large monolith applications but really shines in distributed or microservices-oriented applications. An easy example of the traceability is when you open a web page on a web browser and the Network tab in the Inspector shows you how much time each request takes (Figure 29-1).

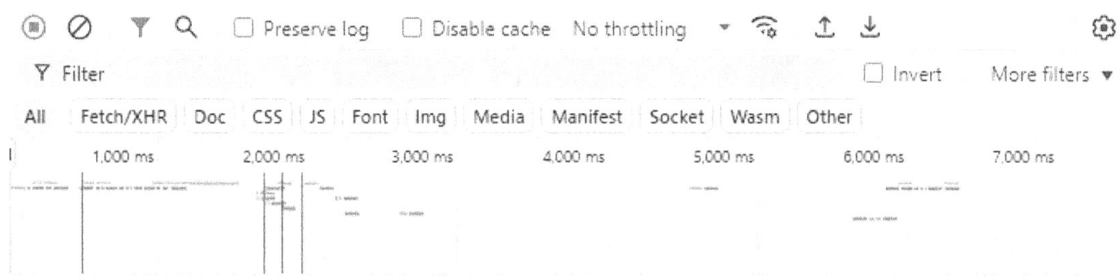

Figure 29-1. *The requests timeline as shown in the Google Chrome DevTools to show when a request was initiated and when it completed*

The inspector tab shows more details when you select the requests, but this timeline-view shows when each request was initiated and when did it end. If your web application is performing poor, you can use this tab to check the services or requests that are slow and improve their performance. You can also see when a particular request is throttling the entire web page and prevents it from loading or prevents other requests from starting.

The pattern of traceability with the server-side requests is the same. You use a timeline-view of all the services that a request is sent to, including the start time, the end time, the time it took to process, including any dependencies, and then where did it go to next. The timeline view gives you a view on what services are called, in which sequence they are called, which service takes a long time to process and forward the request to the next service, and so on and so forth.

Adding the instrumentation and tracing depends on the project that you are building (Desktop, web, mobile, etc.) and the dependency that you are adding (Sentry, Azure Application Insights, etc.). If you are using Visual Studio, the installation of telemetry can be a single click, or it can be a configuration that requires changes to your project configuration. To demonstrate, let's use Visual Studio as an example and an ASP.NET Core project to add instrumentation and see how this makes the changes to our project.

When you start a project without any observability or dependency added, your application configuration looks like this (Figure 29-2):

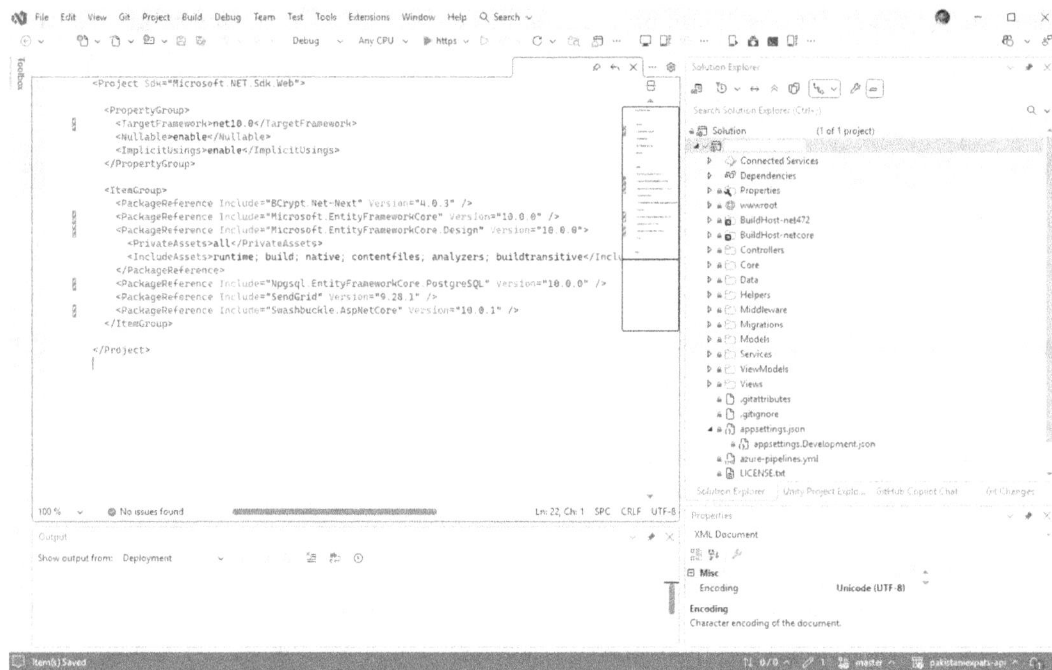

Figure 29-2. *A bare minimum application package. We can add the packages that support instrumentation here to configure them in the application*

Visual Studio enables you to add the services directly to your project. Figure 29-3 demonstrates how to connect your app to the Azure Application Insights.

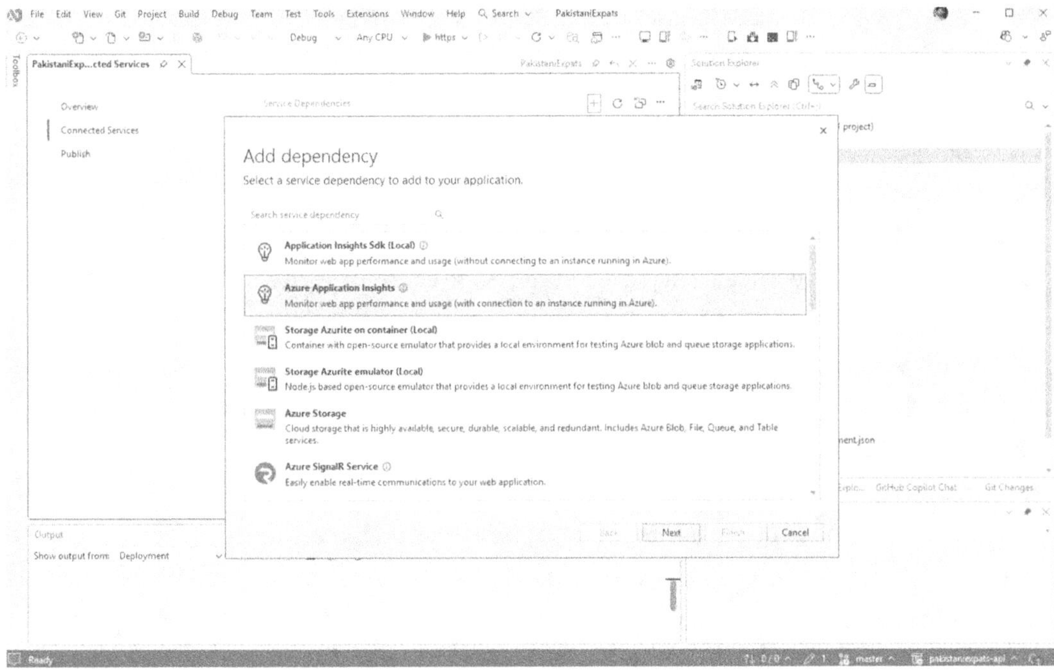

Figure 29-3. *The available services within the Visual Studio window can be used to configure and set up the services for your application instance*

Once you are done, an Application Insights connection string will be added to your project configuration. The connection string will be read on runtime to set up the instrumentation. In an ASP.NET Core application, adding OpenTelemetry is as easy as adding this line:

```
// Add the OpenTelemetry and configure the Azure Monitor for your
application.
builder.Services.AddOpenTelemetry().UseAzureMonitor();
```

Run the application to validate the telemetry collection.

Read more about configuring tracing for your ASP.NET Core web applications here on Microsoft's official website: `https://learn.microsoft.com/en-us/dotnet/core/diagnostics/distributed-tracing`. Also, for cross-runtime applications and systems such as where you are mixing between .NET, Node.js, and other server-side runtimes, consider using the OpenTelemetry support in Azure Application Insights. Read this page to learn how to enable this: `https://learn.microsoft.com/en-us/azure/azure-monitor/app/opentelemetry-enable?tabs=aspnetcore`.

You can use traceability frameworks such as Jaeger,[1] or OpenTelemetry[2] (abbreviated as: OTel) to add traceability to your applications. While traceability provides a solution-level view of the network traffic, the integration happens at the service/application level. When your application sends telemetry to the infrastructure, you can observe how different services receive and process the requests.

Remember: .NET Core has a set of extensions of services and libraries for distributed applications, including traceability, part of the Aspire (`https://learn.microsoft.com/en-us/dotnet/aspire/get-started/aspire-overview`) project. Aspire project works with non-.NET frameworks, and services as well. The best feature of Aspire is the opinionated packages that make integrating different services with each other much easier—such as giving access cache systems, databases, access and authentication with APIs and other backend services.

While it is also possible to bootstrap a framework's own collection of the traceability per request or service, you can customize this behavior to get more control over each of the execution. At the core of each traced request is

- Context:

  - A trace is connected to the request when it enters the system.

- Hierarchy:

  - A trace is never a single event.

  - The first activity ID is served as a root trace.

  - A trace has a parent trace (root) that was the first capture moment for this request, and the trace ends when a trace does not have a child trace.

- Span:

  - Span is a unit block of the trace and includes the information about a specific processing of the request.

  - Contains the start time for the event and the end time for the event.

---

[1] Learn more about Jaeger project here: `https://www.jaegertracing.io/`
[2] Learn more about OpenTelemetry project here: `https://opentelemetry.io/`

Each framework provides ways to configure and attach more details to each of the span unit in the traces to give more context. For OpenTelemetry, checkout this matrix of features supported for the telemetry: `https://github.com/open-telemetry/opentelemetry-specification/blob/main/spec-compliance-matrix.md`.

As you process each request, your services can add metadata to the span to add more insights and contexts to help your observability tools to understand and visualize the natural flow of traffic and the common problems as they arise.

As with any other diagnostics tools and frameworks, it is often best to sample the inputs and telemetry coming to your infrastructure. If your service handles a million requests per hour, and each request generates about 10 traces, that yields 10 million per hour. That is data, in some cases structured data, stored on your infrastructure. That data storage costs a lot and, in most cases, does not yield better results than using a sampled telemetry collection in place. Sampling ensures that while the data transmitted is reduced, the collected sample is a statistically representable collection of the telemetry to present the full picture. Read more about how OpenTelemetry samples the telemetry before transmitting it: `https://opentelemetry.io/docs/concepts/sampling/`.

Sampling is useful when your servers generate too much trace information that usual logs and traces become very dense that a set of logs can be represented by a single trace.

Further Reading

Tracing is one of the signals used in OpenTelemetry, and works together with the metrics and logs to provide a full picture of the system. Read about the data collection and telemetry instrumentation on OpenTelemetry website: `https://opentelemetry.io/`.

Add an OpenTelemetry instrumentation to an existing project. If you do not have an Azure account, you can create a free account to get started with free Azure Monitor account.

CHAPTER 30

Visualization

IT Operations teams create and use dashboards and metric charts to track the live performance of the application. Now that we have added telemetry, tracing, and monitoring to our application, it is the right time for us to visualize and see the trends. Visualization complements logging—while logging is used by the developers to study what is happening in code, visuals help the Ops to check any hiccups or bottlenecks.

Application Insights,[1] Google Analytics,[2] Datadog,[3] and many other service providers enable you to visualize the data. Open-source services such as Grafana[4] provide nice visuals, grids, dashboards, and ability to crunch and visualize the timeseries data to make quick decisions—manually or with automation.

In this chapter, we explore how visualization simplifies the objective of reviewing the application state and discovering weak links. Visualization can be done in many ways, using built-in charts, third-party dependencies, or custom platforms.

During the development, you use logs to track the progress[5] in your application. In staging environment or production environments, your applications write too many logs—thousands or hundreds of thousands of logs per hour. I've worked with teams that would produce hundreds of thousands of logs—often verbose or info-level[6] logs.

---

[1] Azure Application Insights is a service provided by Azure Monitor. Check it out here: `https://learn.microsoft.com/en-gb/azure/azure-monitor/app/app-insights-overview`.

[2] Google Analytics is another online visualization tool for metrics and telemetry, check it out here: `https://developers.google.com/analytics`.

[3] Check out Datadog service here: `https://www.datadoghq.com/`

[4] Check out Grafana here: `https://grafana.com/`

[5] Debugging is also important. However, debugging is used to identify when something goes wrong at a specific point in your source code. You debug by setting a breakpoint and running the application with a debugger, mostly provided by the IDE or the SDK. I am personally in favor of debugging, because debugging can expose the internals of your program and not just the flow of your script.

[6] Read about the level of logs here: `https://sematext.com/blog/logging-levels/`

Checking these logs is extremely crucial to approve the latest changes or decide to roll back the changes if there are problems.

What do you look at when you see a visualization (Figure 30-1)?

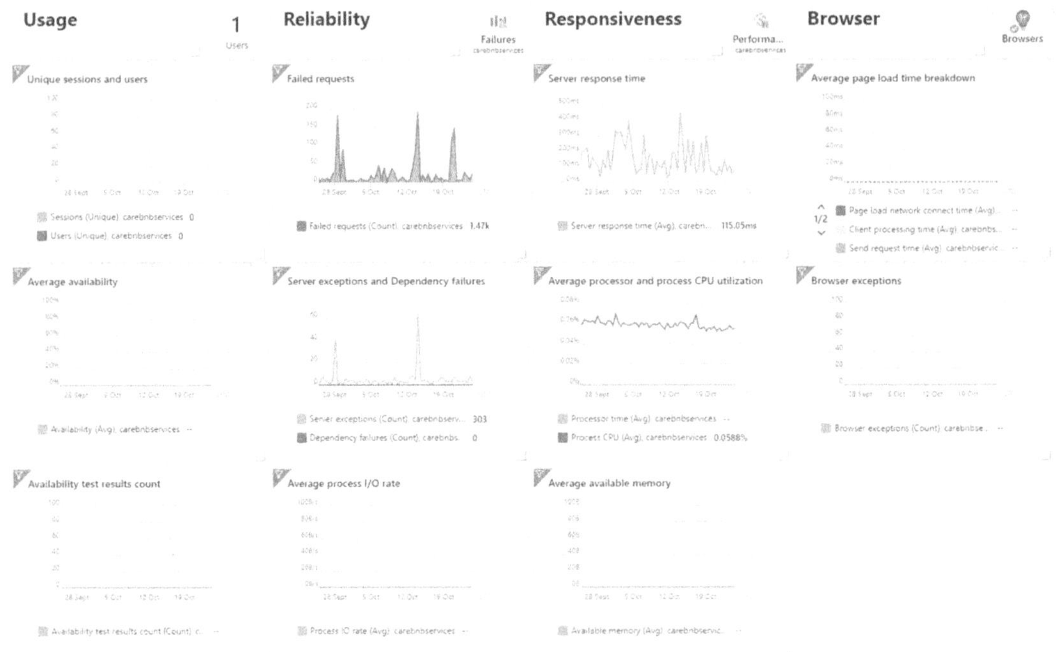

Figure 30-1. *A dashboard showing the application performance over the course of a few weeks, including failure*

The dashboard is not to brag, but to get a view of the internals of the application. The first time you launch a service, the spikes in the service and the user traffic do give a goosebump but from there onward you must focus on getting next features live.

Another important element is to keep the visualization as small and simple as possible. The skill is not in adding more blocks but to process and translate the metrics into readable insights. When things break at night, no one is going to enjoy the 8x6 grid that requires a heavy cognitive payment to process and analyze the important data. But, if you provide insights on what is going south, what is failing, and what needs to be checked, that would speed up the recovery process. To keep things efficient

- Keep the dashboard simple with 5 or less than 5 boards on it.

- Use red color to denote degraded performance and green color to denote the availability range.

- Use colors to represent the performance of metrics as well; if "9ms" metric is a success, render it in green.

- When the graph line is not sloped, the color must be muted; gray.

- Do not use your brand colors to denote the success. It is difficult to teach new members and joiners what success looks like.

It is very important to keep the user-experience in mind when designing and rendering the visualizations. The user is your customer who needs to process the information available on the dashboard. For a .NET engineer, the visualization platform is less important, but the metrics shown is more important. The metrics are often the entry point to dig deeper. Which cell would you click?

- Live Users: 8.2k

- Failed Requests: 3.7k

The size of the data (e.g., 8.2k) matters less, the context matters most. Since you are on the dashboard, you likely need to look at the failed requests and see a pattern. And, for an on-call[7] Engineer, you need to see if this 3.7k failed request collection is a recent spike or a regular trend. In the dashboard above, the **Failed requests** cell had three spikes. The dashboard takes 30 days' worth of data and thus this likely points to a weekly release causing a minor spike in the requests that fail and then go back to normal. This could mean that the service faces some disruption during release, potentially a down time. Note that some environments track regular and wanted problems as failed requests too—for example, *a 404 not found is also a failed request, even for a robots.txt.*

Visualization is used for other formats as well, such as tracing, metrics, resource health, and more. Grafana is the leading platform for building visualizations. Today, almost every platform offers a built-in solution to visualize the current state of affairs and that's fine for most cases. For cases where you need to support an unknown scale, you should focus on a cloud-powered visualization platform that crunches the numbers "for you." Grafana is a great tool for such a use case. You can get started[8] with Grafana

---

[7] The Engineer who is responsible for handling any support tickets for any product or handle infrastructure related concerns is known as on-call Engineer. Also known as Duty Engineer. This is different from Tech Support or Customer Support, in that they do not always work with "customer." But they just check the metrics and trends of the web application and take action when things go bad.

[8] Learn more about Grafana's offering here: `https://grafana.com/grafana/`

without an account and play around to see the difference between reading long threads and rows of logs, and seeing something show up on your screen.

Take a look at the following log output (Figure 30-2):

```
▌ TOTAL RESULTS

  checks_total........: 12860   79.912017/s
  checks_succeeded...: 100.00% 12860 out of 12860
  checks_failed.......: 0.00%   0 out of 12860

  ✓ status was 200


  HTTP
  http_req_duration...............: avg=1.41ms min=0s med=1.21ms max=23.45ms p(90)=2.35ms p(95)=2.8ms
    { expected_response:true }....: avg=1.41ms min=0s med=1.21ms max=23.45ms p(90)=2.35ms p(95)=2.8ms
  http_req_failed.................: 0.00%   0 out of 12860
  http_reqs.......................: 12860   79.912017/s


  EXECUTION
  iteration_duration..............: avg=1s     min=1s med=1s     max=1.04s  p(90)=1s     p(95)=1s
  iterations......................: 12860   79.912017/s
  vus.............................: 31      min=7            max=100
  vus_max.........................: 100     min=100          max=100


  NETWORK
  data_received...................: 1.6 MB  10 kB/s
  data_sent.......................: 977 kB  6.1 kB/s
```

Figure 30-2. *The K6 library allows developers to track the progress of different endpoints of the website and measure the server performance*

The logs demonstrate the details and provide a very complete overview of the system performance. The challenge is that it does not show the trends of the traffic and the bottlenecks. Now, compare Figure 30-2 with Figure 30-3 which shows the traffic trends across the traffic and performance.

Figure 30-3. *A visualization of the traffic trends and demonstrating how the server handled the traffic*

This figure shows a traffic trend that shows that as the traffic moved forward, the server was able to keep up with the load. It does remove all the information about the average, median, and other ranges, but it shows a history of the service. These visualizations were generated using K6 (to study the stress and load performance of an application) and the graphs and logs were generated by the open source library.

The graph shows a clear picture, while the logs provide more in-depth and deep information about the technical state of the system. If you are aiming for in-depth review, go for the logs, while the graphs and trends charts show a high-level. The high-level state is useful for when the services and systems are operating normally.

Application Maps

One interesting area for visualization is how your services communicate with other services across the infrastructure. An application map gives a view of each service or web application and shows the impact that each dependency has on the overall service status—such as response time. The goal of the application map is to

- Show and highlight how many services does our application depend upon.

- How much time does each service take to provide a response—thus contributing to the latency.

- Measure which services are the most time-consuming.

- Identify if your services have their own dependencies that are causing a choke point.

The application map can show incidents or downtimes, but the application map will not be a good platform to use as the raw source to identify, detect, and resolve incidents.

Now, in the chapter, let's see how we can add alerts to the monitors so they notify you when something goes wrong.

Further Reading

The main and most used visualization platform is Grafana (`https://grafana.com/`). Create a free account on Grafana and explore the dashboards that are available. I do not expect you to perform an action, just take a look around and see what dashboards, charts, and graphs are available. Note how different web apps are grouped and clustered to provide an overview of the services.

K6 (`https://grafana.com/oss/k6/?plcmt=oss-nav`) is an open-source library developed and distributed by Grafana to load and stress-test your applications. While the objective of K6 is not to visualize the traffic, K6 and Grafana work hand in hand to help you (1) visualize how the traffic moves across your services and (2) provide you with a complete picture of how the service will operate in near-production environments.

CHAPTER 31

Adding Alerts

The red-green dashboards look really amazing, but when do you press the red button and wake the developer up? The first second when the graph dips? The moment the entire graph turns red? When your Slack starts to blow up?

Alerts are very powerful in notifying when something is not right. Systematic way of identifying when something is wrong helps the operations team make an informed decision. For example, it is a common practice to measure the poor performance over a time to identify that something is wrong, instead of just the first sign of an error. If your application encountered an exception, this is not the right time to raise an alarm. The right time to raise an alarm is when your application has been facing multiple exceptions of same type over the last few minutes, or when the response from servers has been very poor for the last few minutes, etc. The alerts for such behavior can—and should—be configured in the monitoring application. Otherwise, your Ops would be spending most of the time on their calculators averaging the data out.

In this chapter, we will explore when and how we can add alerts to our monitoring systems. We will also explore how to connect the sources where we receive the notifications.

Alerts are mainly beyond the scope of a .NET engineer, as you do not configure the alerts yourself in the .NET apps, nor do you usually receive them in your application. The alerts we are going to talk about in this chapter are the ones for operations teams in their dashboards.

The Engineers in start-up ecosystem, or teams where you do not have a dedicated SRE resource or an operations Engineer, often must wear those hats. At this point, it does not matter whether you write .NET code or Go, or Java, or a new language no one has heard of. You are responsible for making sure that the alert that was sent your way is addressed. The alert can come from

- A system that is no longer moving forward.

- A monitoring system that detected an incorrect response.

© Afzaal Ahmad Zeeshan 2026
A. A. Zeeshan, *Building Mission-Critical Applications with .NET 10 and C# 14*,
https://doi.org/10.1007/979-8-8688-2347-3_31

- An angry client who is unable to use your product.

- A reminder to fix the problem you were supposed to fix in the last Sprint.

An alert is a generic term used to describe a notification or a reminder. Your teams, or even yourself, depend on a sidecar system to always check the health of the systems and notify you when something goes wrong. If your Engineers spend more time on operations, they spend less time writing the features that will take your business ahead of competition. That was very obvious. But what is less obvious is that you do not need to make a dedicated distinction between those who create problems and those who solve the problems. We already discussed the "hero engineer"[1] concept and it is indeed a very crucial one again. It is clear beyond a shadow of doubt that not every Engineer writes perfect code, wants to write the code that doesn't break, or doesn't contribute technical debt, or participates in post-mortems, joining the team retrospectives to learn what went wrong, what we will do better, and what we will stop doing. As a team.

Lastly, the alerts for the teams are different from the alerts for the on-call Engineers. On-Call Engineers have one objective and one objective only: put the fire out. And they do it by any. Means. Necessary. And this does include doing things that are often avoided during business-as-usual. Examples include

- Skipping linter checks in your code

- Avoiding proper commit messages and description for the pull requests

- Not waiting through the entire CI/CD validation

- Bypassing any manual checks that would slow down your patch to reach the production

But, while the On-Call Engineer does skip all these steps to quickly put out the fire, one thing you must never do: forget the mess you made. You "broke the glass"[2] and left the broken shards on the floor to put out the fire. Do something about it.

- Are you the one responsible for cleaning up the floor? Do it.

---

[1] Read more here: `https://incident.io/blog/no-capes`

[2] Read more about how "break glass" protocol helps maintain the security objectives: `https://www.strongdm.com/blog/break-glass`.

- Are you not the one responsible? Label it before you move forward so that the right teams can step in and fix it.

A simple example of labeling can be to just indicate that this commit or merge was a patch and thus did not follow the standard procedure. In the next sprint or the current spring, put more time in fixing this technical debt that you created before it snowballs into a big problem. If you do not have the ability to prioritize it in the current sprint, put an alert on it so that it becomes painful. Engineers—and teams—run away from pain, so put yourself in that position, position of pain, where you do not want to be and you will fix the problems and pay off the debts in time.

Alert or No Alert?

It is often said that there is no such thing as overcommunication. But, is there an over-alert? There are so many things that can be said here, but I guess the right answer comes from the one "alerted." If you are the one being alerted during day and night, then yes, do you think there is ever a time when there are so many alerts? Often, Engineers that are not responsible for On-Call procedures are quick to complain that the dashboards do not send enough alerts. While the On-Call Engineers complain that there is often too much noise, repeat alerts or notifications, server-side events, often mislead and give false positives to trigger a response for something that was not even critical. While alerting is important, it is more important to alert the right person and give the right information:

- Share the shard, application instance, service name and/or the request ID so that the problems can be traced back.

- Share the exact problem that occurred, not just a generic "service crashed."

- If possible, give a list of options that the On-Call person can try.

  - Check the feature flag configuration state.

In some environments or platforms, it is not possible to send a message larger than a specific size. Especially if your platform sends out a message via short message sending (SMS), extra characters cost more. If you use online-only platforms where you use push notifications, then the message length is comparably cheaper, the message can be embedded with rich content, and enable navigation between different services; such as incident.io, Jira/YouTrack, etc.

The metrics dashboard is mostly among the first things to be reviewed when an incident happens. During a war, your metrics dashboard, SSH access, hotfix pipelines are the most important tools to (1) understand what is happening in the system and (2) apply a patch to the system to fix the ongoing problem.

Once your team is ready to fix the problem, alerts become a noise since you are already reviewing the dashboard and seeing the patterns and trends across the user traffic and the success ratio of your service. It is often a good practice to either disable the specific alert or mute it for a set time duration.

Programmable Alerts

Today, everything has an SDK and an API that you can use to connect to it or send notifications to it. If your on-call Engineer is wearing a watch you can just nudge them to wake up and watch when something has gone rogue. PagerDuty is one such example, the platform is used by all major leaders across the industries to send alerts for when things get real. They provide an API, and so what stops you from building an integration? Using the API you can send in notifications to the PagerDuty platform and also read notifications and perform actions on your own events. Here is an example flow, to connect your Google Tasks with the PagerDuty platform through Zapier (Figure 31-1):

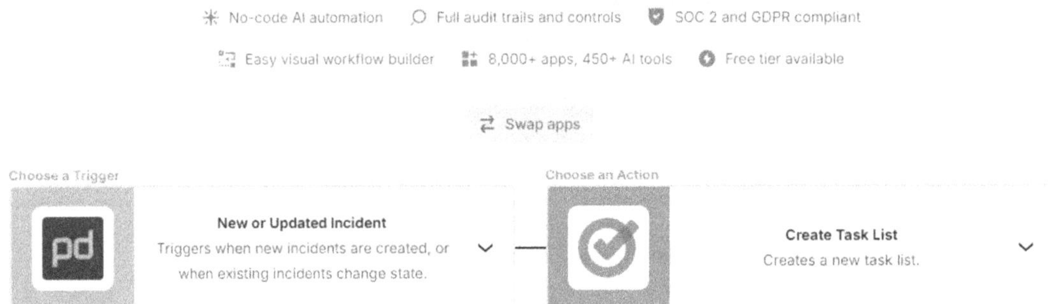

Figure 31-1. Integration between PageDuty and Google Tasks based on the events as IFTTT

Of course, Zapier is one such platform that allows you to go no-code or low-code and build the integrations between different platforms. You can build your own platforms to move the events from one platform to another, to simplify the process for your engineers.

Microsoft Azure Monitor, which we have been talking about in the last chapters, also supports alerts. You can create a new alert for your Azure Monitor based on different dimensions. Figure 31-2 demonstrates how to create alerts for your resources and receive them:

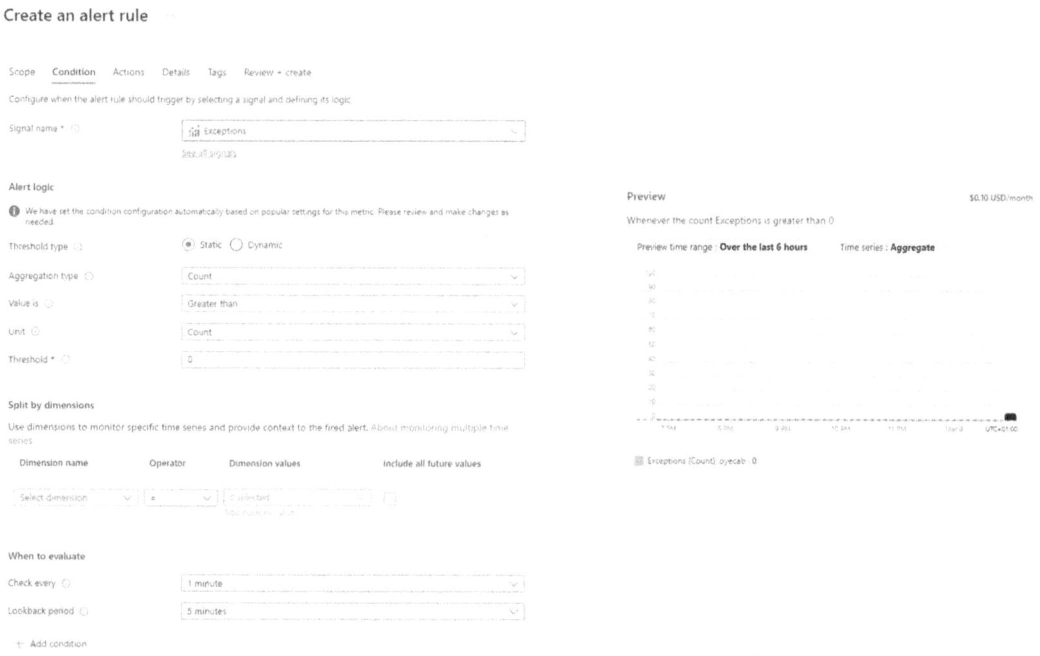

Figure 31-2. *The Azure Monitor interface to create alerts for our services based on criteria*

Azure Monitor allows you to configure the actions that can be taken. By default, Azure Monitor can send out emails to the right groups who must be notified. While Slack and custom integration is not supported out of box for Azure Monitor, you can use and build custom solutions such as Logic Apps to broadcast the notifications. Check out this documentation guide to learn how to build this: `https://learn.microsoft.com/en-us/azure/azure-monitor/alerts/alerts-logic-apps?tabs=send-email`.

The alerts are a good way to communicate the problems and hiccups in a system. Alerting is fine, and like we learned it is okay to communicate more. However, as soon as the alerts communicate a problem that will impact your customers or impact the business in any way, that is the scope of incident management. In the next part, we will learn about incidents and how to manage them for .NET apps.

PART VII

Firefighting

CHAPTER 32

Firefighting Rules

When in Rome, do as the Romans do. When firefighting, do as the firefighters do. We Engineers have two prominent aspects:

- We have very big egos. We believe we cannot make mistakes.

- We love the code we write and consider it to be perfect and flawless.

This causes us to divert the pointing-finger toward the other components. We blame the recent incidents on the latest software update from our vendor—who in turn blame it on their vendor; a vendor within the vendor problem.

A firefighter does not put the blame on the house owner. They are there to do one thing, and one thing only: put the fire out. The insurance company, law-enforcement, house owners, they all come into the picture afterward. We can call it "postmortem."

In this chapter, you will learn about firefighting rules[1]—how simple they actually are—and how you can use them in your regular operations.

We prepare food every day, and that includes burning some fire, things getting hot, somethings burning, and smoke, and stuff. But not every smoke leads to a fire alarm. Sometimes smoke is fine and you turn on the exhaust, and sometimes you open a window to let extra smoke or heat go out. And sometimes, the extras are not enough. The smoke is too much that the fire alarm goes off. Sometimes, the smoke is not enough, but the fire alarm (or the smoke detector) detects that the smoke contains more harmful matter in it and that the quantity does not matter anymore and it goes off.

The fire alarm going off is also not that bad. Right? You can check for the burning stuff and get this out of the situation and then you turn the fire alarm off.

Remember: Do not turn off the fire alarm if the smoke is still present or being made, or the item is still on fire. When in danger, always call your local emergency number.

---

[1] Check out the rules for fighting fires from University of South Carolina: `https://www.sc.edu/ehs/training/Fire/07_rules.htm`.

You never know when something can be very dangerous, even fatal. Fire alarm is the symptom of knowing something is burning but it is not the root cause. The root cause is the food burning in the pan, or something else. You should only turn off the fire alarm once you are certain that danger has been averted.

The biggest challenge seen in incident handling is not that there is no one to solve the problem, but that there is often the same person (or group of people) who are always solving all kinds of problems. This leads to a rather big problem where everyone thinks that it is not their responsibility to solve a problem because someone else will show up to solve it.

In this section, we will focus on two things:

- Root cause

- Mitigation

Often, they go hand in hand, that you fix the root cause or sometimes it is something that you do not see as easily or clearly. There are various ways to look at these different dimensions and we will break it down together as we explore hypothetical scenarios and practices to step into the feet of engineers receiving the fire alarms—or fire drills, and then getting to work to identify what is actually the problem, how to fix it, and then getting to fixing it. The steps for firefighting in engineering teams includes

- Raising the alarm

- Isolating the incident

- Getting the right people in

The first rule when you detect that something is wrong is to raise the alarm. It is better to be sorry about a wrong alarm than not having raised an alarm and ask for professional help. If you detect or observe, or a monitoring dashboard shows that your service is not working fine or the customers are facing problems, you should raise the alarm. In engineering, the alarm could mean

- A message in the infrastructure channel highlighting the issue and raising the concerns with the right team members.

- Use a runbook or automation to create an incident or issue thread on central systems such as Jira or ticket boards.

- Join or call the firefighting rooms (also called war rooms) and loop in the right subject-matter experts.

- An email on an internal communication group to raise the alert so everyone responsible for handling the issues is aware.

The alarming phase is just the starting point for the resolution. The issue could be a temporary one and may have been caused by the recent deployment and the resolution could be the rollback or a patch/hotfix to the recently released feature or service. But sending the message out in the team or shared channels makes finding this problem quick, faster, collaborative, and organized. Identifying that the problem was not major, you can tag the issue with all the relevant information such as severity, accountable team, postmortem details, communication for external or internal stakeholders, etc. and close the issue. And with that, you can close the issue by leaving the war room and leaving it ready for the next issue.

As a second step, make sure the issue and the problem is isolated. In a complex system, multiple problems can happen at the same time. This is fine. But a team focused on incident#653 should not be blocked by incident#235 and vice versa. During the incident resolution process, a team makes changes to see if the problem gets worse or the situation gets better. Keeping all the incidents separate is not always possible, especially if you have only one war room or only one site-reliability engineer. But keeping the incidents separate helps focus on one problem at a time. The incident resolution is a very complex process and one with very high cognitive load as well. The stakes are high, and since the impact is causing problems for the customers, not only the development or engineering department is concerned about it. Leadership is also pushing their nose into the war rooms to learn what is happening and when the problem will be fixed—that is because they are also getting calls from the customers, asking the same questions!

Food for thought: when the patch for incident#653 makes incident#235 resolution worse, is it a high severity incident#235 or do we need to create a new incident? I'd like to hear your thoughts, please share with me on Twitter/X @afzaalvirgoboy.

Even though this is an overarching theme of collaboration, this is the most important one. In every company, there are many people who are interested in solving a problem or at least learning how other experts are solving this problem to understand the architecture or the solution used in the organization. Very quickly it turns into a circus, where the "hero engineer" is at the center of the attention and everyone makes assumptions about their actions. No matter how quiet everyone tends to be, the whispers are enough to break the train of thought for the subject-matter expert. This is why it is important to thin out the herd and only allow the people at work to be part of the group. You can solve this by

- Recording the session, and force-muting every participant on the meeting.

- Giving the session participants the authority to shut people off who are only contributing noise.

- In complicated issues or incidents, try to break into focus groups that each solve a specific problem and communicate the status back.

Read the roles and responsibilities definition on the incident.io: `https://incident.io/guide/foundations/roles`.

When you gather the right people to work together, you get the job done quickly. The most important members in the incident resolution team are

- A subject-matter expert (can be a group)

- A communication manager (outlines and writes the activity events)

- A captain or a commander who orchestrates everything (an outspoken person who knows how to control the group)

In simple incidents, these roles can be taken by a single engineer, or the team that owns the web application. For complex incidents, this has to be shared across different team members where they each focus on their own responsibilities and do them perfectly. The person responsible for ensuring the activity of events is recorded does that. They write down

- When the incident started?

- When was the incident identified?

- When was the incident impacting customers or internal services?

- When was the root cause analysis started?

- When was the root cause determined, and what was it?

- What are the teams doing and how many teams are working on this?

- What is the ETA for a resolution?

- What communication has been made to internal or external partners and customers?

- Has a patch or hotfix been made?

- Who is monitoring the service performance during the incident? After the incident?

- Was the service-level agreement broken? Any communication made?

And so many other questions that each provide a clear information about what is happening and what needs to be done and by whom. They are not responsible for doing this, but noting it down. The subject-matter experts, for example, are responsible for bringing the services back to acceptable levels. Teams and organizations can have their own dedicated roles and responsibilities as well.

Now before we wrap up this chapter, another important thing to remember is that you do not fight every fire with water. Throwing a bucket of water at a fire to put it out may work, but not in all cases. In most cases, it may even be dangerous or fatal—such as if the fire is caused by electrical causes. So, before you do anything, even if the symptom says "throw a bucket of water," always conduct a thorough investigation of what is happening, what the problem is, what the source is, and then devise a plan to put the fire out. And do not shy away from breaking down walls, getting the carpet dirty, jumping out of the window on a mattress, all that is possible when you are focusing on the right objective: put the fire out.

This theme will resonate in this section as we will explore how firefighting in software world is so similar to firefighting.[2]

In the next chapter, we will use the knowledge we gained in this chapter to define what is an incident, what should your team know about the incident, and what does the incident communicate to your team. It is important to learn that every hiccup does not require the team to start to panic and lose their balance. The goal of identifying the incident is not to start the blame game, but rather to prepare the team to bring the platform back to its operational state.

---

[2] In no way to downplay either team or heroes. Just talking about the commonalities on how one craft's practices are used in a different industry.

Further Reading

Before you go and start reading the next chapter, I recommend that you watch the incident management procedures in place with Red Bull's Formula 1 team where they identify, resolve, and get back in the race by "communicating" effectively. Read a breakdown here: `https://archive.fosdem.org/2025/schedule/event/fosdem-2025-6599-what-can-we-learn-from-formula-1-incident-management/`

Computer science and software engineering take a lot from other disciplines. While this part focuses on firefighting and emergency responders, it is also important to note how the medical system can influence our understanding of emergency situations and how to deal with them. This article about nurse calls highlights how we can best allocate the resources to the right areas to avoid a sudden spike in incidents and emergencies: `https://impulsecctv.com/blog/nurse-calling-systems-emergency-response-hospitals/`

CHAPTER 33

What Defines an Incident?

Production is a very sensitive environment, and any hiccup can cause a lot of disruption from a business perspective. As Engineers, we need to establish what is an incident and what is down time. Not every exception needs a team of five to bring the platform up again. Sometimes a response is delayed because of reasons beyond your control. If you depend on an external party, your application can be down because of their downtime—this is why you must always consider reviewing underlying SLAs that your platform depends on.

In this chapter, we focus on

- Introducing the impact of an incident (e.g., severity)

- The impact of tooling on incident detection

Once you know there is an incident, how do you react? Should you react? Is there a way to handle things proactively? Spoiler: incident resolution is mostly a reactive business. If you knew an incident would happen but still rolled out the release, this is not an incident problem, but an Engineering culture problem.

The most thrown-around term in large enterprises is "business as usual." Things break, new features get published, and teams get formed as new 6-month long initiatives are started. The only thing that keeps everyone sane and on the same page is knowing that the services are operational and the customers are not yet creating support tickets in hundreds.

An incident—*also known as issue, problem, outage*—is an event where your customers are unable to use your service to complete their jobs. Of course, there are other ways and reasons to define an incident differently as well. Incident.io, one of the leading service providers for incident managers, provides a different definition, check it out here: `https://incident.io/guide/foundations/defining-an-incident`.

© Afzaal Ahmad Zeeshan 2026
A. A. Zeeshan, *Building Mission-Critical Applications with .NET 10 and C# 14*,
https://doi.org/10.1007/979-8-8688-2347-3_33

Teams use a metric called "severity"[1] indicating how bad the incident is. The severity of an incident is how urgent it is for the business to fix this incident before things get worse—in terms of customer relationship, or service or infrastructure degradation. There are several ways to deduce the "severity" of any incident, but there is no hard-and-fast rule.

- Is this an internal incident or an external incident?

- Do we breach the service-level agreement? Did this incident cause it to be breached?

- Are customers unable to continue their business operations?

- Is there a heartbeat at least?

A common notion is to pick a value from a range of severity levels. Usually, from 1 all the way up to 5. It is commonly accepted to put severity 1 (or severity-0) for high and urgent incident that requires all teams to drop what they are doing and fix the platform, and severities 3, 4, and 5 to non-urgent matters. Severity 5 is usually kept for internal-only problems where the cause and impact does not affect the customers or external parties. Such are the examples of an internal email system outage used to share internal weekly updates, or degraded performance of internal training and learning management system. Given that these are not business critical, they can be solved in the next sprint.

Teams also use their own internal SLIs and SLOs to track when something is an incident, or when the performance has been degraded but is still within allowed limits. While any bad performance or misconfigured behavior of the application requires a quick fix, the incidents are handled with the utmost care and urgency. And during an incident, you typically expect the right teams to drop what they are doing and bring the platform back to a stable state. If you ignore the incidents, the platform always goes to a worse state. If your platform continues to serve the customers, and customers are not impacted—then this is not a high severity incident and does not require your teams to drop everything and fix it first. It can be fixed on the next business day. This is the ideal state for a platform, where your platform either self-heals[2] and gets back to a normal

---

[1] Read more about Severity of an incident here: `https://incident.io/guide/foundations/severities`.

[2] Read about self-healing on cloud-native foundation website: `https://glossary.cncf.io/self-healing/`

state, or contains the problem with cloud-native architectures to prevent using the service. This can be done by

- Short-circuiting the architecture and ensuring the requests do not travel to the faulty services and systems

- Removing the faulty services from our internal service discovery platforms or DNS systems so that the traffic is automatically routed to healthy nodes

This mature level of infrastructure cannot easily be achieved, and one of the goals of our postmortems is to move our infrastructure as close as possible to this state where our systems are aware of themselves, and services that **(1)** they depend on and **(2)** consume them. The biggest challenge for this is not the tooling but the interconnectivity of tooling and the services. For example, if you use message-broker systems and one of the brokers fails. How would your API know that it can no longer accept new requests because the internal communication is down? To contain this problem and abstract it from the customer, your application infrastructure must observe when the brokers go down and either remove the unhealthy nodes from the service discovery or route the traffic to a different service to act as the communication broker.

In the earlier chapters, we discussed the use cases of specialized software-development life cycle pipelines, where we allow skipping certain checks and push the code to production quickly. During an incident, that fast pipeline becomes the tool used by engineers and teams, or the on-call teams to quickly patch the fire and keep the platform stable and running.

Navigating an Incident

The incident navigation happens differently, depending on whether it is a live incident or an old incident—being postmortem'd or retrospective'd. When the incident is live, you need to navigate the incident to understand the situation and to understand who is owning it or fixing it.

The process for an incident navigation during a postmortem or a retrospective is different. The situation is not as serious as when the incident was still live. The customers are not waiting for a patch and the service is operational—at least for the context of this specific incident. During a postmortem or a retrospective, your goal is to study what went wrong, why did it go wrong, why was this not seen in the software-development life cycle, which teams were impacted, and how to add guardrails around the applications or infrastructure to make sure this does not happen again.

It is also important to pay off any technical debt accrued during this incident. An incident is usually closed when the service gets back to normal; however, the incident ticket must not be closed until the technical debt added to the system or the repository is also paid off. The retrospectives are an opportunity for your teams to make sure that a similar incident does not happen, and to learn about the non-technical damage done by the specific incident. In my experience, I've seen engineering teams talk about incidents in terms of databases, firewalls, webapps, and deployments. They miss out the single most important part: customer relationship. Many times teams identified an incident, worked on resolving it, resolved it, closed it and then did a monthly retrospective to learn how to make the tech stack stable and error-free in future. But they did not take the customer experience into account. Several times customer success managers, sales engineers, account managers, complain that each incident puts a crack in their relationship with the customers. One account manager shared a story of how a two-week old incident had just caused a passive negative experience for a customer who was arriving for a contract renegotiation phase and, due to the incident, the account executive needs to do more to make sure the relationship stays the same and the customer signs the contract extension. One of the ways in which we solved this problem was bringing technical and non-technical (commercial) teams together and talk about challenges and learnings from each incident. This very simple initiative was very well received from both departments as they were able to understand what the other department has to do for every operational step and how everyone department impacts the overall customer relationship greatly.

Now, let's talk about navigating an incident as it happens.

Further Reading

Before you proceed to the next chapter, I advise you to read about two of the high severity incident types and how organizations tackle them. The first one is the zero-day vulnerability which is a security incident that may compromise the performance of your application but will surely impact the regulatory compliance and the brand image of your organization or application. Read about the zero-day vulnerabilities on IBM's website: `https://www.ibm.com/think/topics/zero-day`. The second category is DDoS, while this type of attack does impact the brand, its primary focus is the performance and operations of the system and to bring the system to a halt. Read about DDoS on IBM's website: `https://www.ibm.com/think/topics/ddos`.

Each incident has a designated severity rating that indicates and communicates (with internal as well as external parties) the impact that the incident had on the services. While the range is commonly from one (1) to five (5). The sort order (ascending or descending) is a cultural, preferential, and historical choice. If your teams agree to designate severity 1 to the highest impact, then that is same as another incident in a team which designates severity 5 to their highest impacts. Read about the severity levels, reasons, and motivations behind the range on Splunk's website: `https://www.splunk.com/en_us/blog/learn/incident-severity-levels.html`.

As we will also learn in the next chapter how each impact has a huge cost in terms of brand but also financials and customer trust, read this guide from Atlassian on the cost of a downtime for your business: `https://www.atlassian.com/incident-management/kpis/cost-of-downtime`.

The site reliability engineers (SREs) use error budgets. The error budget is your ability to move fast while making sure you break less. `https://sre.google/workbook/error-budget-policy/`

CHAPTER 34

Identify the Root Cause

Do you know why a lot of incidents are handled by a company's senior Engineers and not juniors? Because they know the platform in-and-out. It has nothing to do with the experience with language, runtime, or the database engine used. This quickly becomes a syndrome called "hero engineer."[1] It is great to have hero engineers in your company. But for hero engineers, it very quickly becomes unfair.

The detection/identification phase for an incident takes problem identification into account. Unlike regular day operations, for incidents, you think more before you take the first step. The first action can take you closer to the root cause or take you very far away—which becomes an expensive maneuver. This is why it is of utmost importance to identify the underlying reason of the fire, before putting it out. Put simple: know the source of the fire before you throw water on it.

In this chapter, we will review a timeline of an incident.

- How an incident is encountered by customers or caught by our internal teams and systems.

- We explore a practical way to using the Five Why's to identify the root cause and also demonstrate how and where you can deviate from the norms.

- The prioritization of the incidents can make or break a healthy and growing application and the customer trust.

For your company to have an excellent incident response structure, minimize the number of hero engineers, and maximize the opportunities for others to step into the role of a hero engineer.

---

[1] Check out this blog post by incident.io on challenges of the hero engineer: `https://incident.io/blog/no-capes`.

It is weekend, 7 pm in the evening, half the team is either having dinner with the family, putting their kids to bed, or coming back from a weekend picnic. The other half is already preparing for the Monday and making sure Monday is smooth. They check their emails for anomalies, Slack channels for any urgent or abnormal notifications, and plan their agenda in the calendars. The devil strikes at the strangest of hours. Your dashboard shows the first dip in one of the charts. The incidents or issues do not announce themselves. You must detect them based on the situation and the impact caused.

T-0: The Downward Trend

Incidents can be detected in many ways.

1. Your operations teams can detect a misbehaving application.

2. Your customers open a support thread to ask for help.

3. Your monitoring alerts send out panic emails and notifications to the teams to alert them of the situation.

Once this happens, the first thing to do is not to assess the root cause but the impact. Identifying the root cause takes a significant amount of time, manpower, and system understanding, and if you start doing this for every incident, then you would quickly burn through the time of "hero engineers." That is why you must first assess the severity of the incident to allocate the effort to it. If the incident is critical (severity 1 or 2; remember that we assign 1 or 2 for high severity and urgent matters, 3 for same day or same sprint incidents and severity 4 for business as usual, whereas severity 5 is for internal incidents that can be handled at the earliest opportunity), then your teams must deal with it first thing. If the incident is not critical to business or commercial success of the company or customers, then you can assess it at the first available opportunity; it can be the next hour, next day, or next sprint. Once you have noted down the severity, then the actual work of incident resolution starts. The first person who detects the incident or raises the alarm is responsible for getting everyone and everything together.

- They take the role of incident captain—also called incident commander, incident lead, incident manager, you get the idea.

- They loop in the right subject-matter experts responsible for the web apps that are facing down time.

- They create the communication channels—Slack, Google Docs, third-party platforms, etc.—to effectively communicate the activity in the incidents.

- They take on this role until someone steps in with more experience in managing incidents, or if they assume a different role themselves.

The root cause analysis is the next important step in incident resolution. The root cause is the first thing that broke the system. While the final straw broke the camel's back, it is not the final operation on the system that broke it. It is usually something that happened earlier in the system that is having the impact now. The stress and strain on a system that has accumulated over time actually contributes heavily to the incident on a system. Naturally, this often comes down to

- A recent feature pushed out to the system that does not have credentials or configuration released on the infrastructure.

- An untested code branch that reads a null value, or does not validate the size of the array before reading the elements.

- A network certificate expiration or invalidity that contributes to failed requests.

- A database being under pressure from different websites and web applications and providing degraded performance under load and stress.

- An internal or scheduled maintenance in a component that makes certain parts of the infrastructure unavailable.

A root cause is often difficult to identify. If your customer is unable to finish the purchase on the ecommerce platform, how do you know it is because the new function is reading a property on a null-object? You have to drill down various layers and levels of the services and read the code, check the logs, review the tracing to identify the actual root cause. One of the best working practices is the five whys.[2] The five whys is a practice of asking "Why" until you identify the root cause of the problem.

- Why #1: Why is the customer unable to complete their purchase?

    - Because they are unable to proceed on the checkout page.

---

[2] Read more about the five whys here: `https://en.wikipedia.org/wiki/Five_whys`.

- Why #2: Why is the customer unable to proceed on the checkout page?

  - Because the checkout component receives an error from the backend systems.

- Why #3: Why does the component receive an error from the backend systems?

  - Because the backend system is unable to complete the request and provide a successful response to the API gateway.

- Why #4: Why does the API gateway not receive a successful response?

  - Because the address management system is unable to find the address.

- Why #5: Why is the address management system unable to find the address?

  - Because the address management system is reading a field that does not exist.

This is definitely a rhetorical situation, and real questions would differ and you may encounter the root cause at question #3 or it may take a few more questions to reach something concrete that needs to be fixed. Asking the right questions leads you and your teams to the right problem that must be fixed to avoid this incident from occurring again. Now we identified that the problem was because the latest feature is checking a field that does not exist and fixing this problem would help the systems provide the right response. In an alternative officeverse, it could be that the answer to Why #4 is that the internal database is down and the system does not receive a response from it, then your next question and the resolution procedure will be very different.

Fix the Code

With the root cause identified, the next step is to patch it. During an incident, aim for speed over perfection.

Important: the break glass protocol is a very useful in cases of code emergencies. This gives the teams access to move their code from the safest and fastest way out of the messy situation and to a stable state. It is very natural for the code authors and engineers to abuse this break glass protocol for a speedy delivery of their features to the production. To avoid this, do not move the break glass protocol away from their access but make it punishable by making them accountable for misuses and abuses of this protocol. In real life, we see a similar pattern, we have fire hydrants and other tools in access in different areas and everyone is able to access it. The access is only during the state of emergency and not during regular days; if they do, they are accountable for their action: in terms of fines, etc. For developers, you make it difficult by having this indicated in their code reviews, alerting their team leads, or sharing a leaderboard of "glass breakers."

At this moment, you do not need to remove the pipes and install new ones. It would work if you just put a big tape on the pipes. In code language, it would be wise to hardcode some conditions and logic to avoid scenarios that are breaking the application. Manual testing is okay as long as it offers the agility and speed to ship the patch to production. The code may not use the fancy design patterns and may require further refactoring in the next iteration. If your tech debt grows, let it grow for now. The author must label or tag the code indicating that this contribution contains code that is not ready for review and critique but is solving a different problem. When you break the glass to put the fire out, the shards fall on the floor, and you do not go for the broom right away. Similarly, the code needed to fix the problem does the same thing. It adds a little mess. The responsibility of the incident lead is to make sure every problem identified is fixed, patched, and that the system vitals are back to normal. You can review these vitals on a dashboard as the changes are pushed to the production, or you can have a communication coordinator assessing the situations with the customers—if the customers are the ones impacted by the incident. Once the problem has been averted, study the ongoing patterns for any further anomalies—with your systems or with other customers. This continues for a while until you—as a lead—can close the incident after concluding the system vitals, patch status, activity reports, and next action items.

If you must take anything from this chapter, it is that the safety rules of the engineering—linters, code smells—have been lifted and your only objective is to bring the platform online. By. Any. Means. Necessary.

P.S. If you were disgusted by my suggestion of avoiding linters, know that the oldest working trick that still works today is to turn the system off and on again. Quickly.

Prioritizing Incident Management

At any given time there are several incidents ongoing in any organization. They may all have a different severity, urgency, or impact and different teams would be working toward their resolution.

For business continuity, you should put the customers first unless the customer-facing incident is impacted by an internal outage. Then you fix the internal outage first and then build the solution for the customer-facing incident.

1. Customer-facing or external services take the first priority in resolution.

2. Infrastructure issues that have a chance of causing recursive incidents or causing cracks in other parts of the infrastructure.

3. Incidents that have quickly burned all your error budgets and are causing you to go over your service-level agreements.

4. Experience-related incidents, where a customer is unable to perform an action or must do repetitive tasks to get something done.

5. Internal incidents that break non-operational or critical systems, where a manual step can be taken.

Note that while the prioritization is important to keep in mind, often you may have to prioritize things differently. For example, if an internal system breaks that is responsible for communicating the status of your services and their health, the highest priority should be given because now your customers will start flooding your support teams with requests if something does go south. In such cases, where the customer has a blind spot about the status of your services, they will send in emails and support threads even when your services are not facing any downtime—*they have no way to tell if they are down or not.*

An interesting topic is when your teams have detected that the impact is not huge and decide not to fix the incident right now. It is still important to keep the incident in front of the teams so they do fix it. If an incident remains in severity-5 for too long, give it a bump to severity-4 after a few weeks so that teams prioritize it. It is entirely natural for lowest priority things to have a snowball effect and turn into severity-3 or severity-2. By that time, it takes more effort, more resources, and are often expensive to resolve in terms of resources needed and the damage done. Use the example of an internal service status page. Even though this page is to be used by internal teams and has no business impact or customer problems, if this keeps on being pushed for the next sprint, there would be a day when the customer starts demanding the status report for your application. At that point, if you do not have an acceptable response, the customer will be unhappy, and your teams will then have to prioritize this effort as high or urgent and they will have to drop what they are doing right now.

A smart way to do this would be to exponentially reduce the time needed to fix an internal problem. This should not be taken as a rule of thumb—as it would depend on the size and context of your business—but this can be a good practice:

- Severity-5 incidents move to severity-4 after three months.

- Severity-4 incidents move to severity-3 after one month (or four weeks; or two sprints).

- Severity-3 incidents move to severity-2 after one sprint.

The severity-2 and severity-1 have a different pipeline of urgency and are resolved as they are encountered and detected by the teams. Naturally this gives the teams about 4-ish months to fix an internal outage before it gets troublesome. This also builds a culture of paying off technical debt before the collector comes.

Now, for the cases where you have resolved the incidents. You should have two outcomes in most cases:

1. A component that has technical debt contributed to it

2. A list of actions recommended to avoid this incident in future

These two action items are important and to be resolved, but they often have different timelines. For the component that was on fire and has been fixed with a most-likely poor quality code for a patch. This must be resolved in the next commit to the system that must take all the good practices and style guides in account. The initial commit must be tagged with technical debt term, and must be clear to everyone in the owning team and dependents that the code contains a decided and well-known practice just to fix the problem. And now that the problem has been fixed, we are making a decision to fix it properly and thus the author is publishing a change that must be reviewed for good quality. This must happen as soon as possible and often within the same sprint.

Secondly, for the list of actions that were discovered to be fixed. Your team may or may not be the right team to fix them all. But these must be taken up quickly to ensure that the incident does not occur again. Repeat incidents are more dangerous than isolated instances of incidents as they give more room for error, push the systematic cracks to their limits, causes customers to lose trust and make it more difficult to bring the platform—and the business—back on stable ground.

In the next part, we will explore tangential topics that can increase your productivity as a .NET engineer and a C# developer. These topics and concepts include application deployment and development models, such as monolith or microservices, how you structure and orchestrate your database, and more.

Further Reading

To wrap up this part, I would advise you to learn about how .NET manages and handles the incidents and feedbacks for their framework. Review their SECURITY.md policy on GitHub for .NET: `https://github.com/dotnet/sdk/blob/main/SECURITY.md`

PART VIII

Repeat

CHAPTER 35

Monolith vs. Microservices

Microservices took the (Engineering) world by storm a decade ago. Every business wanted it. Every business was not ready to have it. Tech teams wanted to migrate their repositories, source code, to a disconnected/team-oriented modules setup.

The biggest challenge with Microservices was its biggest win: the ability to separate the concerns into smaller modules. While that gives a lot of value to a product much bigger in size and complexity, for starters, it was a chaos.

In this chapter, we will look at

- Microservices and why do we need to use microservices if so many organizations still use and heavily rely upon the monolith approach to writing software.

- The challenges faced by microservices, and how you should train and upskill your teams to onboard them on a microservices-driven architecture.

- The regulatory challenges and how you should look at the microservice vs. monolith race from a compliance perspective to give your teams the right speed and the right guardrails.

Microservices is not a newly invented approach to developing and deploying the applications. The older service-oriented architecture, modular design, N-tier, Onion architecture, or clean architecture were an early response to a common problem faced by modern applications.

- Multiple teams working on different aspects and areas of the application in their own separate roadmaps.

© Afzaal Ahmad Zeeshan 2026
A. A. Zeeshan, *Building Mission-Critical Applications with .NET 10 and C# 14*,
https://doi.org/10.1007/979-8-8688-2347-3_35

- The CI/CD pipelines not being concurrent or parallel but in complete isolation. Often leading to differently versioned binaries.

- Incidents, issues, and downtimes of one component of the overall application causing downtime in unrelated areas of the product. Think of the shopping cart system going down just because the email system was facing degraded performance.

The tipping point was the dependency on one or two legacy modules that were slow to build, poorly tested, and required manual delivery and deployment. This led to slower deployments for components that could very easily be deployed via CI/CD pipeline.

Breaking Points

In this chapter, instead of preaching the benefits of microservices or why you should continue with your monolith, I would take a different approach. I would share certain breaking points for you to consider if you must use one or the other.

This challenge of migrating from monolith to microservices is very fascinating for me, and I like to think of this as fixing a blown-out tire on a running car.

#1 Teams and Team Size

In the book, Team Topologies,[1] authors recommend businesses to structure their teams according to the business needs and products they are shipping or using (for in-house products). Note that this is not the first time that the computer science field has heard of this pattern. Conway's law[2] introduced this concept, that the businesses have a bias to produce the products that mimic their own internal corporate structure. This law is universal. I have not seen a company that has evaded this law and has a healthy culture. If we use the team size, the communication channels between the teams, the inputs and outputs, and the data flow as the guiding principles, then we can start to see "seams" across the source control.

---

[1] Team Topologies is an amazing book for anyone starting into Leadership roles or trying to understand how to best align the teams with the business mission. Check out the book and resources here: `https://teamtopologies.com/`

[2] `https://martinfowler.com/bliki/ConwaysLaw.html`

The biggest benefit we get by identifying and accepting these seams is we get better software development practices. Alright, put the "number wizard" to the side, just think about the ownership problem of the code. If you have five different teams taking care of your product's source code—they all use the best practices of modern Engineering—if there occurs an incident, who is responsible for that? Since they all are responsible/owner of the product, no one is responsible. In scenarios when blame is being put on people, nobody will want to step up.

By using this breaking point, you make it easier for teams to identify their ownership space regions. Every team can then drive the adoption of best practices in their own space. The roadmaps and pipelines can be developed and deployed on their own. If there is an incident in feature B, the team owning feature C will not be in a downtime. This also contributes to the improved knowledge transfer[3] between the team and reduces the hero engineer scenarios.

The challenge with this approach is, to fully make use of this approach you also need to physically put a seam between the teams. You cannot have team A shouting at team B to speed up their product release roadmaps, just because team D is two versions ahead. Nada. That does not work. If you identify this as a problem, then instead of teams, you can focus on tangible products.

#2 Multiple Products

As your organization grows into the complex zone, the biggest challenge you identify is different areas of your platform being brought down—or being completely blown out in an incident—if you use a central repository, such as a monolith or a monorepo. At this stage, organizations try to put the legacy systems into maintenance mode and avoid adding any further code to the spaghetti regions.

Tip   While you stop adding more spaghetti, sometimes your Engineers add parmesan to the already messy spaghetti bowl to make it taste better. Food for thought.

---

[3] I cannot stress enough that code reviews are not only a means to add guardrails on your code repositories but also to share the knowledge between team members on what is happening in the repositories.

It is here that you spot the window of opportunity to decide that moving forward we will separate the repositories. The biggest challenge here is the central code features that every product depends on, get further spaghettified. This event then becomes the moment where you start building new products outside the monorepo. The central platform lives as it always did, maintained by the same team, but new products then become a customer and not a partner. This offers your teams the flexibility to extend the features and services on their own roadmap. These features and services can be patched, updated, developed, and maintained on their own time while the central platform continues to be developed and maintained in the older manner. It is important to highlight that it is not easy to de-spaghettify a messy bowl. As an Engineer, we are pulled toward the messy bowl to try to solve it, but a business doesn't care about a bowl of spaghetti that they cannot serve.

Question yourself this: would you like a bowl of spaghetti with the spaghetti perfectly lined up as parallel strands and sauce in a separate bowl, with cheese that you need to grate yourself?

The challenge in breaking down a system based on the products is simple: you are in control. If you are in control, you will push the timelines to a later moment to update the system. More on this in a moment.

#3 Separate Roadmaps

A lot of software is versioned, and to ensure data consistency and ensure the system works as a bundle, the right version of the service needs to be available. You should consider keeping dependent systems in a monolith that will not work if the versions break or if a service only ever advertises a single version.

Here are a few challenges:

- When do you release your service if it depends on version X of service Y?

- You released your service because version X of service Y was made available, but how do you handle rollbacks in service Y?

- Should you put your features and new code on hold if the service Y team decides they want to hold their release until the next quarter because of business changes?

Like I said, if your service Y can advertise multiple versions, the challenge is not as drastic, because your service can continue to function with service Y doing their roadmap planning.

To flip this, it is also a good pointer for us to make a choice for products that do not depend on each other to be separate services in their own repositories, with their own teams, their own roadmap, CI/CD pipelines, and rollback policies.

#4 Regulations and Compliance

Continuing from the "Multiple products." A very interesting trick used by many organizations in putting a "seam" is using the compliance and regulatory bodies as a guiding principle. Why do Engineers want to move to microservices? In short: they want speed. They want to

- Research and prototype quickly and with little effort.

- Develop the component quickly and be able to remove the component from the platform when no longer needed—with little to no impact to the database systems.

- Publish the applications to the testing or production environment without waiting for other services to go live.

- Test and validate their assumptions and code on their own roadmap.

Microservices provide these, and Engineers want that. The challenge comes when Engineers try to tinker with the regulated systems.

If you are a backend engineer for a medical services application, and your application goes down when a medical staff member was providing critical care to a patient, you would be having problems. In a regulated industry, the regulators control what happens. They control how much downtime you can have, how much data you can have, how much data you can lose, and when you can remove a feature without prior notice to the customers or partners.

This becomes a guiding principle for your teams to make a call: are they ready to handle the sticks that come with the regulatory license requirements? If your product does not have regulatory requirements, you can break it off and move it to a separate repository.

#5 Best Language Choice

Let's switch the mind from the perspective of breaking down an existing application into different parts and look at another opportunity. A lot of time you try to add an extension or a feature to an existing application but adding that in the initial language is not the right approach, that is the opportunity to choose the microservice.

It may not be clear, but if you build your product with different runtimes, such as .NET with Spring, or Ruby and Go, etc., you are already treading the pathways of microservices—just not at the 10,000 services level. A simple example would be, building your backend service in TypeScript, front-end with Dart/Flutter, database layer with Prisma/ORM. You add Java services that use Spring framework components and then use C/C++ libraries for data/number crunching, etc. and finally, to top it off, you use Go for infrastructure automation. That is a blend of different languages, and they need teams and Engineers who are equipped with the skills in these languages and runtimes. The parts of the platform can be developed in their own timelines, and the components will be deployed in their own roadmap, and they will be improved and maintained in their own way.

At the higher-level, it may contribute to slow speed (how to make sure the right version is available before you release your component?) but with this, you not only get speed but also direction. Now, your database module is no longer responsible for sending out email notifications. Because that is not its responsibility, and you can scale each component separately.

In my opinion, this is the best use case of switching the languages, runtimes, and frameworks. This also contributes directly to the reduction of cognitive load on your Engineers and encourages the use of the right tool for the right job.

The discussion about monolith and microservices is the same as the conversation about SQL and NoSQL. They both have their benefits and they expect a lot of consideration from the user. In the next chapter, now we will review the differences as well as the scenarios where we should use SQL or where NoSQL-based databases provide us with more value.

Further Reading

AWS is a leading organization that is always pushing the technical boundaries for their services, infrastructure, and solutions. A while back they learned the lessons of "over-engineering" and had to move their cutting edge architecture back to a monolith to save on costs and simplify the architecture. Read how and what this means for an application that grows beyond a few engineers here: `https://www.docker.com/blog/do-you-really-need-microservices/`.

Microservices are not without their flaws, and while they are not exactly a "sin," this article on InfoQ should give you an idea of what practices you should be avoiding in microservices, if you are planning to adopt microservices: `https://www.infoq.com/presentations/7-sins-microservices/`.

Last, but not least, the most important code repository to read that still uses a monorepo approach to bringing teams and services together is the Google's repository. While the repository is not available, lessons are available. Read about Google's story on their website: `https://research.google/pubs/why-google-stores-billions-of-lines-of-code-in-a-single-repository/?utm_source=hw.glich.co&utm_medium=referral&utm_campaign=what-are-microservices`.

CHAPTER 36

SQL vs. NoSQL

Egyptians built their pyramids in a triangular shape not for the speed of it, but everlasting nature of it. The decision of SQL vs. NoSQL comes down to the same reason: do you want to build quickly, or do you want to build once and run it for decades to come? SQL (ANSI SQL[1]) has been alive for almost half a century and still takes modern database query languages to the cleaners. While NoSQL database engines offer speed, agility, and modern features bundled in a single executable, the old-school SQL aims for legacy—*no, no, I don't mean it's for the legacy systems only*. SQL-based systems, databases, have been live for more than a decade and the platforms will still scale for the next decade.

This chapter focuses on teaching

- The reason why SQL is still here, even thought is a multi-decade old standard of writing queries.

- The purpose, motivation, and benefits that you get from using NoSQL, and what NoSQL actually means.

- Practical guidance to deciding when you should use SQL vs. NoSQL and also a database engine that offers you best of both.

The data modeling and data persistence layer cannot be delayed until production. For every application, enterprise or not, the data layer is designed and developed during the development of the application. This layer makes or breaks the application—by enabling a successful data capture and service provisioning, or crashing due to data loss and inconsistency and difference in the data models expected by the application.

---

[1] https://azure.microsoft.com/en-us/resources/cloud-computing-dictionary/what-is-sql-database

Software Engineers, for any programming language, need to keep their SQL knowledge sharp and active at any moment. When you are prototyping new business opportunities, productivity toolsets, or customer experience experiments, you need to think about the data storage. Where are you doing to store the information, how are you going to crunch the data and provide services to the customers? Note that, I am scoping the regulatory services out and we are not explicitly talking about the regulatory requirements for storing and processing the data—GDPR, etc.

The SQL-engines enable your teams to use ACID compliant database engines, such as MySQL, SQL Server, PostgreSQL, etc. to develop your applications on stable and available engines. The complexity of SQL comes from the verbose and boilerplate nature of the SQL queries. To fetch the data in ten modules, you need to execute the same query ten times and parse the output. The problems start when you change the structure of your objects (in C# programs) or the database schema. Suddenly you now need to update ten queries. Relational engines offer the flexibility to write stored procedures— *but this changes your expertise domain from backend to database.*

NoSQL was a movement against the rigid nature of SQL engines, and to give the flexibility to the developers and Engineers to ingest and access data in any manner. The most used NoSQL database, MongoDB, offers a native embedded experience for JavaScript-like applications. MongoDB stores the data in JSON documents. JSON is a well-known standard for data transfer among applications, while keeping the data in human readable format.

Interestingly, this movement spawned a lot of other NoSQL engines:

- Key-value: Redis, Memcached, etcd, etc.[2]

- Graph databases: Neo4j

- Document: MongoDB

Most cloud providers also offer their own versions of these NoSQL databases. AWS, Azure, Google Cloud, and Oracle, all offer NoSQL database offerings. There are various other types of NoSQL database engines, such as column store, time-series, etc. NoSQL has become a synonym for anything that is not old-school relational database for data storage.

---

[2] No pun intended.

The NoSQL nature of these engines assist quick prototyping at the cost of scalability. NoSQL—just like SQL—works great in some cases and does very bad in other cases. Relational database engines go very nicely to manage the relationships, and you can have multiple tables each having a parent-child relationship. The same cannot be said for NoSQL databases. The best feature of MongoDB is that you can create documents of any structure and then parse them on the runtime. The documents contain everything that your apps need to perform an operation. If you need relevant information or data, you can embed that information in the main document. MongoDB, while allows embedding child documents directly inside the parent document, makes it very difficult to scale beyond a certain length. MongoDB offers us to build documents with references[3] instead of embeddings. And that is when we go back to square one and build a "referential"[4] database.

PostgreSQL: For the Win

I have found the perfect balance between the world of SQL and NoSQL with PostgreSQL. It offers the stability of an SQL/relational database in the form of an object relational database, while also supporting dynamic data in terms of JSON—*or special data structures such as geospatial data.* PostgreSQL is supported by the Npgsql[5] NuGet package and provides a native C# driver for the PostgreSQL database server.

The leading authority on everything PostgreSQL is their own official website: `https://www.postgresql.org/`.

Short-Term Critical?

The criticality of a system does not only mean that it is supposed to provide the same service over the course of a decade. Do you remember 2020? A lot of COVID-19 apps were being created. These apps would allow you to

---

[3] `https://www.mongodb.com/resources/products/fundamentals/embedded-mongodb`

[4] Referential integrity is a core concept in relational databases: `https://www.ibm.com/docs/en/informix-servers/15.0.x?topic=integrity-referential`

[5] `https://www.npgsql.org/`

- Find where other groups are right now, who have been vaccinated,[6] or who have not been vaccinated?

- Learn about the sickness trends across different countries and what are the travel policies?

- Discover which application do I need to download and how can I show that I am vaccinated to get the entry?

- Check all the latest country-level requirements for different ages, household rules, and general healthcare?

Where are those applications now? Do you have any?

I remember, in the Netherlands the government provided a QR application that you would download your vaccine certificate on and then use it to get access to various locations. I uninstalled the application more than a year ago and the application is no longer needed. The application, which was once critical for access, and used by millions of users every day, is no longer needed.

Using this example, for an application that is only going to be used for a year or two, should you really be worried about long-term performance and availability? I am speaking in terms of years, of course.

COVID-19 and early 2020s was just an example. A lot of examples are valid, even today. A lot of sports venues create and publish their own applications to provide services. FIFA, ICC, Olympics, and many other federations and organizations provide customized apps per event or tournament. While maintaining the data for long-term data crunch is important, in the moment, the most important thing is: customer experience.

NoSQL provides that flexibility to prototype the database around your application's structure.

Now in the next chapter, we will explore what WebViews are, when and how they are used in an application to (1) onboard more customers and (2) reduce the overall development overhead from the development teams. We will also discuss the situations where using a WebView does not contribute any value and, in fact, degrades the quality of the application and the solution that we are building.

---

[6] On an important note: I am only talking about what was happening, I am not making a case for or against vaccines in this or following statements. :)

Further Reading

Historically, MongoDB was the first database to commercialize the concepts of NoSQL and mass-produce and distribute a database that allows users to simply inject copies of JSON documents and then query them as needed. If there is a subject-matter expert with authority, it is MongoDB. Read how MongoDB distinguishes between SQL and NoSQL: `https://www.mongodb.com/resources/basics/databases/nosql-explained/nosql-vs-sql`.

The problem that NoSQL solves is its biggest problem. There is no one NoSQL database that can provide a service or solution for all the NoSQL-related problems. In the chapter, we discussed a few NoSQL databases that each solve a particular challenge but we benchmark them against others (such as key-value databases against document-based databases) they perform poorly. Read about different NoSQL database types, what problem they each solve, and how you can use them in your architecture here: `https://docs.aws.amazon.com/whitepapers/latest/choosing-an-aws-nosql-database/types-of-nosql-databases.html`. This article on Microsoft Azure is a great resource if your cloud platform is Microsoft primarily: `https://azure.microsoft.com/en-us/resources/cloud-computing-dictionary/what-is-nosql-database`.

The design of the database schema is equally important for NoSQL databases, and must never be left to uncertainty just because the system or the architecture is not in its final phases. This MongoDB document guides on the process for designing a NoSQL database schema that provides scalability, but also ensures performance for the current workloads without compromising the data quality: `https://www.mongodb.com/resources/basics/databases/nosql-explained/data-modeling`.

CHAPTER 37

WebViews

Ionic framework was among the first few to launch the hybrid application development experience. They offered the flexibility to port your web applications to mobile applications and target both audiences from the same source control. Just like microservices, hybrid development approach has been abused a lot. I am all for the approach to develop and deploy the apps from the same source code. But I am all against the idea of using WebView to bundle and embed your website as a mobile app.

The core objective of this chapter is to educate you on why we need WebView, and why this need evolves into a malpractice where everything becomes a WebView. The biggest challenge is that the customer experience and the native integration is compromised. You will also learn about a few ways using which you can avoid the pitfalls of WebView overuse.

P.S. If you would like to release your web app on a mobile without effort, consider using Progressive Web Apps[1] (PWA) framework. As for WebViews, let's keep it for less than 1% of the use cases where it is not possible to either do things via a PWA or a native control.

Web browsers are not a new trend; it is a very old piece of software. Modern companies try to take a jab at the concept of a web browser and create something unique. But this chapter is not about the concept of web browsers but the practice of using web browser software as an embedded component in your UI application. This gave a few benefits to the engineers:

- Web browsers are capable of opening and previewing certain file types. If you were building support for PDF files, a very safe bet was to simply open the file in the web browser. iTextSharp, and other PDF processors were either too complex, lacked features, or were expensive in terms of license.

---

[1] https://web.dev/explore/progressive-web-apps

© Afzaal Ahmad Zeeshan 2026
A. A. Zeeshan, *Building Mission-Critical Applications with .NET 10 and C# 14*,
https://doi.org/10.1007/979-8-8688-2347-3_37

- You do not need to parse the HTML content to preview the results of an API—remember that not many applications and platforms offered RESTful support back in the early 2010s. API-first approach is rather modern.

- You can customize the experience of your customer in the embedded browser based on the authentication credentials from the app.

As you start using the WebView, you realize that you are also sharing the code from the web application and migrating a lot of authenticated/shared components in the web application instead of the mobile application. The trend then becomes the migration of code from your native mobile application to the shared web application. When you need to use the shared code, you import the WebView and render the application.

Ionic Framework

It is 2015, and you are building native applications. For every feature that you publish on Android, you must write the code on iOS repository as well. This is the worst, as long as you are only publishing to Android and iOS, and do not support any Desktop platforms—macOS, Windows, or Linux, etc. The advent of various consumer platforms, like Android, iOS, and third-party platforms such as Symbian, Windows Mobile, etc. were all only adding to the injury. The front-end "mobile" engineer now needs to make sure every customer on all the platforms has the same experience. The frameworks like Ionic, provide native bindings for the most used features and platforms, but not for everything.

If you'd like to read more about the history of WebViews and how Android project provided initial versions of WebViews and how it matured into what we have today, check out this article on Medium (`https://medium.com/@johan.jungbeck.bbc/the-dark-age-of-webview-a-history-of-android-and-javascript-support-in-apps-4c01522d7e54`).

Today, we have so many platforms of choice to develop our applications, that it's not even funny anymore. But I do not blame the developers of these platforms; a developer must do what a developer must do, in fact, I blame the giants who had the opportunity to provide a central platform[2] to developers to develop and distribute cross-platform applications but didn't.

What Is Wrong with WebView?

Nothing.

If anything, WebView enables everyone to **(1)** reuse the code on any platform, even if the platform is not supported by the original implementor of the cross-platform development platform, **(2)** use the browser capabilities to process different types of data, such as reading PDF files, playing audio/video, and validating data, such as certificates.

The biggest challenge with WebView is that while a WebView is simply a web browser on all the platforms, the challenge comes from the fact that every browser has its own engine that renders and parses the HTML and CSS, and even JavaScript differently. There is a reason why we have the Can I Use (`https://caniuse.com/`) project in the first place. WebViews tend to solve the problem of making our apps cross-platform, but how can they, when they are not a one-platform based on the same specification? In short: they only add insult to injury and do not make your apps look and feel native.

When Should I Use WebView?

Never.

The problem originates not from the fact that developers use WebView, but because developers overuse WebView. I am not saying you should not use a WebView (even thought I just did in the previous paragraph). In fact, in some cases, do use a WebView. For example, if you are using a complex flow of data transfer in a regulated environment, it is recommended to keep the code in a shared space that can be changed as needed. One example is payment handling. The payments landscape is highly regulated, and very strict.

---

[2] If you are interested in building cross-platform applications, I recommend using Flutter. It has a good developer experience and provides a good support for various platforms. However, I am not sure if this is the right platform for the next five years given how Google is investing their resources. But there is no problem in trying. :)

Many times, when you make a payment, you are required to verify that it is indeed you making the payment. The online payment platform that I use, uses a custom flow to verify the payment by sending a notification to the app. During this time, the payment confirmation page needs to be open to listen for payment updates and then redirect me to final step—to claim the items. In this scenario, platforms show a web page for the confirmation that stays open until the payment is confirmed or rejected and then the page closes. I have not seen an application be able to replicate this flow in a native behavior—*unless the payment gateway is also owned by the application*. Since this security behavior is different and unique to every payment gateway, it is difficult to replicate this for every provider and maintain it. So, a simple WebView that navigates to the verification page is simple yet powerful enough.

Microsoft's investment in the Machine Learning space and AI has provided a lot of interesting tools, tricks, and services. While we are not going to cover Generative AI in this book as per the scope of the manuscript, in the next chapter, we will explore the Machine Learning technical ecosystem that is available to C# developers and how you can use the models that are prebuilt, pretrained, and available on an as-needed and pay-as-you-go model.

Further Reading

I used the example of payments as a scenario where it makes sense to use WebView. While that is true and a real-world use case of the WebView technology, it does not mean that a WebView is mandatory to have a successful payment or payout flow. Read this article to learn how to approach highly regulated and sophisticated workflows and manage to provide a native service: `https://cybersecurity.asee.io/blog/webview-payment-gateway-and-native-3ds-sdk/`.

WebViews is available for legacy, back-porting, and "emergency" scenarios. Otherwise, it is advised to use more modern ways of rendering and offering external web-based content to your customers; for example, an API is a better alternative to providing RESTful services to your customers. Google Chrome's WebView documentation outlines more ways in which you learn how to utilize the WebView and what other methods are available for you to use. My favorite approach is the Custom Tabs on Android: `https://developer.chrome.com/docs/android/custom-tabs`. It solves two problems: (1) the user data is secure and your application only accesses what the user allows it to and (2) the interface and UI/UX is maintained as per the user's default preferences, so the WebView doesn't feel like a bloatware. Read more on how this can help you and your team to provide amazing customer experiences across the devices while reducing the load on the development teams.

CHAPTER 38

Machine Learning

I have a disclaimer: I was not sure about writing this chapter at all. AI is taking everything by storm, including book authoring. But if you are reading this chapter, or this book, it means you still care about the human-generated experience. Also, the OpenCV project is still ongoing, so who am I kidding?

.NET offers first-class Machine Learning[1] development experience. For most startup-focused and indie-projects, the ML services are available as packages or services, such as Azure Machine Learning.

If you are using Generative AI to develop your apps, provide services to customers, or add features to your application, feel free to skip this chapter. This chapter has nothing to do with the trendy Generative AI. In this chapter, I point out how to use Azure as an AI services platform for your .NET applications.

It has been more than a decade that a lot of machine learning platforms have emerged, a lot of plug-and-play services have been made available to your applications for various smart services. If you want to use vision-services, text-analytics, video-moderation, everything is available for a penny a request. Note that it is critical to quickly prototype, roll out, and rollback as needed by your business and customers. This requires the best-in-class pipelines and monitoring controls.

ML.NET

Let's address the elephant in the room first. ML.NET.

ML.NET offers

---

[1] https://learn.microsoft.com/en-us/dotnet/machine-learning/

- Baseline classes that you can use to define your sources, run the algorithms to train your models, and provide output for test/production input.

- The model classes that enable you to prepare and transform the input data.

- ML.NET works with TensorFlow, Pytorch, and other general deep learning libraries so you can use the source code that you wrote for ML.NET.

- Model validation code that provides you with the opportunity to test the quality of the model before you publish it for production.

For simpler applications, you can even train the models directly from within the Visual Studio environment. Check out the **Model Builder** (`https://dotnet.microsoft.com/en-us/apps/ai/ml-dotnet/model-builder`) from ML.NET in Visual Studio. The ML.NET Model Builder is available free of cost and works with any application in the .NET platform. While the model training and deployment can happen offline on your own machine, the data sources can come directly from the databases—local on your database, or from remote environments such as cloud. You can try this tutorial (`https://dotnet.microsoft.com/en-us/learn/ml-dotnet/get-started-tutorial/intro`) to get started with ML.NET.

If you are building a general-purpose application that requires basic AI/ML services, ML.NET provides the baseline foundation.

Last, but not least, the best benefit of using ML.NET in your .NET applications is the automated ML (`https://learn.microsoft.com/en-gb/dotnet/machine-learning/how-to-guides/how-to-use-the-automl-api`), which deduces the model generation procedure.

ML.NET, however, does expect you or your engineers to know the basics of machine learning. While you can import the models and use them, if you are training your own models, it is of utmost importance to understand how models are trained and how to debug the performance or accuracy of the models.

Azure AI Services

I take it that you do not have a dedicated machine learning team that creates and publishes models for your applications to use. That's not a problem at all. You do not need to have a dedicated machine learning team. Cloud platforms, and many other providers offer services. I will talk about Azure—since that is my personal go-to, but this is not a recommendation, endorsement, or any of that sort for the legal/trust reasons. I will try to mention services offered by other providers as well, but all in all, the services offered are same in all platforms.

To get started, Azure AI Services (`https://azure.microsoft.com/en-us/products/ai-services`) provides a set of AI-enabled services that you can consume either via an SDK, or via API, or similar methods. Note that the models could be specifically licensed to an enterprise and may not have the same development experience across the platforms. Azure AI Services is a rebranding of Azure Cognitive Services, which provides RESTful models for all generally needed AI services. You need text analysis? You got it. You need vision and video services? Azure AI Services supports that.

You can get started with the Azure AI Services (also known as Foundry Tools) on the official website: `https://ai.azure.com/explore/aiservices`. The website demonstrates a few ways in which you can use the intelligent services for the operations that you need to perform. For example, extracting content from the documents, processing the speech content, extracting and removing the personally identifiable information, and much more.

Azure As Machine Learning Platform

The key aspect of Azure as a Machine Learning platform is the infrastructure that Microsoft provides with Azure. The Azure platform brings top-notch security, highest quality infrastructure and networking capability, fleet of GPUs and compute, and high-speed storage to deliver the models. As Microsoft delivers this infrastructure, you are relieved of the need to design and build the infrastructure for your models.

Azure also enables you to make your ML features available across your own apps, or apps of your customers. The features store enables teams to publish their models and then advertise them across the apps and models that need the trained capabilities. While the biggest benefit you have is avoiding duplicate model training, with Azure, you also don't have to think about or plan for the underlying infrastructure—Microsoft Azure has already invested in that area.

Notebooks on Azure

Data scientists use Notebooks—I am talking about the Jupyter notebooks, of course— to work on their objectives. The data needs of most of these notebooks is, simply put, "large." Azure offers the platform to host your notebooks and share them with others for collaboration. Google also offers their own service to host notebooks (`https://colab. google/`).

That said, the ecosystem of Machine Learning, AI, and Azure is so vast that just recently Microsoft released the Microsoft Foundry (`https://azure.microsoft.com/en- us/products/ai-foundry`) platform on Azure that offers all the latest and cutting edge models for deployment and consumption. To respect the scope of this book, and to make sure the content of the book does not become outdated or stale, we're not discussing the AI-portfolio of Microsoft products here.

In the next chapter, we will explore a separate topic. The topic of open source is part of the "soft skills" because open source expects more people skills than your regular enterprise jobs. Open source has evolved, and open source is now the source of power for various software and architectures. I cannot think of a company that operates with zero open source projects, dependencies, frameworks, runtimes, or libraries. Let's take a look at what open source means for .NET, for Microsoft's ecosystem, and for us the C# developers.

Further Reading

If you're interested in learning how Microsoft's .NET Machine Learning capabilities can be used in production, look no further than the official documentation for .NET and the Machine Learning section: `https://dotnet.microsoft.com/en-us/apps/ai/ml- dotnet`. The website demonstrates different use cases of the ML.NET library and what sort of business logics you can handle using the library, out of the box. Since ML.NET also integrates with TensorFlow, you can also retrofit the library with community-driven projects.

While the ML.NET, and other models are here, the community-driven frameworks and platforms are also of great quality. I still actively use Accord.NET (`http://accord-framework.net/`) framework for some tasks, especially around pattern recognition, and signal processing, and use EmguCV (`https://www.emgu.com/wiki/index.php?title=Main_Page`) for OpenCV processing in .NET programs. While for new projects, I would recommend using either prebuilt models, if you need you can use the Accord.NET library to build your own models and use them. The benefit of using Accord.NET and other custom frameworks is that you don't need to pay a monthly fee and you fully own the models and can use and reuse them.

CHAPTER 39

Open Source and Community

I have another honest disclaimer to make: companies support Open Source and Community as a "good-to-have" and not an important—I am not even saying a mandatory or required—purpose of their business. It will be extremely difficult to find a company that does not use any open-source project or service and is a Tech-first company. The benefits and applications of open source extend beyond just the Tech, and we see the use cases in non-Tech systems as well—think of HR, sports, fashion, and more.

The biggest challenge in adopting, accepting, and relying on Open Source is its inability to focus on "your" objectives. That is where Community comes in. Your involvement with, and relationship with the Community can be a "make it or break it" element for Open-Source adoption and contribution from your organization.

Open Source and Community are a pivotal part of the .NET strategy of Microsoft. Microsoft open sourced not just .NET platform but various other components to onboard Community and external contributors for this ecosystem. On the one hand, it seems as if the business is giving up its competitive advantage, on the other, it is increasing the surface area of the crop yield—now anyone can build, test, and deploy their solutions to proprietary and premium services offered by Microsoft, such as Microsoft Azure.

This goes without saying, this chapter is not a legal advice. For your situation, and to understand how to best use and work with Open Source, or if it is even allowed, consult with your legal department or advisor.

As we get closer to the closing of the book, I hope you have a better understanding of why .NET is a good choice for your applications, business platforms, and products, and what would make .NET a wrong choice. While .NET does offer a lot of services for

© Afzaal Ahmad Zeeshan 2026
A. A. Zeeshan, *Building Mission-Critical Applications with .NET 10 and C# 14*,
https://doi.org/10.1007/979-8-8688-2347-3_39

improved developer productivity and developer experience, if you cannot find the right SDKs, right platforms, right Engineers, .NET is not going to solve the problems for you. This is why I would like to close the topic on the note of discussing Open Source and the Community support that you would have with .NET.

Microsoft is the primary provider of SDLC toolsets for .NET ecosystem; from work planning (Azure DevOps) to development environments (Visual Studio) to build tooling (dotnet CLI, MSBuild, etc.) to version control (Azure DevOps, GitHub) to deployment environments (Microsoft Azure) to observability platforms (Azure Application Insights), and more, like Azure AI Services, etc. This ensures that your applications always have the integrated experience and right dependencies available. This is not true for a lot of other runtimes/frameworks, where the development environments are provided by one vendor, while the language or runtime specifications are owned by another, and the hosting environments are a third-party solution. Ensuring that the right services, right versions of the deployable runtimes, right roadmap are available is very crucial and critical if you want to be in control.

That said, Microsoft open-sourced .NET platform to become transparent in their framework roadmaps and language strategy, and to invite the community to play a central role in the growth of the platform. The .NET Foundation[1] is the place where stakeholders and partners gather to speak about current and ongoing progress of the platform.

Incoming Open Source

At the very basic, everything in .NET is basically incoming Open Source for you. The .NET SDK (`https://github.com/dotnet/sdk`), runtime (`https://github.com/dotnet/runtime`), and other components are all available as source code repositories on GitHub that you can download and even build yourself (`https://github.com/dotnet/sdk/blob/main/documentation/project-docs/developer-guide.md`). Note that the products that Microsoft builds and ships often have a different license and sometimes contain custom telemetry that is sent back to Microsoft. You can always disable the telemetry collection.

---

[1] `https://dotnetfoundation.org/`

The packages available on NuGet are also open source in most cases; however, NuGet is not an area completely owned and run by Microsoft when it comes to the packages that are available. This is why a lot of times you will see packages that are not MIT licensed. The Json.NET (Newtonsoft.Json: `https://www.nuget.org/packages/newtonsoft.json/`) package is MIT licensed, while Serilog (`https://www.nuget.org/packages/Serilog`) is Apache-2.0 licensed. Keep this in mind when accepting and using any community-driven package, as the license may or may not allow you to use the package. The biggest risk, as already discussed, comes from the development and delivery of the software. Since the packages are developed, contributed to, and maintained by the public it gets very difficult to track who is contributing what. Zero-day vulnerabilities are a big trend across all the Open Source projects, no matter the size and complexity of the software.

DevSecOps has a common practice of evaluating the license terms before accepting any dependency—direct or indirect dependency. Snyk is a platform that enables you and your teams to check the license terms for dependencies (`https://docs.snyk.io/manage-risk/reporting/dependencies-and-licenses/view-licenses`) in your CI/CD pipeline. At this stage, it is very important to involve your legal and risk teams to ensure that your Engineers are aware of their responsibilities.

A common example of this behavior was the Visual Studio Code editor, the code repository itself is licensed under MIT (`https://github.com/microsoft/vscode/blob/main/LICENSE.txt`), while the built binary is released with Visual Studio Code license (`https://code.visualstudio.com/license`). This is not a showstopper—the software is still free to use, for personal or commercial jobs, but if you are serving the binaries of VS Code to your customers, you need to be clear in the terms and licenses with all parties involved.

Outgoing Open Source

The .NET platform is MIT licensed, and thus you can distribute the apps that you publish on top of the .NET platform. In my experience, the MIT-license (`https://opensource.org/license/mit`) is just the best-enough license for a majority of the Open-Source projects.

Contributing a Project

I can tell from experience; nothing feels better than contributing something back to the community. The community that helped you achieve your goals, now being helped to achieve their goals. The projects that you contribute don't have to be the fanciest or complex projects. Something very simple can start the conversation. A lot of projects start as a basic functionality that is needed by, in most cases, the developers themselves. The most downloaded project on NuGet, Json.NET, has a rather simple scope: parse and serialize C# to JSON and vice versa.

Almost a decade ago, contributing a project to the Open Source was like giving up your project and leaving it on Community's goodwill to drive the adoption and development of the project. Today, that is not the case. A lot of projects start as open-source repositories and then super-exciting companies spawn around to provide the support. Odoo (https://www.odoo.com/) is a very recent example of such a company that enables businesses to operate on their Open-Source tech stack. The code is available open source for anyone to use, and the hosted services are also available for anyone to sign up for. However, commercial products and offerings are made for large scale organizations.

In tech space itself, we know of a lot of companies that built an open source project and then created a company that would provide services and consultancy—Databricks, Prisma, etc.

Contributing to an Existing Project

It is that sometimes you use an open-source project and that project lacks a feature, or you'd like to contribute something to either improve the performance or to cover another edge case. In such a scenario, you'd like to contribute something to the project. That is always possible, and not only possible but also welcome.

The biggest dilemma for a lot is whether you can contribute the code that you wrote on your work time—intellectual property, or if you become responsible for the maintenance of the code, module, or the project. The answer depends on the license of the project. And it is of utmost importance that you review the license terms. In simple, MIT repositories—.NET platform, ASP.NET Core, etc. are all MIT licensed and thus they allow you to contribute code, but you are not the owner of the project just because you contributed something. You cannot claim any liabilities or warranties for damages.

Oh, and this project can also be the .NET platform. Remember that .NET platform is open source as well, and the contributions are welcome to this platform.

Community

The community gives a "sense of belonging" to the members. Like bees to a flower, members flock toward a valuable resource automatically. Everybody knows about Linux today, but who knew about it in its first year? That is what community is all about. Today, Linux has a bigger size of consumers than its community. You are part of the community if you "consume" or "contribute" to it—using a platform puts you at a different stage (`https://pm2alliance.eu/forum/the-3-cs-of-open-source-engagement/`) of the community. If you use a platform, you are part of the community. The maturity of your organization depends on how you interact with the Open-Source platform and its community.

The community of the project is not a constant, in fact, it is ever-growing and ever-evolving. One decade a project has a specific group of audience in its community and the next decade is a different turn, and so on and so forth. This makes gauging "community" for any particular project difficult. If you'd like to understand what your community looks like, look at the PRs, issues, and discussions for your project or dependencies.

And now this brings us to the wrap for the part, where we explored the complimentary topics and subjects for .NET projects. The goal of this part was to deliver extra knowledge and reading material for .NET and C# developers to sharpen their skills. The topics that we discussed in this part do not directly improve or degrade your C# programs, but they allow you to think in terms of systems and design an architecture that scales without pains. The goal of this book and the manuscript is also to help you write code and build solutions that scale, without keeping you up at night (every night) and can be understood by new engineers in your team. We now wrap the topic and suggest we continue this conversation beyond just the book. I am available on X/Twitter @afzaalvirgoboy, and would be happy and in fact welcome your feedback and questions for topics in this book, .NET, C#, or modern engineering practices.

Further Reading

This chapter barely touches the surface of the topic of community, open source, trust, and contributions. The subject of open source software and the history of Microsoft and other players in the market is too huge to cover in one chapter. The book *Program Management for Open Source Projects* is a good start if you'd like to learn about the Program Management perspective of the open source. For practical aspects of open source, such as writing the code, building trust, managing security and safety of the community and the project, you need to get in the trenches.

Index

A

Accessibility, 32

Accord.NET framework, 5

Active Directory, 134

Agile manifesto, 46

Aikido, 185

Alerts, 257–258
    labeling, 259
    on-call Engineers, 258
    programs, 260–262

Android, 302

Apache JMeter, 143

API documentation
    as contract, 121–122
    automation, 121
    Swagger, 119–121

Application maps, 255

Applications, 228

Artifacts, 169–172, 174

ASP.NET, 233
    Core, 40, 41, 46, 51, 95, 105–107,
        217–220, 245, 247
    Web apps, 13, 42
    Web Pages, 31

Async/await keywords, 94–96

Asynchronous programming, 93

Automation, 202

Azure AI Services, 309

Azure App Service, 135

Azure App Service's Deployment
        Slots, 194

Azure Artifacts, 181

Azure DevOps, 6, 7, 170, 177, 181, 185

Azure Functions, 47, 49, 50

Azure servers, 135

Azure Storage, 234

Azure Virtual Machines, 234

B

Backend Engineering, 92

Backend Systems, 92

Best-in-class development, 32

BigInteger, 78

Blazor, 51

Blocking, 92

Bot limitations, 129–130

Branching strategy, 205

Break glass, 151, 280

BrowserStack, 144

Bug, 224

C

C#, 118

C# developer, 284

C# language, 65, 94

C# programming language, 20–24

C# programs, 317

C++ compiler, 26

C/C++ libraries, 292

Cached artifacts, 180–181

Caching services, 173

Cardinality, 233, 237–239

Checksum-less software, 187

Chronosphere, 236

CI/CD pipelines, 33, 150–151, 159, 167, 227, 233, 234, 239, 288

CI/CD processes, 111

CI servers, 165–166

Client-apps, 39, 221

Cloud-hosted screens, 128–129

Cloud-native architectures, 273

CNAME linking, 135, 137

Common-language infrastructure (CLI), 21

Communication, 269, 281

Community, 313, 317

Community-driven open-source, 142–143

Community-driven package, 315

Community-led framework, 10–12

Complexity, 41

Consumer platforms, 51–52

Consumption, 234

Contracts, 117–118
    central agreement, 122–123
    documentation, 121–122

Conway's law, 8

COVID-19 pandemic, 297, 298

CPU usage, 235

Criticality of system, 297–298

Cross-platform, 63

Cross-site scripting, 175

Crypto wallets, 69

CSS selectors, 129

Customer experience, 33

Customer-facing incident, 282

Customer-owned platforms, 224

CyberArk, 134

D

Database connections, 228

Datadog, 236

Data layer, 178

Data modeling, 295

Data source, 83

Data state management, 85

Data usage
    field keyword, 87
    record types, 86–87

DbContext, 77, 83–85

Debugging, 202, 244, 251

Delivery, 118

Dependency hijacks, 187

Deployment, 113, 118
    building, 68–69
    distribution, 69–72
    options, 166

Desktop apps, 51, 58–59, 62

"dev branch", 216

Developer experience, 156

Development environments, 26–27

DevOps, 46, 68, 113, 150, 173, 184, 185, 188, 191–192, 197, 233
    application architectures, 193
    HTTP request, 193
    uptime *vs.* downtime, 192–195

DevSecOps, 112, 315

Discovery, 118

Distributing platforms, 221–224

dotnet CLI, 156

Dribbble, 67

Duty Engineer, 253

Dynatrace, 236

E

Edge-networks, 36

Elasticity, 195

Emergency exits, 151

Engineering department, 35
Engineers, 117
Enterprise patterns, 42–43
Entity Framework (EF) Core, 80, 81, 173
Environment, 213–215
    in ASP.NET Core, 217–220
    dev branch, 216
    feature behavior, 214–215
    release branch, 217
    repository, 215
Event-driven programming, 92
Events, 91, 101
    async/await nature, 94–96
    default execution path, 91
    HTTP call, 93
    messages, 97–98
    natural execution flow, 96–97
    program-space events, 94
    server-applications, 92

F

Failed requests, 253
Fan-out updates, 71
Faulty services, 273
Feature configuration, 214–215
Feature flags, 223
Feedback, 127
Field keyword, 87
Figma, 67
Fire alarm, 265–267
Firefighting rules, 265
    engineering teams, 266
    fire alarm, 265–267
    issue and problem, 267
    knowledge, 269
    overarching theme, 267
    professional help, 266
    responsibilities, 268–269
    roles and responsibilities, 268
    root cause, 266
    subject-matter expert, 268
Flakiness, 144–146
Flaky-free test suite, 127
Flexibility, 203
Framework-dependent
        applications, 163–164
Framework-dependent
        deployment, 163–164
Framework-dependent environments, 35
Freemium scalability, 144

G

GET/pets/{id}, 50
Git-based repositories, 219
Git flows, 205, 210
Git history, 209
GitHub, 6, 155, 170, 177, 185
GitHub repository, 145
GitLab, 6, 170, 177, 185
    Auto DevOps, 143
    Feature Flags, 214
GitOps, 150, 200, 201
GitOps Pro Max, 208–211
Git repository, 209
Git version control, 179
GitX Flow, 206
Glass breakers, 281
Google Analytics, 251
Google Search Console, 136
Google Tasks, 260
Go programming language, 177
Grafana, 236, 253, 256
gRPC, 107–108
GUI-based Desktop, 52

H

Hero engineers, 277, 278
Hosting infrastructure, 108–109
Hosting platforms, 12–15
HTTP polling, 104
HTTP request, 235

I

Incidents
    alarm, 278–279
    business as usual, 271
    code fixing, 280–281
    downward trend, 278–280
    five whys, 279–280
    management, 282–284
    navigation, 273–274
    postmortems, 273
    response structure, 277
    rhetorical situation, 280
    severity, 272
    teams, 272
Infrastructure as Code (IaC)
    architecture, 202–203
    automation, 202
    benefits, 201–202
    development and growth, 199
    lock down, 203–204
    terraforming, 199–201
    virtual machines, 201
Infrastructure level, 243
Infrastructure management, 195–198
Infrastructure teams, 207
Infrastructure validation, 134–135
Innovative cultures, 35–36

Integrated dashboard, 229
Integrated development
    environments (IDEs), 26, 37
Interpreted programming language, 159
iOS, 302
IronPython, 38
Iteration, 177–178
iTextSharp, 301

J

JavaScript, 38, 159
JFrog, 144

K

K6, 256
Kafka, 98
Keep-Alive header, 104
Known platforms, 33–34

L

Language, 18, 43
    assessment, 24
    C#, 21–24
    development, 19
    .NET framework, 17
    opinionated approach, 20
    use case, 20
Lazy loading, 62
LINQ, 88–90
Localization, 32
Local network, 31–32
Log output, 254
logger-8.3, 178

M

Machine learning (ML), 304
    Azure platform, 309–310
    ML.NET, 307–308
Main branch, 150
Man-in-the-middle attacks, 187
Manual testing, 127, 281
Master passwords, 114–115
MAUI projects, 63–66
Message Bus, 97–98
Messages, 97–98
Metrics dashboard, 260
MFC-derived application, 19
Micro ORMs, 85, 86
Microservices, 43–46, 287
    language choice, 292
    multiple products, 289–290
    regulations and compliance, 291
    separate roadmaps, 290–291
    teams and team-size, 288–289
Microsoft, 3, 19, 75, 141, 176, 314
Microsoft Azure, 47, 234, 237
Microsoft Azure Monitor, 261
Microsoft.Data.Sqlite, 173
Microsoft .NET, 3, 10, 12
Microsoft Foundry, 310
Migration, 34
Minimum viable products (MVPs), 9
Mitigation, 266
ML.NET, 307–308
Mobile platforms, 222
Model Builder, 308
Model validation code, 308
Modern software systems, 122
MongoDB, 299
Monitoring approach, 235, 239–240
MQTT-compliant queue storage, 97

MSBuild, 155–157
Multilanguage solutions, 164–165
Multi-threaded data processing, 228
"My-something-app", 135
MySQL, 80

N

Natural execution flow, 96–97
Navigation, 273–274
Negligible, 198
.NET 9.0, 34
.NET 10, 166
.NET applications, 111, 167, 307
.NET Aspire, 42
.NET CLI, 169
.NET code, 257–258
.NET Core, 7, 11, 38
.NET ecosystem
    assessment, 15
    community-led framework, 10–12
    developer experience, 9
    development experience, 6–10
    hands-on experience, 4
    hosting platforms, 12–15
    mobile development, 5
    offline applications, 4
.NET engineers, 159, 253, 257, 284
.NET Foundation, 24
.NET frameworks, 25, 32, 37, 55, 57, 65, 74,
        162, 174, 211
.NET guide, 131
.NET packages, 77
.NET platforms, 96
    customers, 39
    enterprise patterns, 42–43
    microservices, 43–46
    server applications, 40–42

.NET platforms (*cont.*)
    serverless, 46–47
    touch-screen devices, 39
    types, 40
.NET projects, 35
.NET runtime, 163–164
NetSparkle, 70
.NET team, 176
Network behavior, 229
New database, 210
Non-enterprise systems, 214
NoSQL database, 295, 296
Notebooks, 309–310
NuGet, 6, 156, 179, 315
NuGet repository, 168

O

Object-relational
    mappers, 79
Observability, 236–237
On-call Engineers, 258, 259
Open Source
    and community, 313, 317
    existing project, 316
    incoming, 314–315
    outgoing, 315–317
    projects, 316
    repositories, 316
    SDLC toolsets, 314
OpenAPI, 117, 120
OpenAPI NuGet package, 121
OpenCV, 307
Open-source packages, 142–143
Open-source project, 141
OpenTelemetry, 249
OutOfMemoryException, 91, 94

P

PagerDuty, 260
Parallel builds, 166
Parser-5.5, 178
Passwords, 114–115
Plug-and-play solution, 35
Polling, 102–105
Polyglot Engineer, 26
Post-conference-hyped-up-gossip, 45
PostgreSQL, 80, 146, 297
Pre-mortems, 229–230
Private dependencies, 175
Programmable alerts, 260–262
Program-space events, 94
Progressive Web Apps (PWA), 301
Pulumi, 200
Punystructure, 208
Python, 38, 87, 159

Q

QR application, 298

R

RabbitMQ, 98
R&D budgets, 35
Real-time apps
    ASP.NET Core, 105–107
    hosting infrastructure, 108–109
    Polling *vs.* Server Push, 102–105
    remote calls, 107–108
Red-green dashboards, 257
Redis, 109
Release branch, 150
Render-heavy application, 62
Repository, 150

Responsive-design, 33
Restoration, 168–169
ROBOT automation scripts, 128
Root cause analysis, 279
Ruby, 159

S

Sampling, 249
Scalability, 39, 109, 128
Scaled-up version, 129
Security, 111
    delivery, 112
    deployment, 113
    detection, 113
    development environment, 112
    passwords, 114–115
    vulnerability, 222
Self-contained deployment, 160–162
Self-contained package, 35
Self-hosted version, 209
Semantic versioning, 208
Separate folder, 40
Sequential builds, 166
Serializer-1.9, 178
Serverless, 46–47, 97–98
    inputs, 48
    output, 48–51
    workloads, 42
Server platforms, 40–42
Server Push, 102–105
Server-side applications, 39
Service-level agreement (SLA),
    122, 233, 240
Severity levels, 272
Short message sending (SMS), 259
SignalR, 106, 109
Site reliability engineers (SREs), 275

Slack channels, 278
Soft skills, 310
Software, 31
    development, 118
    development life cycle, 111, 151, 186
    documentation, 117–118
    Engineers, 25, 296
    Engineering, 177
    history, 37
    innovative cultures, 35–36
    known platforms, 33–34
    migration, 34
    .NET framework, 32
    quality, 67
    supporting services, 36–37
    tools, 142
Source code, 227
Speed, 204
Splunk's website, 275
SQL database, 295, 296
SQL query, 149–150
SQL Server, 31
Stability, 149, 204
Staging branch, 150
Staging environment, 237
Startup, 208
Stock market, 55
Supply-chain security
    community-led environments, 183
    delivery, 186–188
    development and building
        phase, 185–186
    quality control, 186
    software, 183
    source code, 184
Supporting services, 36–37
Swagger documentation, 119–121
System.Data namespace, 78

T

Tangible binding, 198
Team Topologies, 288
Telemetry, 243
TensorFlow, 5
Terraform, 199–201
Testability
    bots, 129–130
    platforms, 127
Testers, 127
The Mono Project, 10
"The Wild West", 133–134
Third-party dependencies, 173, 174
Third-party testing
    flakiness, 144–146
    Freemium scalability, 144
    open source, 142–143
    software-development
        approach, 141
TorchSharp, 12
Touch-screen devices, 39
Traceability, 244–249
Triggers, 50

U

UI-driven apps, 56–58, 92
    consumer-side, 73
    cross-platform, 63
    customer experience, 73
    deployment, 68–72
    design, 66
    Desktop, 58–59
    detection, 73–74
    development, 67–68
    MAUI, 63–66, 74–75

    requirements, 56
    Windows, 59–63
Usage, 234
User-interface, 129

V

Version-2.0, 178
Versioned zone, 138–139
Virtual private network (VPN), 114
Visual Basic, 20, 59
Visualization
    application maps, 255
    dashboard, 252
    development, 251
    logs, 252
    objective, 251
    recovery process, 252
    tools, 239
Visual Studio, 7, 25, 37, 61, 64, 155, 157,
        180, 245, 246, 308
Visual Studio Code, 16, 37, 157
Voice-enabled automation, 39
Vulnerability, 224

W

Web applications, 51
WebSocket protocol, 104
WebView, 301
    challenge, 303
    developers, 303
    Microsoft's investment, 304
    online payment platform, 304
Wheel reinvention, 175
Win32, 19
Windows, 3, 59–63, 96

X

Xamarin framework,
        5, 63–66
XAML-driven Windows
        Presentation Foundation, 60
X-as-Code, 199
XMLDoc, 118–119
XML file format, 155
XPath, 129

Y

YOLO, 138, 213

Z

Zapier, 260
Zero-day vulnerabilities, 82, 274
Zero-downtime release, 194
Zero-Everything culture, 113

GPSR Compliance
The European Union's (EU) General Product Safety Regulation (GPSR) is a set
of rules that requires consumer products to be safe and our obligations to
ensure this.

If you have any concerns about our products, you can contact us on

ProductSafety@springernature.com

In case Publisher is established outside the EU, the EU authorized
representative is:

Springer Nature Customer Service Center GmbH
Europaplatz 3
69115 Heidelberg, Germany